Museums of World Religions

Bloomsbury Studies in Material Religion

Bloomsbury Studies in Material Religion is the first book series dedicated exclusively to studies in material religion. Within the field of lived religion, the series is concerned with the material things with which people do religion, and how these things—objects, buildings, landscapes—relate to people, their bodies, clothes, food, actions, thoughts, and emotions. The series engages and advances theories in "sensuous" and "experiential" religion, as well as informing museum practices and influencing wider cultural understandings with relation to religious objects and performances. Books in the series are at the cutting edge of debates as well as developments in fields including religious studies, anthropology, museum studies, art history, and material culture studies.

Christianity and the Limits of Materiality, edited by Minna Opas and Anna Haapalainen

Figurations and Sensations of the Unseen in Judaism, Christianity and Islam, edited by Birgit Meyer and Terje Stordalen

Food, Festival and Religion, Francesca Ciancimino Howell

Material Devotion in a South Indian Poetic World, Leah Elizabeth Comeau

Qur'anic Matters, Natalia K. Suit

The Religious Heritage Complex, edited by Cyril Isnart and Nathalie Cerezales

Museums of World Religions

Displaying the Divine, Shaping Cultures

Charles D. Orzech

BLOOMSBURY ACADEMIC
LONDON • NEW YORK • OXFORD • NEW DELHI • SYDNEY

BLOOMSBURY ACADEMIC
Bloomsbury Publishing Plc
50 Bedford Square, London, WC1B 3DP, UK
1385 Broadway, New York, NY 10018, USA
29 Earlsfort Terrace, Dublin 2, Ireland

BLOOMSBURY, BLOOMSBURY ACADEMIC and the Diana logo are trademarks of
Bloomsbury Publishing Plc

First published in Great Britain 2020
This paperback edition published in 2021

ISBN: HB: 978-1-3500-1624-8
PB: 978-1-3502-6713-8
ePDF: 978-1-3500-1626-2
eBook: 978-1-3500-1625-5

Series: Bloomsbury Studies in Material Religion

Typeset by Deanta Global Publishing Services, Chennai, India

To find out more about our authors and books visit www.bloomsbury.com and
sign up for our newsletters.

To Mary Ellis Gibson

Contents

Figures

Preface

In the summer of 1969, in order to make money for college, I took a job at Old Sturbridge Village, a popular open-air museum.[1] Located in Sturbridge, Massachusetts, "the village" had started as an antique collection of the industrialist Wells family and, after the Second World War, was transformed into a replica of a late eighteenth- to early nineteenth-century New England village, complete with working mill, blacksmith's shop, and farm. The creation of the village entailed, over time, the purchase, disassembly, and reassembly of buildings from across New England, until a village of some fifty-nine structures was assembled. It is populated with reenactors who by day go about the village as if they live in the late eighteenth century. In the evening they drive home into the twentieth and now the twenty-first century. Occasionally, I thought about the oddity of a museum village, constructed of real eighteenth-century homes and shops and barns, populated by twentieth-century people pretending to be living in 1795. Was it real? How so? Was it a mere simulacra? If anything, it was a twentieth-century arrangement of eighteenth-century objects for twentieth-century purposes.

My interest in museums continued through college and postgraduate degrees, but took a backseat to my professional focus as a specialist in East Asian Buddhism and its South Asian predecessors. The nature of my research kept me engaged with images and rituals and, inevitably, with collections of Buddhist and Daoist images held in museums in Asia, Europe, and in the Americas.

Teaching Buddhism, Asian religions, and various courses on theory and method in the study of religion in North Carolina, I was one of a small group of scholars contacted by Amanda Hughes and Caroline Wood of the Ackland Museum of Art to participate in a three-year series of seminars funded by the Luce Foundation on religious objects held by the Ackland and the possibilities of engaging local religious communities with the museum. The impetus for the project was, in part, due to the plans to increase the size of the museum. The Ackland has a rich collection of religious objects including one of the best collections of South Asian religious sculpture in the United States. How should it be displayed? Was there a way to better integrate local communities into the museum? As a result, Hughes and Wood assembled a group of scholars, curators, and religious leaders to address the issue. The three-year "Five Faiths" colloquium resulted in a handbook for museum professionals edited by Amanda Hughes and Caroline Wood, *A Place for Meaning: Art, Faith, and Museum Culture.*[2]

Ten years later, I moved to the University of Glasgow as Reader in Religion, Conflict, and Transition. There, along with teaching of Buddhism, Asian religions, and various courses on theory in the study of religion, I began an involvement with the St. Mungo Museum of Religious Life and Art as part of programming provided to the museum by my colleagues from Theology and Religious Studies. At the same time, it became increasingly clear that new criteria of the Research Excellence Framework (REF) in the UK specifying that scholarly research have demonstrable "impact" made it very difficult to acquire funding for projects related to my research in medieval Chinese Buddhist liturgy. But my interest in Buddhist and, more broadly, religious objects ensconced in museums led me back to the role of religious objects in their new homes. This interest was also enhanced by conversations with my colleague Victoria Harrison (Philosophy and Education, the University of Glasgow) who had led seminars and workshops on religious objects, museums, and philosophy,[3] and with Bruce Sullivan of Northern Arizona University who asked me to write on world religions museums for his volume *Sacred Objects in Secular Spaces.*[4]

My acquaintance with the St. Mungo Museum of Religious Life and Art led me to explore the genesis of museums of religions, and more specifically museums of religions structured by the principles of the "comparative science of religion" and the popular category "world religions." I soon discovered that such museums of religions had their origins in the comparative disciplines of the late nineteenth century and were thus of a piece with the emergence of global empires and the development of the field of religious studies more broadly.

This study treats five major museums based on comparative principles: the Religionskundliche Sammlung in Marburg, Germany; the State Museum of the History of Religions in St. Petersburg, Russia; Le Musée des Religions du Monde in Nicolet, Québec; the St. Mungo Museum of Religious Life and Art in Glasgow, Scotland; and the Museum of World Religions in Taipei, Taiwan. These comprise Part Two of this study. Although there are other museums that treat religions, these five museums are unique in sharing a worldwide scope and were designed expressly according to knowledge regimes arising from the nineteenth- and twentieth-century comparative religion agenda.[5] Further, these museums all conceive of their current mission as a form of social intervention with the aim of promoting religious tolerance.

Part One prepares the reader to examine these museums by setting them in the context of comparative studies of religion and in recent theoretical discussions concerning our understanding of objects and material religion. My aim is to set out the interpretive episteme of comparative religion through which knowledge about "religion" and "religions" has been produced and circulated, and to suggest alternative ways for museums to mount exhibits of religious objects. Before delving into the five museums, I briefly treat the London Missionary Society Museum, The Pitt Rivers Museum, and the Horniman Museum as illustrations of comparativist techniques of display developed in the late nineteenth and twentieth centuries.

Each museum I examine can be said to be a material definition and narrative which constitutes the object "religion." This approach resists the dominant paradigms and discourses about religions in which spirit and transcendence are primary realities while matter, physical objects, and activities are secondary and derivative. Throughout I have tried to keep a focus not on what the objects, displays, and buildings might "mean" but rather on what is actually present. In this regard I have tried to follow the advice of Bruno Latour that the primary task is to describe all the actors and to trace their activities.

Each of the five museums in this study is really a composite of permanent collections, special exhibitions, and online virtual exhibits and resources. Each museum is a product of modern comparativist understandings of religion and of local politics and notions of identity. I have avoided a lockstep or procrustean approach—each museum has similarities to others as well as its own unique historical and cultural environment. So, the treatments are not completely identical.

The web is now host to an amazing array of sites dealing with "world religions" from those put up by sectarian traditions to college, high school, and GCSE certification sites, to sites provided by the British Museum and the Ashmolean Museum.[6] These virtual exhibits raise questions that go far beyond what can be dealt with in this study, the focus of which is solidly fastened to material objects.

Acknowledgments

Works of scholarship are usually conversations masquerading as monologues. Many people have contributed to this conversation. Discussions began and have continued with my colleagues Gregory Price Grieve, Derek Krueger, and Eugene Rogers of the Religious Studies Department at the University of North Carolina at Greensboro. Victoria Harrison, formerly in Philosophy and Education at the University of Glasgow, now at the University of Macao, prompted me to think more broadly about museums. I have benefited from conversations with George Pattison, David Jasper, Lloyd Ridgeon, Heather Walton, Scott Spurlock, and Mia Spiro—all of Theology and Religious Studies at the University of Glasgow. At Colby College, where I have presented some of this material, I have enjoyed questions and comments from Shalini Le Gall, Dan Cohen, David Freidenreich, Nikky Guninder K. Singh, and David Jorgensen. Bruce Sullivan, formerly of Northern Arizona University, shares both my interest in Buddhism and my interest in museums. Crispin Paine, arguably the authority on religion and museums, has enthusiastically shared his knowledge. Special thanks are owed to my history of religions mentors at the University of Chicago: Joseph M. Kitagawa, Wendy Doniger, Jonathan Z. Smith, Frank Reynolds, and Tony Yu. The insightful comments provided by two anonymous readers led to numerous improvements in the text. I thank them for their contributions.

This project has given me the opportunity to meet many museum curators and professionals. They have been gracious in sharing their knowledge and insights. Amanda Hughes and Caroline Wood, formerly of the Ackland Art Museum, invited me to participate in the Ackland's "Five Faiths" project; Mark O'Neill and Harry Dunlop of Glasgow Life shared their knowledge of the St. Mungo Museum and their expertise more broadly. In St. Petersburg, Marianna Shaknovich of St. Petersburg State University has been an indispensable source of insight about the development of the State Museum of the History of Religions, while Ekaterina Teryukova, the deputy director of the museum, has been unstinting in sharing her knowledge and time. Ekaterina Volkova has twice guided me through the museum. Edith Franke, director of the Religionskundliche Sammlung, and Konstanze Runge, formerly the curator, have welcomed me to Marburg and helped me to understand the complex role of the museum. They have also been wonderful hosts on my visits to Marburg. In Nicolet, Noémie Déschamps, formerly head of expositions of Le Musée des Religions du Monde, spent several hours with me answering my questions about the history and operation of the museum. Mathieu Fortin who is in charge of the educational operations of the museum has graciously helped with arrangements of visits and provision of images. Michèle Paradis who helped found the museum provided valuable insights concerning the early goals of the museum. Chen Kuo-Ning, director of the Museum of World Religions in Taipei, and Fan Min-Chen were essential in helping me arrange a visit and have a detailed tour. I also thank each of the museums for providing images and permissions for their use in this volume.

Preliminary research and travel for this project has been supported by research incentive grants from the University of Glasgow and the Carnegie Trust. A major research fellowship from the Leverhulme Trust provided funds for travel and release from teaching and administrative duties in 2016–17. Colby College has made further travel to the UK possible. I am indebted to these institutions—the project would not have been possible without their support.

Editors at Bloomsbury, especially Ms. Lucy Carroll, Ms. Lalle Pursglove, and Ms. Camilla Erskine, have been very supportive, patient, and understanding. Leela Ulaganathan, senior project manager at Deanta Global, expertly guided production.

Finally, I wish to thank Professor Mary Ellis Gibson for reading the entire manuscript and for her support, conversation, and insight, and Emily Orzech for her encouragement.

Part One

Displaying the Divine:
Religious Objects and Comparison

Comparative Religion and World Religions Museums

Museums devoted to religions are new and, for many people, exotic kinds of places. Where did they come from? Unlike church treasuries, such institutions are designed as public places, and they perform complex social and political roles.[1] Museums devoted to religions—*plural*—to comparative religion, or to world religions are inseparable from the notion of religion itself. Yet many visitors to these museums would be surprised to hear that the idea of a thing "religion," encompassing what Catholics, Vaiṣṇavas, Shi'ia Muslims, or contemporary Wiccans do, is a relatively recent innovation. In the sense we think about them in the early twenty-first century, both religion and museums are products of the global empires that emerged in the eighteenth and nineteenth centuries.

The title of this book, and particularly the three words—World Religions Museums—presents many difficulties. Two of the museums I study here—Le Musée des Religions du Monde in Nicolet, Québec, and the Museum of World Religions in Taipei—designate themselves museums of world religions. All of the museums and many of the exhibits I will discuss in the following chapters use the term "world religions" in their self-descriptions or offer tours and exhibits about world religions. Some of the museum curators I have talked with reject the term as an inaccurate characterization of their institutions. But even those museums that eschew the term are forced to produce materials for schools and to mount exhibits that have adopted the widespread and popular category. Perhaps a more accurate designation for the institutions I treat in this book would be "Comparative Religion Museums," but this has the appearance of a technical jargon. World Religions is now instantly recognizable in English and appears immediately meaningful. Thus, I have chosen to problematize the term "world religions" rather than to banish a term now so firmly ensconced in popular consciousness and media.

This chapter will examine the emergence of the comparative science of religion and the notion of world religions, its theories, its intellectual and material construction, and its circulation in conferences, exhibitions, textbooks, and museums. I will argue that the comparative religion approach—forged as an adjunct to empire and now canonical—is beset by contradictions and ambiguity. In contrast to anthropology, a field that also arose in the context of colonial empires and whose object of study is human beings, comparative religion, also known as history of religions, or religious studies, originated as the shadow of Protestant Christianity and its object of study is "divinity," "spirit," or the "transcendent."² Thus its founding assumptions hobble the study of objects, distort the public presentation and understanding of religions, and pose problems for teachers and museum curators. In the next chapter I will consider new approaches to objects as "religious" and provide a different way of thinking about objects in museums. Part Two of this volume examines five museums based on the comparative religion approach and suggests alternative ways to frame museum displays of religious objects.

The Idea of Religion(s)

Are the objects placed in museum collections and exhibits focused on "religion," to be understood as exemplifying religion, or religions? Is there a single underlying reality designated by the term "religion" of which the objects in question are so many instantiations, or are there many different cultural forms or systems which *we* have chosen for analytic purposes to designate as religions? The question, and the taxonomic disparity it indicates, takes a central role in the emergence of the notion of religion from the Enlightenment onward. The distinction between religion and religions bears directly on how museums frame their objects—on how they label them and how they configure them.

In a 1982 essay, Jonathan Z. Smith made the provocative argument that religion is a recent invention:

> If we have understood the archaeological and textual record correctly, man [*sic*] has had his entire history in which to imagine deities and modes of interaction within them. But man, more precisely western man, has had only the last few centuries in which to imagine religion. That is to say, while there is a staggering amount of data, phenomena, of human experiences and expressions that might be characterized in one culture or another, by one criterion or another, as religion—there is no data for religion. . . . Religion is solely the creation of the

scholar's study. It is created for the scholar's analytic purposes by his imaginative acts of comparison and generalization. Religion has no existence apart from the academy.[3]

This claim at first seems counterintuitive. After all, the term "religion" is now used worldwide wherever English is spoken or written. English language newspapers in South and East Asia use the term "religion," and the English websites of religious studies programs can be found at universities around the world. Yet, despite the almost universal adoption of the term in English in the modern period, even a cursory look at the history of the term demonstrates that this usage is new. Premodern usage of the term "religion" overwhelmingly refers to Christian and mostly Catholic vows or the taking of holy orders.[4] The first documented use of the plural term "religions" appears in 1593 in the work of the Anglican theologian Richard Hooker as a term encompassing Protestants and some Catholics.[5] In short, the English terms "religion" and "religions" in their current usage begin as higher order classifiers made necessary by changing sectarian political demands in England brought about by the Reformation. In the course of the great colonial expansion that followed, the taxonomy of religion was deployed to encompass beliefs and practices worldwide.

Max Müller (1823–1900), often cited today as the key figure in the creation of the comparative science of religion (*religionswissenschaft*), predicted in 1870 that "a science of religion, based on a comparison of all, or, at all events, of the most important religions of mankind, is now only a question of time."[6] But which religions were "most important" and what exactly is religion? What work does the designation "religion" or "religions" actually do? Why compare religions at all? How can religions be compared? To what ends? As currently used in textbooks and museums, religion functions as a system to distinguish whether this or that practice or idea is "religious" or not. Two ritual practices can thus be classified as belonging to the taxa "religion," be compared, and be deemed similar, and, if not, one or both might be excluded. For instance, in one museum repetitive behavior involved in Christian prayer is deemed religious, as is Buddhist meditation, as is the repetition of the name of god in Islam. All three are deemed to have similar aims. Religion as a taxonomy, therefore, lays down a hegemonic comparative grid, and comparison is the mechanism that produces a homogenous space as well as its own object of study, "religion." From this point of view, before this taxonomic innovation there was no generic "religion" corresponding to its modern usage. There was only truth versus error, orthodoxy versus heterodoxy—a heterogeneous space.

For some, the new understanding of religion appeared to validate rare earlier ecumenical notions. A quotation attributed to Sikh Guru Gobind Singh (1666–1708), prominently displayed at the Museum of World Religions in Taipei, proclaims: "The same Reality is the creator and preserver of all; Know no distinctions between them, The monastery and the mosque are the same; So is the Hindu worship and the Muslim prayer. Humans are all one!"[7] Gobind Singh's perspective has gained considerable currency with the twentieth-century advent of ecumenical ideas. For many—including many visitors who have left comments at the St. Mungo Museum of Religious Life and Art—all paths lead to a single truth. That truth in its current incarnation has been "formulated by theosophists, Christian ecumenicists, comparative religionists, and the 'perennial philosophy' of Aldous Huxley."[8]

Not everyone, however, is flattered by such ecumenical assertions. Museums of world religions must contend with a legacy comprising Gobind Singh's "all religions are one"; mediated positions deriving from the historicizing of Christianity; and the counterclaims of orthodox exclusivist traditions. Although Christian missionaries were among the main contributors of data to the new comparative science of religion, the implication of a science in which Christianity is classified as one religion among other religions—even in comparisons designed to promote the superiority of Christianity—was not lost either on partisans of Christianity or on its critics. Early work by Pierre Bayle (1647–1706) who had the temerity to criticize pagan myth on the basis of rational and historical criteria was itself criticized for the implied comparison between pagan myths and Christianity. From the perspective of the defenders of the uniqueness of biblical faith, Bayle's work "supported Christianity as a rope supports a hanged man."[9] The rejection of comparison implied in the notion of "religions" was parodied by Henry Fielding in *The History of Tom Jones, a Foundling* (1749) when the Revered Thwackum opines, "nor is religion manifold, because there are various sects and heresies in the world. When I mention religion, I mean the Christian religion; and not only the Christian religion, but the Protestant religion; and not only the Protestant religion, but the Church of England."[10]

Between Gobind Singh's optimism about a unitary truth underlying all religions and Thwackum's sectarian certainty lay the muddy waters of Bayle's rationalism and the Higher Criticism of the Bible. It is no wonder that George Eliot's answer to Fielding's Thwackum, the Reverend Casaubon, labored unsuccessfully for decades on his forever incomplete "key to all mythologies." *Middlemarch, A Study of Provincial Life* (1871–72) lampoons the efforts of the Reverend Casaubon to finish his magnum opus.[11] The leveling and historicizing implications of comparative method for Christianity were hard to avoid. The theologian Ernst Troeltsch (1865–1923), writing in his *The Place of Christianity among the World Religions* (originally published in 1923, shortly after his death), concluded that all religions are culturally contingent and therefore that Christianity is merely one among the world religions (though it may be the best for "us").[12]

In concert with ecumenical and perennialist assertions, religious studies, in producing a homogeneous comparative space, has long asserted that religion is a category sui generis and that the sacred or the holy cannot be reduced to culture, anthropology, psychology, history, cultural studies, and so forth. This assertion has been the touchstone of the field of religious studies throughout the twentieth century.[13] As it now exists, many of us who study religions do so with tools borrowed from these other disciplines. But the fact that the category is a scholarly construct does not necessarily obviate its usefulness in studying cultures past or present.[14] Indeed, as T. Griffith Foulk points out regarding the analysis of Chinese Buddhist lineages:

> It is sometimes objected that historians, especially intellectual or religious historians, should not impose their own categories on the foreign cultures they study. . . . However, when it comes time to explain and interpret what one has learned using one's own language and operating within the constraints of one's own academic discipline, it is manifestly impossible to use only concepts borrowed from the foreign tradition that is the object of study. In plain English, it is absurd to argue that because medieval Chinese Buddhists never drew a distinction between lineages as semi-mythological entities and schools as historical ones we should refrain from imposing that distinction on them.[15]

Foulk's caution applies to other labels as well, such as "Buddhism," "Hinduism," and "Confucianism," all of which have been shown to be synthetic terms that emerged in encounters with the West, and all of which have been widely adopted.[16] Nevertheless, if we are not careful, the unspoken (or spoken) assumptions that accompany a category can lead to problems. "It is impossible not to conclude," writes Timothy Fitzgerald,

> from reading Sharpe's reliable account of the origins of the modern study of religion in his *Comparative Religion: A History* (1986) that the guiding concept lying behind the thought of almost all the founding fathers, and usually quite explicitly stated, is that of a transcendent intelligent Being who gives meaning and purpose to human history.[17]

Thus, "comparative religion in its various guises as the science of religion, the phenomenology of religion, and religious studies has been fundamentally imbued with theological principles of the liberal ecumenical kind."[18] This is not to say that the notion of the transcendent or the sacred cannot be a proper object of study. Rather, for historians its proper context is human, not divine realities.

For those who reject any comparison among religions, there is but a single truth—all other "religions" are fictions, and any other form of religion than their own is a form of blasphemy at worst or ignorance at best. Yet for those who accept the category "religions" and the comparison that underlies it, the many religions can be understood as more or less adequate refractions of a single underlying truth. For others who accept the category, all religions are viewed as purely historical—the products of cultural and scholarly construction. Museums of religions based on the comparative or world religions model inhabit this ambiguous and contradictory space. While the theological assumptions of the field are now well understood in the scholarly community, such assumptions continue to have an impact on the understanding and treatment of religious objects in museum displays, and on visitors who view these objects. In short, if the proper object of the study of religion is the transcendent, what then of religious objects?[19]

World Religions

In one way or another each of the museums I treat in Part Two of this study employs the category "world religions" and assumes the comparative religion project. In doing so, these museums aim to promote cultural education, interreligious tolerance, and dialogue. But they are doing so on the basis of knowledge regimes that embody contradictions and ambiguities.

If "religion" is a problematic category, "world religions" is yet more problematic. What differentiates a world religion from another sort of religion, and how many world religions are there? Are there three, five, seven, eight, ten, or more religions so designated? What are the criteria for inclusion in the set of world religions? Is inclusion reserved for those religions with the largest total number of adherents? What is the cutoff point, below which a religion is not a world religion? Is membership in the set reserved for those religions having a global reach (Islam, Christianity, Buddhism) through missionizing and a universalist message (as opposed to religions that are based on ethnicity such as Hinduism or Judaism)? Is the status conveyed by a tradition's reliance on texts?

The most common current lists of world religions include Christianity, Islam, Buddhism, Judaism, and Hinduism, and it is these five which comprise, for example, the permanent exhibit at Le Musée des Religions du Monde and which dominate many textbook treatments.

Many museum visitors will take the notion of world religions for granted. Certainly, many educational structures have prepared the public to view world religions as a natural category. The world religions model is pervasive in North American and European university and secondary curricula and is now being emulated worldwide. It is often used to structure academic departments.[20] Thus, in Britain it is common to find departments of "Theology and Religious Studies" whose two wings offer courses pertaining to the "Abrahamic religions" of Christianity, Judaism, and Islam, and the "World Religions" (usually Buddhism, Hinduism, and Chinese religions) respectively.

After the Second World War, European and North American universities, colleges, and schools saw the widespread establishment of religion departments—many of which have now been renamed as religious studies departments—with the change indicative of a curriculum departing from traditional theological education models. Court rulings in the United States concerning the separation of church and state banished theologically based curricula from public institutions while allowing education *about* religion in those very same public institutions. Thus, in the pivotal case *Abington v. Shempp* (1963) in which prayer in public schools was deemed unconstitutional, Associate Justice Tom Clark wrote:

> It might well be said that one's education is not complete without a study of comparative religion or the history of religion and its relationship to the advancement of civilization. It certainly may be said that the Bible is worthy of study for its literary and historic qualities. Nothing we have said here indicates that such study of the Bible or of religion, when presented objectively as part of a secular program of education may not be effected consistently with the First Amendment.[21]

Influential programs for the comparative study of religion were already developing at private institutions of higher learning. The 1963 ruling opened the door for public universities to institute programs in comparative religions as well. By the late 1960s, the University of Chicago, Harvard, Princeton, University of California Santa Barbara, and others were graduating PhDs trained in comparative religion or the history of religion (as it was known at Chicago). At the same time, these and other institutions trained young scholars in the historical, sociological, and anthropological study of religion as a part of culture.

Although one might have primary competence in American Christianity or in Hinduism, for example, these programs prepared students to teach broadly and comparatively, introducing students to the history of the field and its emergence in the nineteenth-century comparative disciplines. Students often found jobs in small colleges or regional universities where it was expected they would teach introductory and survey courses in world religions. Thus, "comparative religion" or simply "religious studies" became the broad disciplinary umbrella in the second half of the twentieth century, and "world religions" became the popular face of comparative religion.

Textbooks produced for the English-speaking world from the 1950s onward tell the tale both of the growing place of world religions in the curriculum and the growing critique of the category toward the end of the twentieth century. Among the most popular are texts such as Huston Smith's *The World's Religions* (originally titled *The Religions of Man*, now in its fiftieth anniversary edition) and Willard Oxtoby's *A Concise Introduction to World Religions*.[22] The titles demonstrate a certain uneasiness with the term "world religions," and some texts offer the same organization rebranded using the same phrasing—the world's religions—that Max Müller used more than a century earlier. The uneasiness is well founded, but the more inclusive sounding "the world's religions" is an evasion. The contents of such texts seldom depart from the categories established at the end of the nineteenth century. The term "world religions" was recently chosen for the title of *The Norton Anthology of World Religions*. Its two volumes cover Hinduism, Buddhism, and Daoism (volume 1) and Judaism, Christianity, and Islam (volume 2).[23] A search of the Amazon website results in some twenty volumes on world religions, and it is notable that Amazon classifies all such books under the heading "Comparative Religion (Books)."

If we examine a recent and, generally, excellent textbook, *Religions of the World: An Introduction to Culture and Meaning* (2011) produced under the general editorship of Lawrence E. Sullivan (a scholar trained at Chicago who led the team from Harvard that helped design the Museum of World Religions in Taipei), we can see the more inclusive-sounding term "religions of the world" being used instead of the term "world religions."[24] The initial chapter, "Indigenous Religious Traditions," was written by Robin M. Wright. The chapter begins by signaling discomfort with the world religions paradigm and with the notion of religion itself.[25] Nonetheless, the book's structure—single chapters on Indigenous Religions, Hinduism, Buddhism, Jainism, Sikhism, Daoism, Confucianism, Shinto, and Judaism, followed by individual chapters on Early Christian Foundations, Roman Catholicism, Orthodox Christianity, and Protestant Christianity, and then followed by individual chapters on Islam, Zoroastrianism, and new religions—begs several questions. Why a multi-chapter treatment of Christianity but not of Islam or Buddhism or Jainism or Judaism, and so on? Why begin with "Indigenous Religions" followed by chapters on Asian religions, followed by Judaism, then chapters on Christianity, and so on? Is the structure historical? Is it in some sense developmental? Is it some combination of both? Sullivan explains in the preface that the book's structure divides the world geographically into religions originating in South Asia, East Asia, and the Mediterranean (the "Abrahamic" religions of Judaism, Christianity, and Islam). In addition are the "indigenous" traditions.[26] Despite the geographic pluralism, the world religions typology has since the nineteenth century tended to encode a hierarchy. Religions are treated as "Abrahamic" or "Asian," and as originating in the Near East (Judaism, Christianity, Islam), South Asia (Hinduism, Buddhism), and the Far East (Confucianism, Daoism, Shinto). The remaining "little traditions" are grouped variously under the categories such as "tribal," "minority," "animistic," "primitive," or "indigenous" religions if they are accorded the status of religion at all. The world religions typology can all too easily be understood as implying a hierarchy—whatever the intent of the author—since given limited time (or, in a museum, limited space) these "little traditions" are dealt with cursorily, as simple precursors to religions proper, or not at all. This division resembles that of world religions texts stretching back a century and originates with the comparative science of religion in the colonial period.

In addition to the problems of inclusion and exclusion world religions textbooks, like world religions museums, must deal with the issue of comparison. The description of the textbook on the Amazon site claims that such world religions texts typically take "either historical or phenomenological approaches," and that "this new survey text for comparative religion . . . successfully marries traditional approaches with analysis drawn from anthropology and sociology to explain the making of meaning in leading religious traditions."[27] Some of the chapters are more historically oriented, others more phenomenological, yet others have a more anthropological or sociological focus. The anthropological forms of analysis involve attention to ritual process, life-cycle rites (rites of passage), and so on that have been hallmarks of comparative religion and anthropology since the work of Arnold van Gennep in the early twentieth century.[28]

In Sullivan's textbook, for instance, the widely used typology of "life-cycle rites" or "rites of passage" appears in some of the chapters. This typology is a prominent feature of many introductory courses and textbooks on world religions and of the museums I examine in Part Two of this study. The life-cycle rites typology compares rituals by appealing to broad similarities. Thus we find rites classified as conception rites, prenatal rites, birth rites, maturation rites, marriage rites, death rites, and so on. In this taxonomic regime Confirmation is classified with Bar and Bat Mitzvah. What does this actually tell us about these rites? Are we to assume that the meanings of the Catholic Confirmation and the Jewish Bar Mitzvah are the same? In what way are they the same? How are they different? Even more problematic, can the investiture of the sacred thread (*upanayana*) for upper caste Hindu boys be equated with or substituted for Confirmation and Bar Mitzvah? Are the similarities illuminating, or does the comparative grid flatten all difference by reducing all three rites to the lowest common denominator—coming of age rites?

The shape of these secondary and university textbooks and of religious studies programs reflects the institutionalization of and market for world religions and the virtual canonization of the comparative science of religion. Since the 1980s there have been a series of critiques of the world religions model, but such critiques have been slow to erode institutional wisdom.[29] Although such comparative tools are now canonical, it is imperative that we step back and understand the history of their development, the assumptions and blind spots entailed in them, and what might be the consequences of deploying them in exhibits of religious objects.

World Religions and Ideal Types

Why is there such confusion and discomfort surrounding the designation world religions? The difficulty lies—in large part—with the fact that "world religions" as a *typological scheme* is haunted by nineteenth-century theological and social-evolutionary biases. Typologies are used in many fields and are designed by observation of similarities and differences of appearance, function, or other characteristics to help classify phenomena into manageable groups and to discern or assert underlying connections and regularities. Like the periodic table in chemistry or Linnaean classification, typologies are an attempt at discerning universal regularities. Typologies were used in the early church to draw relationships between events and figures in the Hebrew Scriptures that were seen as prophecies of New Testament events. They are still widely employed in Christian liturgy. For example, many Christians regard the offering of Isaac as a type of Christ's sacrifice, or Jonah's sojourn in the belly of a fish as a type of Christ's death and resurrection. In the development of comparative religion various typologies have been proposed, including types of religions (world religions, ethnic religions), types of rituals (calendrical, life cycle, etc.), types of religious authority (reformer, prophet, priest, seer, magician, etc.). Some comparative religion theorists have argued that carefully constructed typologies can help us perceive the sacred reality that is hidden by the multiplicity of phenomena. Others see the development of typologies as heuristic tools for managing historical data and deny that typologies have any ontological validity.

Typologies and their creation and application have been a core feature of the study of religion from its inception. When Kant in his *Religion within the Limits of Bare Reason* (1793) posits that a natural religion based on reason alone is the truly "universal world-religion" (*weltreligion*), he distinguishes an ideal type (religion) from its instantiations (religions).[30] A similar distinction between ideal types and instantiations is found in *The Metamorphosis of Plants* (1790), the work of Kant's contemporary Johann Wolfgang von Goethe.[31] For Goethe, the distinction was as follows:

> If I look at the created object, inquire into its creation, and follow this process back as far as I can, I will find a series of steps. Since these are not actually seen together before me, I must visualize them in my memory so that they form a certain ideal whole.[32]

Whether one regards such an ideal whole as the product of strictly mental composition, whether it is taken as evidence of genealogical or evolutionary development, or whether it is considered an ideal type approximating or representing a transcendent reality, Goethe's ideal whole has been an invitation to and an inspiration for theorists of religions.

Nineteenth-century accounts of religion often created typologies that implicitly or explicitly privileged Western, and particularly Christian, religion over all others. As early as 1827 Chantepie de la Saussaye distinguished "religions of the world" from "national" religions, and this distinction was further articulated in Cornelis Petrus Tiele's *Outline of the History of Religion to the Spread of Universal Religion* (1876).[33] There, the "universal" religions were reckoned as Christianity, Buddhism, and Islam, while all others including Judaism and the various Hindu and Chinese religions are categorized as "national." Tiele's developmental scheme moves from animism through national religions through pantheism and monotheism to "universal or world religions."[34] Tiele's goal "was not so much a grouping of religious phenomena as a critical evaluation of what in his view, on the highest level of development, were the essential manifestations of religion."[35]

Like Tiele, most of the founders of the discipline of comparative religion were pastors or theologians. Even Max Müller, widely credited with presenting his new science as free of sectarian influences, assumed a universal sensibility of god:

> However imperfect, however childish a religion may be, it always places the human soul in the presence of God; and however imperfect and however childish the conception of God may be, it always represents the highest ideal of perfection which the human soul, for the time being, can reach and grasp.[36]

Thus, for Müller as for many other advocates of typological analyses of religion, there is a clear developmental hierarchy. What was true in the first generation of theoreticians was also true of the following generations.[37]

Some scholars in the early twentieth century—Rudolf Otto, Mircea Eliade, Gerardus van der Leeuw, for example—deployed typology in an attempt to delineate or intuit the essence of the "sacred"; the sui generis transcendent object of religion by careful attention to its manifestations.[38] Their assumption was that the religions represent historically differentiated refractions of or discrete "steps" or parts of an archetypal reality, and that by careful observation one can build up a vision of that reality. The work of the influential comparativist Mircea Eliade was directly inspired by Goethe's approach to plant morphology.[39] Eliade originally proposed "The Morphology of the Sacred" as the title for what became *Patterns in Comparative Religion*, and his aim was to delineate sacred reality by careful observation of its "hierophanies" or manifestations.[40] Eliade's work focused on finding similarities or patterns behind the multiplicity of religious phenomena. *Patterns in Comparative Religion* treated such topics as "The Sky and Sky Gods," "Sacred Stones," "Vegetation Rites and Symbols of Regeneration," and so on, by arraying an almost encyclopedic range of data from across the globe and throughout human history.[41] As we will see, this kind of thinking is materially instantiated in museums of world religions. In Eliade's words:

> I do not mean that every hierophany and every religious experience whatsoever is a unique and never-to-be-repeated incident in the working of the spirit. The greatest experiences are not only alike in content, but often also alike in their expression. Rudolf Otto discovered some astonishing similarities between the vocabulary and formulae of Meister Eckhardt and those of Śaṅkara.[42]

Here Eliade, discovering a *weltreligion* essence in differing objects, rituals, and texts, judged some experiences more significant than others. Eliade invoked the authority of the theologian Rudolf Otto, who sought to show how objects helped to intuit the "numinous." Otto was the progenitor of the Religionskundliche

Sammlung in Marburg, Germany, treated later. His aim was to present objects from various religions for their value in evoking a sense of the "numinous."

Typology, however, need not be founded on theological assumptions. In contrast to this approach, other scholars following the sociologist Max Weber saw ideal types as purely analytic constructs. For Weber,

> an ideal type is formed by the one-sided *accentuation* of one or more points of view and by the synthesis of a great many diffuse, discrete, more or less present and occasionally absent *concrete individual* phenomena, which are arranged according to those one-sidedly emphasized viewpoints into a unified *analytical* construct (*Gedankenbild*). In its conceptual purity, this mental construct (*Gedankenbild*) cannot be found empirically anywhere in reality.[43]

Rather than trying to use typology to intuit a transcendent immaterial sacred, Weber's sociological approach sees it as a heuristic device used to explore and bring order to the welter of concrete historical data. Weberian typology explicitly denies transcendent ontological claims.[44] From the Weberian perspective, attributing ontological status to a typology runs the risk of confusing sociological and historical analytical tools with prior assumptions based on ideology.

Imperial Science: World Religions and European Universalism

A critique of comparative religion is that, in fashioning its typological systems and comparisons, many of its practitioners have assumed that behind the multiplicity of manifestations lies a unitary spiritual or transcendent reality. Types are then arranged in a hierarchy according to their perceived approach to this transcendent reality. The transcendent reality has all too often conformed to liberal Protestant notions and biases. The selection and placement of objects in collections, as well as their anchoring labels or explanatory text, were subject to existing and emerging knowledge regimes. Jonathan Z. Smith has proposed a Weberian-style typology to capture these knowledge regimes. Smith delineated "four modes or styles of comparison" based on attitudes about colonial "others" (they are "like" or "not like" us).[45] Smith labels these ethnographic, encyclopedic, morphological, and evolutionary.[46] Smith characterizes the ethnographic form of comparison as, at base, "traveler's accounts." "Such comparisons," according to Smith, "are idiosyncratic, depending upon intuition, a chance association, or the knowledge one happens to have at the moment of another culture."[47] Many museum collections were, and some still are, driven by such ad hoc acquisitions and modes of display. Encyclopedic comparisons "offered a topical arrangement of cross-cultural material (arranged either by subject matter or alphabetically) culled from reading."[48] Lists, whether arranged under some arbitrary scheme such as the alphabet or "the use of contextless lists held together by mere surface associations rather than careful, specific, and meaningful comparisons with the interest in exotic content has plagued the encyclopaedic tradition until the present time."[49] A museum organized along such lines resembles a filing cabinet or a library for objects that are stored according to some indexing system to be consulted when necessary. In Smith's scheme, the third type, morphological comparisons, tends to be synchronic and focuses on similarity of structure or appearance and comparisons are drawn between a posited ideal type and individual instances or between individual examples with an eye to the ideal type.[50] A museum or exhibit so organized would group objects based on formal similarity stripping away cultural and historical context.

Finally, evolutionary forms of comparison were inspired by the work of comparative anatomists including Buffon, Cuvier, Lamarck, and Darwin. Such comparisons tend to be diachronic and focus on development. These thinkers "drew the implication that an increased complexity reflected a process of growth, adaptation, and evolution."[51] But the addition of a temporal dimension led to an effacement of the morphological notion of arrangement according to more or less complexity without reference to history.[52] In the development of the comparative science of religion this evolutionary approach tended to equate simplicity of form with temporal priority and complexity with development as "detection of simplicity now yielded historical origins (e.g., 'the primitive') rather than 'logical' Urformen."[53] Thus, while ethnographic, encyclopedic, and morphological forms of comparison can fix on superficial similarities and differences, the evolutionary approach was widely used to affirm transcendentalist and racial biases. No single comparative religion museum over the course of its history fully conforms to one or another of these types. Rather, Smith's scheme can serve as a useful tool to alert us to comparativist agendas behind the displays of religious objects.[54]

The new science of comparative religion and the institutions that disseminated the findings of this science, such as exhibitions, museums, and publications, were the products of global imperialism and were deeply entwined with notions of racial evolutionism. In nineteenth-century comparative religion, accidents of history became dehistoricized and presented as a teleological progress toward the spiritual and away from material. Religious things—objects—at best were thought to point to transcendent reality. At worst, the "fetishes" and "totems" of "savages" were presented as evidence for idolatry and associated with the "backward" or "lower" races.

The methods and theories of this new science were worked out and circulated in what David Chidester has called a "triple mediation" between indigenous "savages" in Africa, exotic colonial subjects in South and East Asia, and the imperial center.[55] "This triple mediation mixed and merged in complex ways in the formation of the study of religion."[56] Methods of comparison and the typologies devised in the imperial milieu still shape the discourses about religions in the twenty-first century and continue to have an impact on how religious objects are displayed.

The emergence of comparative sciences (geology, anatomy, zoology, etc.) took place in the context of expanding European empires in the mid-nineteenth century. The idea of evolution in the theories of Darwin and especially those of Lamarck seemed to offer an explanation for the conditions found in the colonial field. Neo-Lamarckians

> pictured evolution as marking inevitable progress toward a goal. The goal of evolution within nature had been the human being. With this natural model firmly in place, there was little difficulty in imagining that human life was evolving toward a more complex goal—and that some human groups had made more progress toward it than had others.[57]

This popular neo-Lamarckian form of evolutionism appeared more obvious than Darwin's theories and seemed to confirm differences in material culture, and technological development. As John Burris has argued, "The widespread popular acceptance of evolutionary theory in general was primarily due to the fact that it could be used to interpret cultural differences in a way advantageous to the West."[58] Thus, the comparative science of religion tended, in the hands of many of its pioneers, to be deployed in affirming an evolutionary hierarchy in which Western religions were deemed the most advanced, usually because they claimed to worship an immaterial transcendent deity, while less advanced religions worshipped material objects. The argument mirrored that used by Protestants to denigrate Catholics as idolaters.

Although comparative religion opened the road to dethroning biblical religion, Tomoko Masuzawa has argued that world religions took its place as a "reconstituted European universalism."[59] This discourse was shaped by efforts to "distinguish the West from the rest."[60] For example, Max Müller, writing in 1894, discerned eight religions of the world as defined by their possession of sacred scriptures:

There are, after all, not so many religions in the world as people imagine. There are only eight great historical religions which can claim that name on the strength of their possessing sacred books. All these religions came from the East; three from an Aryan, three from a Semitic source, and two from China. The three Aryan religions are the Vedic, with its modern offshoots in India, the Avestic of Zoroaster in Persia, and the religion of Buddha, likewise the off spring of Brahmanism in India. The three great religions of Semitic origin are the Jewish, the Christian, and the Mohammedan. There are, besides, the two Chinese religions, that of Confucius and that of Lao-tse, and that is all; unless we assign a separate place to such creeds as Gainism, a near relative of Buddhism, which was ably represented at Chicago, or the religion of the Sikhs, which is after all but a compromise between Brahmanism and Mohammedanism.[61]

Müller's taxonomy is based on the problematic assumption that all of these traditions regard certain texts as "sacred." But the status of texts both among and within the traditions listed varies widely, and it is clear that the category sacred text is modeled broadly on Christian tradition. Further, by making texts the defining characteristic of religion, Müller excludes the possibility of nonliterate societies having religion. "Savages" in Africa or the Americas by definition had no religion or, at best, no "great religion."

At base, Müller's science of comparative religion implied "that the great civilizations of the past and present divide into two: venerable East on the one hand and progressive West on the other. They both have been called 'historical,' but implicitly in different senses . . . the East preserves history, the West creates history (active). In contradistinction from both East and West, the tertiary group of minor religions has been considered lacking in history, or at least lacking in written history, hence its designation as preliterate . . . these societies are relegated to a position in some sense before history or at the very beginning of history, hence, primal."[62] In short, the apparent admission of "other" religious traditions to the club of religion was accomplished at the expense of equality. All are human perceptions of the divine, but the difference that counts privileges "the West over the rest."[63]

Comparative Religions in Imperial Discourse and Display: From Civilized versus Savage to God versus Fetish

The nineteenth and early twentieth century saw the vast expansion of empires—British, American, German, Dutch, Russian, and Japanese. The historical understanding of imperial activity tends to focus on conflicts, colonies, raw materials, and so forth. But it has become increasingly clear that a key component of imperial projects entailed the creation, collection, classification, production, control, and display of knowledge. Research about the colonies was useful in governing them and led to displays at the metropolitan center in exhibitions and museums. "Imperialism," notes David Chidester, "depended not only on military force, political control, and economic exploitation; it also required accumulating and archiving information." All of the colonial powers—British, Germans, Japanese, and so on—assiduously assembled information on rituals, belief, folklore, and customs of the peoples they ruled.[64] This process was far from being mere curiosity. Developing scholarship on the European past provided templates for mastering both the past and the present of colonial subjects. Thus, as Steven Connor has shown, intellectual mastery of ancient Western mythology held out the promise "of being able to exercise the same power over the subject races who were the producers of such mythologies."[65] Like imperial exhibitions, imperial comparative religion collected, condensed, and displayed the empire as a sign of its global scope and domination. Max Müller, in his lectures of 1870, was not shy about the nature of this endeavor. "Let us take the old saying, *Divide et imperia*, and translate it somewhat freely by 'Classify and conquer.'"[66] David Chidester argues in his *Empire of Religion*:

> In the empire of religion . . . imperial theory operated with a distinction, sometimes explicit, often implicit, between text-based "world religions" and savage religions, a distinction duplicating the bifurcated system of colonial governance that established different laws for racialized citizens and ethnic, tribal, or savage subjects. Imperial theory established different methods of inquiry into the citizens of world religions and the subjects of savage religions.[67]

This comparative science of religion evolved in and was codependent with a vast web of colonial officials, missionaries, botanizers, collectors, traders, and transportation networks, through which the raw materials of the ruled territories were turned into "intellectual manufactured goods" and funneled for display, discussion, and consumption at exhibitions, in international scholarly meetings, and in newly established museums in London, Berlin, Tokyo, St. Petersburg, and elsewhere.[68] Comparative religion was born in what Germain Bazin dubbed the "museum age."[69]

"Cabinets of curiosities" (*kunstkammer*) had proliferated early in the period of the rise of global empires. These predecessors of museums presented "a universe peopled with strange beings and objects, where anything could happen, and where, consequently, every question could legitimately be posed. In other words, it was a universe to which corresponded a type of curiosity no longer controlled by theology and not yet controlled by science."[70] But by the nineteenth century, imperial regimes regarded exhibitions and museums as a kind of dynastic palladia. Like palladia the new imperial exhibitions and museums rendered visibly and materially empire and its newly developing "superior" scientific and technological regimes.[71]

Over the course of the second half of the nineteenth century, imperial regimes also produced a social-evolutionary view of "races." Toward the end of the century and during the beginning of the next the comparative science of religion rendered religious evolution visible and tangible in museums and exhibitions. The paradigmatic exhibition was England's Crystal Palace or Great Exhibition of 1851. The exhibition spawned a series of follow-on exhibitions in Britain, on the continent, in the United States, and in the colonies. In the case of the British Empire,

> Exhibitions organizers and displays were at the core of a participatory system, constructing a tripartite imperial world of "England," "India," or subject colonies, and "Australia," or settler societies. Each provided distinctive and complementary exhibits of machinery, commercial goods, workers, ethnography, and public history. Australia stood for other white-settler communities, such as Canada and Southern Africa; India was the dominant image of subject colonies, which included the West Indies and much of sub-Saharan Africa by the time of Rudyard Kipling's Empire at the turn of the twentieth century. Exhibitions were intended to promote external commonwealth and internal nationalism, differing forms of cooperative federation, rather than competition among and within those communities.[72]

With little or no reference to religion early exhibitions presented "idols" and displayed "savage customs" alongside handicrafts and natural "curiosities." Indeed, it appears that the typology most common in the mid-nineteenth century involved a contrast between "civilized" and "savage" with a growing awareness of colonial others represented by South and East Asian "heathens." By the 1870s, however, new ideas about race and the emerging category "religions" were circulating among scholars and intellectuals. By the time of the Colonial and Indian Exhibition of 1886, held in South Kensington adjacent to the Royal Albert Hall, religions had become a well-established category.[73] The catalog of that exhibition demonstrates a sophisticated comparative use of the term. For example, it notes that "Sikh religion which, like Mahommedanism, excludes all iconic forms, or what are commonly termed idols, from its worship."[74] In discussing displays from New Zealand visitors were informed that a "new religion, called Hau-hau" had been formed.[75]

By the time of the World's Columbian Exposition held in Chicago in 1893 we can see "religions" established as a category distinct from but parallel to "culture" as deployed by the newly consolidating field of ethnology/anthropology. The exhibition, like its British predecessors, functioned as a display of the world as viewed from a newly powerful commercial hub in the United States. Like other such expositions the Columbian Exposition displayed products, natural wonders, cultural artifacts, and technology, in this case from some forty-six countries. It also functioned as something of a human zoo with buildings, temples, and encampments from Japan to Dahomey.

The 1893 World's Parliament of Religions—one of several conferences convened in conjunction with the World's Columbian Exposition—aided in the development, spread, and acceptance of the idea of religions and world religions. The parliament "applied the strategies used to define 'cultures' to identify 'religions.'"[76] Burris notes, "What made the World's Parliament of Religions significant was that in an unprecedented attempt at genuine global inclusiveness, the event's organizers solicited participation from representatives outside the Western Bloc of nations," and that "foreign representatives were allowed to speak without interruption or rebuttal."[77] The very name "World's Parliament of Religions" seemed to signal an insistence on the value of difference, equal representation, and pluralism.[78] Despite this democratic rhetoric and the unusual inclusion of non-Western representatives, Western and largely Christian groups advancing arguments for religion as a singular entity with more or less adequate incarnations dominated the World's Parliament of Religions. These incarnations were arranged in an evolutionary hierarchy, the highest of which worshipped a transcendent deity, the lowest of which worshipped objects themselves—designated variously as fetishes or totems. Ironically, new voices including those from East and South Asia such as Swami Vivekananda adopted the very same transcendentalist arguments and turned them into a gospel of Eastern spirituality set to save the West from its materialism.[79]

The conception of the parliament as a meeting of the "ten great world religions" echoed the sentiments expressed in James Freeman Clarke's 1871 *Ten Great Religions: An Essay in Comparative Theology* that, "while most of the religions of the world are ethnic, or the religions of races, Christianity is catholic, or adapted to become the religion of all races."[80] The emerging consensus surrounding world religions that dominated the parliament was tangible. The events "excluded by category all Native Americans and included African Americans only as converted Christians."[81] A look at the placement of representatives of various groups at the wider Columbian Exposition further confirmed that the civilized/exotic, colonial/savage taxonomy still made the notion of primitive religion a contradiction in terms. Japanese, Chinese, and others had displays in the "White City." But the representatives of Africa and Native Americans were placed at the far end of the Midway.[82] William E. Cameron, writing at the time, reacted thus:

> [Buddhism] is not a religion, but a system of crude philosophy embodying the worship of an idealized type of manhood through idols and symbols. The Chinese have Joss House where their peculiar forms of idolatry are observed. The Zulus, Fijians, and Samoans have weird beliefs, and their ceremonials are such as to strike pity and disgust upon the minds of enlightened beholders. That gross superstition should maintain its existence in the midst of an occasion which shows forth the fullest flower of civilization and Christianity, intensifies the repugnance with which one views the mummeries and grosser rites by which these savages travesty the name of worship. But it is in the Dahomey Village that the grossest and most repulsive forms of fetichism [*sic*] hold sway.[83]

Cameron's special loathing of "fetichism" is an indication that recent theories in anthropology, ethnology, and the now consolidating field of comparative religion were becoming better known. By the time of the parliament, contending theories concerning the evolutionary development of religion and society were a major scholarly concern. Edward Burnet Tylor's evolutionist theories concerning animism as the earliest stage of religion were well known. James G. Frazer had just published *The Golden Bough* in which he discussed the relationship between magic and religion. His continuing researches would result in *Totemism and Exogamy* (1910). Émile Durkheim was beginning his investigations of totemism that would result in his *The Elementary Forms of the Religious Life*. Indeed, as Cameron's comments make clear, the issue of materiality and its relationship to evolutionary ideas was key to an emerging definition of religion.

The idea of the fetish encapsulated a particular kind of fascination and disgust, and the term came to be used in a promiscuous manner across a broad range of popular and scholarly discourses in the nineteenth and twentieth centuries. Fetish as a discourse emerges in the sixteenth-century and seventeenth-century encounters between Europeans and Africans.[84] Charles de Brosses coined the word "fétichisme" in 1757, by which he meant that "the fetish was essentially a material, terrestrial entity; fetishism was thus to be distinguished from cults of celestial bodies (whose truth might be a sort of proto Deist intimation of the rational order of nature rather than direct worship of the natural bodies themselves)."[85] Or, as William Pietz has noted, the fetish involves "the object's untranscended materiality."[86]

The Columbian Exhibition and the World's Parliament of Religions were part of a much wider cultural discourse. The problem of religious evolution was in many ways defined by an emerging dialectic between "savage" religion (if it was to be considered religion at all) and world religions. Beginning in the second half of the nineteenth century, conferences were organized in the metropole as well as in Johannesburg, Calcutta, and elsewhere to discuss the problem of savage religion. These conferences were the predecessors to the World's Parliament of Religions (1893) as well as the progenitors of conferences on the history of religions that commenced in Paris (1900), Basel (1904), Oxford (1908), and Leiden (1912). Fetishism, totemism, and animism were topics of debate central to the emerging definition of religion. The theories debated at scholarly meetings were circulated broadly in publications such as the eleven-volume series Non-Christian Religious Systems published between 1877 and 1905, and access to a vast array of non-Christian texts was furthered through Max Müller's famous *Sacred Books of the East* (1879–1910).[87] The scholarly meetings that had begun in Paris in 1900 were restarted in 1950 after a hiatus during the Second World War. These conferences shaped colonial theory concerning religion, and the conference would later be hosted by the Religionskundliche Sammlung in Marburg in 1960. The meetings of the International Association for the History of Religions (IAHR) continue today.[88] Theoretical and comparative knowledge produced through the comparative science of religion shaped and continues to shape the collection and display of material objects in exhibitions and museums.

Like current textbooks and school and university curricula, the World's Parliament of Religions—rebranded with the title "The Parliament of the World's Religions" and resurrected in 1993 on the one-hundredth anniversary of the original parliament—represents a consolidation of this discourse. The Council for a Parliament of the World's Religions asserts plurality and individual difference:

> The Council for a Parliament of the World's Religions seeks to promote interreligious harmony, rather than unity. The problem with seeking unity among religions is the risk of loss of the unique and precious character of each individual religious and spiritual tradition; this understanding is key to our framework. Interreligious harmony, on the other hand, is an attainable and highly desirable goal. Such an approach respects, and is enriched by, the particularities of each tradition. Moreover, within each tradition are the resources (philosophical, theological and spiritual teachings and perspectives) that enable each to enter

into respectful, appreciative and cooperative relationships with persons and communities of other traditions.[89]

The metaphor of religions as individual representatives in a parliamentary system operating in a single pluralistic society is obvious. Yet, the preservation of individuality under a representative system that champions harmony can result in two difficulties. On the one hand, true difference can be flattened or suppressed in the pursuit of harmony. On the other hand, without effective safeguards, the structure relegates minority groups to permanent second-class status. Such an approach makes it easy, then, to regard such religions as exotic multicultural evidence of the success of the system. Critics of multiculturalism have noted these problems.[90]

Even more troubling, the popularity of the notion of world religions and of world religions courses and the implicit comparison and hierarchy they enshrine reinforce a picture of the world divided into developed, developing, and undeveloped traditions, a picture that uncomfortably corresponds to the dominant political and economic descriptions of the present world.[91] Despite their good intentions, some of the displays I examine in Part Two of this study suffer from precisely this implied hierarchy while simultaneously flattening difference.

Forebears: The London Missionary Society Museum, the Pitt Rivers Museum, and the Horniman Museum

Even as these temporary exhibitions and scholarly and public conferences were developed, "religious" objects were finding permanent institutional homes. The most notable of these in the first half of the twentieth century were the Religionskundliche Sammlung in Marburg, Germany, and the State Museum of the History of Religions in Leningrad, the Soviet Union, examined in detail in subsequent chapters. In 1927, the theologian Rudolf Otto proposed a "university collection for the teaching and study of the history of religions and confessions" to be held at the Philipps-Universität in Marburg, Germany. The first display of objects was mounted in autumn of 1929. During the same period the government in the Soviet Union was establishing "anti-religious museums." The State Museum of the History of Religions was initiated in May 1931, and in November of 1932, it opened two exhibits in the former Kazan Cathedral. These were the first purpose-designed museums of *religions* drawing on comparative theories emerging in the new fields of anthropology and comparative religion. These collections, however, were preceded by several collections that began to collect, classify, and compare religious objects. Examining—briefly—three of these institutions before turning to world religions museums illustrates how collections of objects were enmeshed in knowledge regimes that preceded and contributed to the production of "religions" in the context of empire. These are the London Missionary Society Museum, the Pitt Rivers Museum, and the Horniman Museum.[92] In the course of its history, the London Missionary Society Museum became largely devoted to items we would now label as "religious." On its dissolution many of its objects were acquired by the Pitt Rivers Museum and the Horniman Museum. Thus, the three museums bear a kind of genetic relationship.

Despite the often-remarked hostility of Christian missionaries to the religious practices of peoples in the colonies, missionaries were instrumental in documenting and collecting material objects for the comparative science of religions. Missionaries were key participants in the collection of data for the new science of religion, and it is well known that the civilizing mission of empire was often conceived and rationalized in terms of bringing the enlightenment of Christ to the heathen. Missionaries typically had more contact with local customs than the colonial officials and industrialist collectors.

A'a, now in the British Museum, was one of the "gods" offered to the missionary John Williams (1821) by the inhabitants of Rurutu (now the Society Islands, French Polynesia) as a part of the process of their conversion to Christianity. Williams displayed the "gods" of Rurutu from the pulpit of the church on the island of Ra'iātea, and then had the "rejected gods" shipped to London and put on display at the new London Missionary Society Museum. The museum, founded in 1814, survived until 1910 and, ironically, might be seen as the first comparative religion museum. After its dissolution, much of its documentary material came to be housed at the School of Oriental and African Studies of the University of London (SOAS), while the bulk of the artifacts made their way to the British Museum, the Pitt Rivers Museum, and the Horniman Museum.[93]

The impetus for what became the London Missionary Society Museum was the growing collection of items sent or brought back to the Society's London home by missionaries in Asia, Africa, and the Pacific mission fields.[94] Although the items included what might be termed idols or deities' images or "fetishes," a careful analysis by Chris Wingfield shows that at least for the first third of the nineteenth century the growing collection was dominated not by "idols" but by "curiosities" involving natural history (animal skins and taxidermied animals, such as crocodiles, minerals, etc.).[95] Thus, the museum at its inception was not unlike earlier "cabinets of curiosities" that emerged in the sixteenth century—initially entire rooms, rather than mere "cabinets," in which objects collected by travelers in an ad hoc fashion were meant to provide a miniature sampler of the world.

Over the course of the century the mixture of curiosities at the London Missionary Society Museum gradually changed and came to be dominated by "idols" and "fetishes." This change was, at least in part, produced by items sent to the society by John Williams from Ra'iātea. An "advertisement" in the catalog of the museum from 1826 characterizes the holdings of the museum as follows:

> But the most valuable and impressive objects in this Collection, are the numerous, and (in some instances) horrible idols, which have been imported from the South Sea Islands, from India, from China, and Africa; and among these, those especially which were given up by their former worshippers, from a full conviction of the folly and sin of idolatry—a conviction derived from the ministry of the Gospel by the Missionaries.[96]

Wingfield's analysis suggests that the original focus of the collection on curiosities of natural history and on "efforts of natural genius" was slowly being overtaken by a growing interest in the idols, now arranged geographically in glass cases according to the various mission fields (Africa, China, the Pacific, etc.).[97] This change is evident by the time of the second catalog, dating from the late 1850s. An analysis of the catalog and the image of the museum which appeared in the *Illustrated London News* of June 1859, as well as another image appearing in the *Juvenile Missionary Magazine* of 1860 (Figure 1), demonstrates that, along with a major increase in the number of objects in the collection in the intervening thirty-four years between the two catalogs, the

> numbers of natural history specimens increased by only a relatively small amount; indeed, they had been overtaken in numerical terms by the items classed as "idols and objects of superstitious regard." This numerical shift undoubtedly contributed to the eclipsing of the African collections in favour of those from the Pacific, India and China, where "idols" were more prominent.[98]

How these objects were understood can be gleaned from an article in the *Juvenile Missionary Magazine*, which stated that

> the instruments of cruelty, the weapons of war, and the horrid idols once feared and worshipped, are themselves proofs that old things have passed away, as most of these are relics and trophies—tokens that the wicked customs and abominable idolatries of former days have been abandoned.[99]

Figure 1 "The Museum of the London Missionary Society," *Illustrated London News*, June 15, 1859, p. 605. Creative Commons License: CC BY 3.0.

At this point in 1860 these objects were classified as "customs" and "idolatries"— the category religion was not yet being used. Elsewhere, the *Juvenile Missionary Magazine* informed its young readers:

> Now this museum is altogether different from every other museum in the world. It is a not a mere collection of curious, or beautiful, or valuable things. . . . [Its] chief purpose . . . is to show what men are without the Gospel.[100]

However negative, we have here a comparison between Christianity (the "Gospel") and other religions. Exemplars of those religions—installed by geographic area in glass cases—constituted an incipient comparative religion museum organized in an ad hoc ethnographic fashion. The museum's collection was clearly popular as it was mentioned in the major guidebooks of the period.[101] Indeed, portions of the collection toured, and many items were in demand. Increasing numbers were on loan to the British Museum from the 1880s onward.[102]

The popularity of the museum, changing sensibilities regarding the curating of exhibits, and a change in museum venue finally led to a decision by the mission Home Board to close the museum. In April 1910, Charles Hercules Read got first pick of items to be removed to the British Museum. Thereafter, in May, Henry Balfour procured objects for the Pitt Rivers Museum in Oxford, as did Dr. Harrison of the Horniman Museum. The remaining objects were sold at auction.[103]

Many of the items from the London Missionary Society Museum, including the "god" A'a were acquired by the British Museum. Those acquired by the Pitt Rivers and the Horniman were ensconced in newer comparative regimes—morphological and evolutionary. A brief look at the Pitt Rivers Museum and the Horniman Museum can help put the development of comparative schemes—and their use in museums of comparative religion—in perspective.

The morphological organization of the Pitt Rivers Museum is still evident. Visitors enter the Pitt Rivers Museum through Oxford's Natural History Museum which was the site of the 1860 debate between Huxley and Wilberforce about evolution. The entry to the Pitt Rivers Museum is through a massive wooden door at the rear of the Natural History Museum. Walking through that door one almost seems to be walking into a museum in 1900. This, of course, is not really the case, but enough of Augustus Pitt Rivers' (1827–1900) vision still exists in the museum to at least give the visitor a sense of what it was like.[104] The building is an ornate ironwork structure enclosing a large three-storied space that is girdled with three levels of side galleries. The main floor and much of the side gallery space is crowded with traditional dark wood-framed glass cases. Opposite the entryway a towering Haida totem pole donated by Edward Burnett Tylor dominates the view.

The Pitt Rivers Museum was established in 1884 by Augustus Pitt Rivers on the condition that Oxford provide a purpose-built building for the museum and appoint a permanent lecturer in anthropology. Pitt Rivers was a military man with an interest in the history and development of armaments. He began collecting along these lines and, having unexpectedly inherited a considerable estate began to branch out into collecting artifacts of all sorts—particularly manufactures and handicrafts. He soon became a noted and well-published expert with a growing interest in archaeology and engaged in excavations, initially on his own estates. The Pitt Rivers Museum is not, strictly speaking, a museum of religion, although much of what it contains, including many pieces from the London Missionary Society Museum, has to do with what we now call religion.

For the purposes of this study, our interest is in Pitt Rivers's theories of morphology and evolution. Moving in the circles that included Darwin and E. B. Tylor, Pitt Rivers was influenced by comparative theories. His displays were often arranged according to morphological principles. One might find for instance a case grouping together pots of a particular shape from across the world and across time. His was not the only such scheme, and by the 1860s Pitt

Rivers was acquainted with developments in collections in Paris, Berlin, Leiden, and elsewhere. Gustave Klemm's typological approach was probably the closest to that of Pitt Rivers.[105] According to William Ryan Chapman,

> the special character of Pitt Rivers' collection, however, reflected the fact that it was in the first instance one of comparative technology, not prehistoric implements. Even after he added prehistoric remains, the typologically organized ethnographic series remained the core; his purpose was not simply to help fill in an incomplete archeological series, but to offer a comparably effective historical tool for the study of the material culture of present exotic peoples.[106]

How Pitt Rivers's morphological approach worked is made clear by an illustration he provided for his essay "The Evolution of Culture."[107] The illustration assembles a series of stick-based weapons arranged according to shape into a developmental diagram. The approach is reminiscent of Goethe's approach to plants. About this diagram, Pitt Rivers says,

> I have arranged, on Plate III, drawings of nearly all the weapons used by the Australians, placing them together according to their affinities in such a manner as to show hypothetically their derivation from a single form. As all the forms given on this diagram are drawings of weapons in use at the present time, and there are many intermediate forms not given here, I have not arranged them in horizontal lines, as in the previous diagrams, to show their place in time, but have arranged them as radiating from a central point.[108] (Figure 2)

While some of Pitt Rivers's schemes used evolutionary arrangements—"in horizontal lines . . . to show their place in time"—his interest in morphology dominated the collection. Both schemes organized the weapons and other cultural productions of subject peoples of the empire into a consumable and utilitarian form of knowledge—a form of knowledge that facilitated comparison between "us" and "them" and subjugated the world to the imperial "scientific" grid.

The other museum that acquired a significant number of objects from the London Missionary Society Museum was the Horniman Museum in Forest Hill, South London, near Dulwich.[109] The museum was made possible by the wealth of the Horniman's Tea Company. Fredrick John Horniman, the son of the company founder, was an avid collector who founded the museum in 1901. It has undergone two major enlargements since then, and the museum and its gardens constitute one of Britain's "designated" collections. It is particularly notable for its anthropological and evolutionary exhibits, as well as a remarkable exhibit of musical instruments.

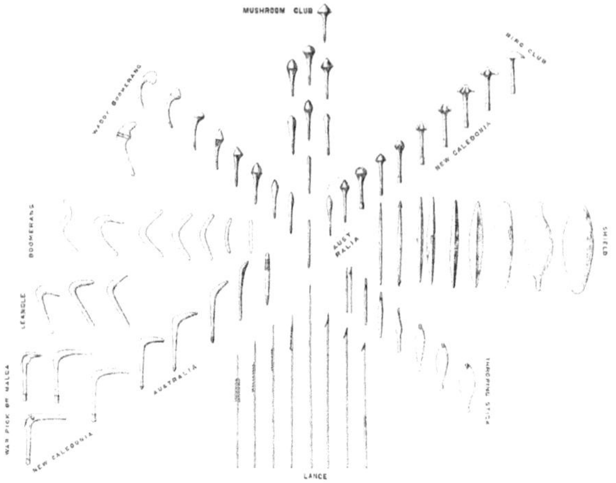

Figure 2 Pitt Rivers, Australian throwing stick chart. From "The Evolution of Culture," plate III, p. 37. Public Domain.

Much like the Pitt Rivers Museum, the core collections in the Horniman were once enshrined in wood and glass cases (some still are). The Horniman is still very much an institution shaped by the evolutionary theories of Darwin and Lamarck. Although the Horniman, like other museums, has undergone serious revisions of its displays, it still has a strongly evolutionary ambiance. Perhaps most striking are the evolutionary displays relating to mammal and hominid skulls, the evolution of dogs, horses, and so on. In these displays material is arranged to suggest a developmental sequence from simple to complex and from earlier to more recent examples. The more troubling displays concerning late nineteenth- and early twentieth-century theories about human races, phrenology, and anthropometry have disappeared. Nonetheless, research on the web still turns up a few images of charts portraying the distribution of the major races.

An examination of the 1921 *Guide to the Collections in the Horniman Museum and Library* provides a glimpse of the museum's earlier disposition. The *Guide* includes extensive discussions of "advanced" and "backward races" as well as descriptions of their relative standing with regard to agriculture, warfare, tools, and so on. "Evolution" is applied to all things—animals, tools, machinery, decorative arts, musical instruments, wheeled vehicles, boats, and humans. Section "XX: Man and the Great Apes" contains descriptions of a number of display cases formerly in the North Hall relating apes, premodern humans, and modern humans.[110] Cases 7–9 were devoted to "Classification of Modern Races." Anthropometry, cranial measurement, and other features are used as the basis of racial comparison and evaluation of evolutionary development. To choose just one example, the *Guide* instructs the visitor as follows:

> Visitors should compare and contrast the Australian aborigine's skull with that of the ancient Saxon. The former will be found to present features which bring it distinctly nearer to the Neanderthal type, and therefore to the ape, than is the large well-formed skull of the Saxon, though the latter is some 1,500 years older.[111]

Discussions of magic and religion, fetishism, and totemism reflecting the prominent evolutionary theories of the time are directly related to human progress. Judgments as to higher and lower forms of religion undergird the discussion, as in this comment on Hindu traditions: "Polytheism is general amongst the people, and it is often associated with still lower forms of magic and religion."[112]

Before the full emergence of religion as a sui generis phenomenon studied in a field distinct from ethnography/anthropology, idols and fetishes were contrasted with Christian belief based on a distinction between worship of the one transcendent god and the mistaken worship of material things. Grouped together by geographic origin in the London Missionary Society Museum, the objects invited comparison with each other but not with the one true religion. By the time Pitt Rivers amassed his collection in the mid-nineteenth century, and by the time the tea magnate John Horniman founded his museum at the opening of the twentieth century, new knowledge regimes based on comparative methods and inflected by evolutionary theory were producing a new episteme in which certain objects were deemed "religious" and were subject to scientific comparison and judgment. Furthermore, Christian understandings of a transcendent god opposed to material creation could be easily elided with evolutionary ideas to yield justifications for Western supremacy that were both religious and racial. Thus, religious studies was born and soon museums of religions were being constructed.

The London Missionary Society Museum is no more, and both the Pitt Rivers Museum and the Horniman Museum have come to terms with the problematic nature of their earlier selves. Indeed, the Pitt Rivers Museum has been at the forefront of UK museums in using its collections as innovative "thirdspaces" or contact zones where contemporary artist-representatives of various formerly colonial communities join curators and visitors to explore the meaning of their own museumification. One can see an excellent example in the exhibit by the Tibetan photographer Nyema Droma titled Performing Tibetan Identities.

Droma used the many "ethnic" portraits of Tibetans held by the museum as a basis for her contemporary portraits of Tibetans in both "ethnic" and contemporary dress to disrupt the continuing ethnic stereotyping of Tibetan people.[113]

Whether in displays of tools, animals, or humans, we are now aware that what is elided by the lines connecting the objects are assumptions about development, superiority, and subordination that were crucial to imperial enterprises and to the early development of the comparative science of religion. This is not to say that all comparison must be rejected. The point, Smith says, is that "comparison is, at base, never identity. Comparison requires the postulation of difference as the grounds of its being interesting . . . and a methodological manipulation of difference, a playing across the 'gap' in the service of some useful end."[114] Placing objects together in a collection is almost never random or accidental. There is always some underlying principle, "some useful end" whether consciously programmatic or emergent. Spatial proximity invites comparison, and comparison, as culturally deployed and enshrined, has typically implied contiguity. If a tradition frames itself as unique (through revelation, etc.), its proponents will likely object to any form of comparison, overt or implied. So any such exhibit of world religions or any museum devoted to world religions must tread carefully. Ironically, although the world religions category is founded on the notion of comparison, museums find they must attempt to design displays that isolate and minimize comparison and carefully drain objects of any danger.

Given the pervasiveness of the world religions typology and its parent comparative religion, how are museums to present religious objects? David Chidester provides one possible answer: "If we are going to retain these imperial ancestors," they must be situated "in the imperial, colonial, and indigenous mediations in which knowledge about religion and religions has been generated."[115] He writes:

> As we review the history of the study of religion, it is necessary but not sufficient to assert that the general idea of religion is a constructed category and that all kinds of ideas about specific religions have been invented. Although the empire of religion was certainly full of ideas, thinking was materially grounded. Therefore, we have to ask: Under what material conditions were these crucial terms in secular modernity produced, authenticated, and circulated?[116]

Chidester's proposal to present a critique based on an historical awareness of the development of these institutions and the theories—explicit and implicit—upon which they are based is certainly one way forward. Critique linked with the story of the life of selected objects can provide impressive learning experiences. The

British Museum's display of "A" provides a viable example, as does Richard Davis's explorations in his *Lives of Indian Images*.[117] Another avenue, which I take up in Chapter 2, is to present alternative understandings of religious objects as objects. Finally, museums can become more inclusive of religious communities and can function as spaces for genuine dialogical encounter. Some of the museums I study later have been exploring just such dialogical forums.

The Body of God and the Matter of Religion

What do the religious images in museums want? What are they doing there? Can we imagine how they might feel being displayed in close proximity to one another? We can venture that, although museums of world religions would not have seemed strange to Max Müller or to Ernst Troeltsch, questions such as *these* would have been baffling. The fact that in the early twenty-first century a growing body of research does take such questions seriously reflects a major shift in our understanding of religion and in the material objects that constitute it. While Chapter 1 examined the critique of religion as a modern discourse associated with the rise of comparative method, this chapter engages recent efforts to fundamentally rethink the nature of religious objects and avoid seeing them as mere material signposts pointing to transcendent reality or as indices of progress on a civilized/savage or racial scale.

Displays of religious objects serve a variety of agendas and ideologies that can be labeled religious, anti-religious, cultural, comparative, aesthetic, and so on. But they have dimensions that escape comparativist, Cartesian, and purely aesthetic views of them. Indeed, the work of Crispin Paine, Graham Harvey, and Amy Whitehead—among others—points to a world in which the sculpted and painted inhabitants of museums have been and may continue to be "persons"—nodes facilitating a web of social relationships.[1] Applying insights from new animist approaches, I argue for a new way of understanding the material of religion. I suggest how world religions museums, as well as traditional museums of art and culture, might reconfigure their displays to render such relations visible and to alert the visitor to the social, ideological, and relational dimensions of the objects displayed.

Śiva and the Virgin at St. Mungo

The St. Mungo Museum of Religious Life and Art is ensconced in a modern Scottish baronial-style building nestled close to the historic Glasgow cathedral and the Glasgow Necropolis. Opened with considerable publicity in 1993, the small and intimate museum consists of three permanent galleries and one space for special exhibits. Two galleries occupy the main floor—one devoted to religious art and one a comparative gallery based on life-cycle rites. On the upper floor is a gallery devoted to the various religious groups in Glasgow. In the words of Mark O'Neill, who was instrumental in the founding and design of the St. Mungo Museum, the aim was to promote "tolerance" in a city long marked by sectarian tension. The Religious Art Gallery is small and striking. Islamic, Christian, and Buddhist images crowd one's visual field. The first time I visited, Buddhist images were framed by a background of stained glass windows, and Salvador Dali's Christ of St. John of the Cross seemed to loom over the Buddha.[2] A small anteroom is dominated by a glorious sculpture of Śiva as Naṭarāja illuminated by Christian stained glass and snuggled up to a pietà.[3] Indeed, shortly after the museum was opened, the Śiva statue was attacked and damaged and, when asked, the perpetrator said that he did it "for Christ."[4] This tension—seen here not only in this event but also in the perceived danger of deities of different religions placed proximate to one another—is key to my analysis of such museums and the comparative method that constitutes their foundational assumptions.

Living with Gods at the British Museum

During visits to the State Museum of the History of Religions in St. Petersburg, Russia, and to the Religionskundliche Sammlung in Marburg, Germany, in 2016, my curator friends described an upcoming exhibit that the British Museum was mounting to which their museums were contributing objects. Indeed, the focus would be on the material of religion, and we were duly anticipating the exhibit. Titled *Living with Gods: Peoples, Places, and Worlds Beyond*, it would be accompanied by a lavishly illustrated companion volume and a BBC Radio 4 series.[5] According to the website,

> beliefs in spiritual beings and worlds beyond nature are characteristic of all human societies. By looking at how people believe through everyday objects of faith, this exhibition provides a perspective on what makes believing a vital part of human behaviour.
>
> Seeing *how* people believe, rather than considering *what* they believe, suggests that humans might be naturally inclined to believe in transcendent worlds and beings. Stories, objects, images, prayers, meditation and rituals can provide ways

for people to cope with anxieties about the world, and help form strong social bonds. This in turn helps to make our lives well ordered and understandable.[6]

There are several assumptions here, not least of which are the sweeping generalizations about "belief," "human societies," "faith," and "transcendence." For example, does looking at a Siberian shaman's costume really show us "how people believe"? These examples illustrate the tension between transcendence and material objects inherent in our notion of religion and the ambiguities museums of world religions must negotiate.

In the mid-twentieth century, theologians and practitioners of the newly emerged field of religious studies worried that growing secularism would see religion all but disappear by the twenty-first century. In communist countries, education and indoctrination would, some hoped, eradicate religion.[7] This was the logic behind the establishment of "atheism" or "anti-religion" museums in the Soviet Union, one of which—the State Museum of the History of Religions in St. Petersburg—is treated in Chapter 4. Despite twentieth-century predictions to the contrary, religion is thriving in our world. Although it has retreated in some places, notably among mainstream Catholic and Protestant denominations in Europe and the United States, resurgent forms of Christianity, Islam, and Buddhism have made our world notably more "religious." Further, and especially in parts of Europe and the Americas, alternative forms of "spirituality" are widespread.[8] What this has to do with the logic of a hegemonic global capitalism has been the object of numerous studies.[9]

Along with churches, mosques, temples, seminaries, zendos, and so on, religion is studied in schools and universities—both secular and religious—and is increasingly enshrined in museum exhibits and in museums to religion. While there have long been church treasuries, the more recent phenomenon are overtly religious institutions attuned to a distinctively religious form of consumption. These include such theme-park museums as *Holy Land Experience* in Orlando, *Haw Par Villa* in Singapore, or the Creation Museum in Kentucky. These are examined in Crispin Paine's recent book *Gods and Rollercoasters: Religion in Theme-parks Worldwide*.[10]

Leaving aside museums focused on a single religion, religious theme parks, or traditional church treasuries, my focus here is on purpose-built museums of comparative religion with worldwide scope and, by extension, related exhibits on religions in mainstream museums that are structured by the typologies of comparative religion and world religions. In the following chapters, I will examine five museums of religions based on comparative principles: the Religionskundliche Sammlung in Marburg, Germany; the State Museum of the

History of Religions in St. Petersburg, Russia; Le Musée des Religions du Monde in Nicolet, Québec; the St. Mungo Museum of Religious Life and Art in Glasgow, Scotland; and the Museum of World Religions in Taipei, Taiwan.[11] But before we turn to the museums, a consideration of recent work on the material turn in the study of religion will help us to frame the questions we bring to these institutions.

What Do Religion Museums Do?

Religion can be seen as a practice involving material things and what people do with them and say about them. Why, we might ask, are there museums of religions? What are they for? How are they distinct from, say, a watch museum or a museum dedicated to football? Obviously, a museum devoted to football will not include all teams or all players. It might include a history of the sport and its development and be illustrated by exemplary and notable players, games, and teams.[12] Such a museum constitutes an ideal object by assembling material objects—artifacts, images, and text. So too, by its choices of objects and framing, a religions museum constitutes an ideal object "religion." Each museum (or display) produces a particular kind of religion for a particular audience with a particular educational goal in mind. Comparative or world religions museums are, then, a kind of cultural discourse in things whose signs are arranged to produce an ideal object for public display, reflection, and discussion.[13]

What does the ideal object "religion" consist of? The description of the exhibit *Living with Gods* from the British Museum webpage is typical of many definitions of religion, evoking Edward Burnett Tylor's nineteenth-century minimalist definition that religion involves "belief in spiritual beings," and adding that religions help people cope with life while pointing to something called "transcendence."[14] Such definitions are based on dichotomies that are cornerstones of European thought: spirit versus matter and subjects versus objects. The spirit/matter dichotomy is a key part of Christian theology and anthropology in which a transcendent god imparts life to dead matter, as in the account of creation found in Gen. 2:7, "Then the Lord God formed man of dust from the ground, and breathed into his nostrils the breath of life; and man became a living being."[15] This bifurcation of the cosmos into living God and dead matter is oddly echoed in certain Enlightenment thinkers. For instance, the Cartesian divide between subject and object, the first alive the second consisting of dead matter is an obvious parallel to the idea of living spirit and dead matter.

How deeply such notions color our perceptions of the world and how difficult it is to even conceive elsewhere. Under what we might think of as the tyranny of the transcendent subject, abstract terms such as belief, faith, spirit, transcendence, and religion alter our perceptions of the everyday world of bodies, materials, and things.[16] Crosses become symbols pointing to something other than themselves in an infinite regress of "signs and wonders."[17] Thus, a museum as a collection of objects—especially a museum of religions—is constituted in the tension between signs and things. What's more, the signs—and now I refer to the labels and explanatory material that frame objects and entire exhibits—endeavor to shape the museum experience. Ironically, many visitors spend the majority of their time reading or listening to the information that accompanies the objects. Between objects and signs, the signs usually win.[18]

This is no surprise. Anja Lüpken, in her perceptive essay "Politics of Representation—Normativity in Museum Practice" puts it thus,

> Musealization is integrating the object into the collection by indexing and classifying it. Museum collections are cultural treasuries where important objects are kept, and where they are ordered in a categorical system.[19]

Further, museums built on an obvious comparative framework such as the ones in this study drive home a message about inclusion and exclusion. Lüpken continues, now quoting Timothy W. Luke, who notes that

> museums help to forge reality, and then they organize the collective rites of this unstable reality's reception that will write authoritative accounts of the past, present, and future in their displays. By doing this, museums serve as ontologues, telling us what reality really is.[20]

A museum, then, involves various dialectic tensions between permanent exhibits and temporary exhibits, objects and images, global and local, objects and the narratives that frame them. James Clifford, studying a variety of museums, draws on Mary Louise Pratt's notion of a "contact zone" to explore the function and dynamics of museums and the cultural encounters that sometimes take place there. Pratt's "contact zone" is a "space of colonial encounters, the space in which peoples geographically and historically separated come into contact with each other and establish ongoing relations, usually involving conditions of coercion, radical inequality, and intractable conflict."[21] Clifford turns these observations to museums:

> When museums are seen as contact zones, their organizing structure as a *collection* becomes an ongoing historical, political, moral *relationship*—a power-charged

set of exchanges, of push and pull. The organizing structure of the museum-as-collection functions like Pratt's frontier. A center and a periphery are assumed: the center a point of gathering, the periphery an area of discovery. The museum, usually located in a metropolitan city, is the historical destination for the cultural productions it lovingly and authoritatively salvages, cares for, and interprets.[22]

Little wonder, then, that "museality" is so often seen not as dialogue but as appropriation. Is there any alternative to this religious and political theater inherited with comparative religion?

Here we can turn to recent work on things as an antidote to a definition of religion fixated on transcendence. Museums are full of things—artifacts—and these things involve dimensions that exceed our framing of them. Here is the list of contents from Henry Hodges's influential book *Artifacts*:

Pottery; glazes; glass and enamels; copper and copper alloys; iron and steel; gold, silver, lead and mercury; stone; wood; fibres and threads; textiles and baskets; hides and leather; antler, bone, horn and ivory; dyes, pigments and paints; adhesives; some other materials.[23]

Visitors to museums often apprehend these artifacts as indicative of ideologies, cultures, and aesthetic ideals, and the objects themselves as stable, and even unchanging. Curators and conservators know better. Matter is active, changing; the objects in exhibits are ever in flux.

Objects, Things, and People: Dismantling Transcendence

When visitors to museums view objects and displays, they participate in an illusion—they, autonomous subjects on one side of the glass, the objects, dead matter on the other side. There is nothing inevitable or natural about this belief concerning perception. We have learned to see things framed in this "scientific" or "objective" manner.

In the mid-twentieth century, the philosopher Maurice Merleau-Ponty characterized "scientific thinking" as "a thinking which looks on from above, and thinks of the object in general."

Science manipulates things and gives up living in them. Operating within its own realm, it makes its own limited models of things; operating upon these indices or variables to effect whatever transformations are permitted by their definition, it comes face to face with the real world only at rare intervals. Science is, and always has been, that admirably active, ingenious, and bold way of thinking whose fundamental bias is to treat everything as though it were an object-in-general—as though it meant nothing to us and yet was predestined for our own use.[24]

Anticipating by some decades advances in cognitive metaphor and the embodied material turn in our understanding of perception and thought, Merleau-Ponty's late work, focusing on painting and perception, amounts to a critique of, and alternative to, Cartesian dualism of mind and body.[25]

> Visible and mobile, my body is a thing among things; it is caught in the fabric of the world, and its cohesion is that of a thing. But because it moves itself and sees, it holds things in a circle around itself. Things are an annex or prolongation of itself; they are incrusted into its flesh, they are part of its full definition; the world is made of the same stuff as the body. This way of turning things round [*ces renversements*], these antinomies, are different ways of saying that vision happens among, or is caught in, things—in that place where something visible undertakes to see, becomes visible for itself by virtue of the sight of all things; in that place where there persists, like the mother water in crystal, the undividedness [*l'indivision*] of the sensing and the sensed.[26]

A consequence of our "objectivist" view is that we often use the terms "object" and "thing" interchangeably, but it is helpful to distinguish these. David Morgan has put the difference succinctly: "Thingness does not depend on us; objecthood does. Objects are intentional things, but may have little to do with what things want or do."[27]

The scientific reduction of complex processes, relationships, things, and technologies to abstract labels and concepts can produce an almost magical precession of signs which some have designated by the term "episteme." Michel Foucault described an "episteme" as a sort of cultural grid that "defines the conditions of possibility of all knowledge."[28] Bruno Latour, working on the social history of science, has spent his career in an effort to expose how such epistemes function through our use of language to nominalize, naturalize, and thus obscure the complex processes and material basis of our existence. In a sense, Latour is interested in *how things become objects*. For example, in his work *We Have Never Been Modern* (1993) Latour traces the emergence of the "modern" episteme to the debate between Boyle and Hobbes concerning the respective spheres of science and politics:

> Boyle is not simply creating a scientific discourse while Hobbes is doing the same thing for politics; Boyle is creating a political discourse from which politics is to be excluded, while Hobbes is imagining a scientific politics from which

experimental science has to be excluded. In other words, they are inventing our modern world, a world in which the representation of things through the intermediary of the laboratory is forever dissociated from the representation of citizens through the intermediary of the social contract. . . . They are like a pair of Founding Fathers, acting in concert to promote one and the same innovation in political theory: the representation of nonhumans belongs to science, but science is not allowed to appeal to politics; the representation of citizens belongs to politics, but politics is not allowed to have any relation to the nonhumans produced and mobilized by science and technology.[29]

Keeping in mind that the object is not a thing, we can see Latour's point that in the modern episteme the object here called "politics" excludes the discourses of the sciences, while the object called "science" excludes appeal to political discourses. By extension it is also evident that in this modern episteme God and spirit are banished to the individual realm of the subject. Thus:

God/Transcendent : World :: Spirit : Matter :: Subject : Object

God indeed has been dethroned by the modern episteme and banished to the realm of the subject which is where William James famously finds him, and proclaims in his Gifford Lectures of 1901–02 that "religion . . . shall mean for us the feelings, acts, and experiences of individual men in their solitude, so far as they apprehend themselves to stand in relation to whatever they may consider the divine."[30] James's definition enshrined the notion of "religious experience" as an authoritative touchstone of authenticity—a touchstone beyond scrutiny because defined as subjective.[31] In other words, a cosmology based on the binary opposition of transcendent spirit and matter is a single concept, as is a cosmology based on the binary opposition of subject and object. Further, the two cosmologies—that of traditional Christianity and that of modernity— are frequently and easily elided. Objects can represent but cannot be spirit or transcendent. Understanding this conflation can help make us aware of foundational assumptions underlying the characterizations of objects as "religious," shaping how they are assembled and framed in museums of religion, and suggesting how we might reframe them to offer visitors the possibility of seeing objects in more than a single light.

In his discussion of the implications of Bruno Latour's work for the study of religion, Adam S. Miller says:

Religion is objective. It is made of objects, practiced by objects, and practiced for the revelation of objects. When estranged from its objective character, religion plays a ridiculous parody. On Latour's view, no single mistake does more to reinforce this bitter parody than thinking that religion is about "belief." Belief is not a religious idea. Belief is a stopgap explanation imposed on religion by those unable to see the too-immanent objects that animate it.[32]

Miller adds that

religion, divided from objects by the traditional claim, anathema to Latour, that Nature is one thing and our beliefs another, is left to either hide inside people's heads or get folded into the emptiness of deep space.[33]

Our typical "commonsense" modern episteme creates the object "religion" and the object "objects" as a paired vision of the world in which one side represents what is deemed primary, alive, and transcendent, the other represents what is deemed secondary and dead. Spirit and matter, the sacred and the profane, are mutually constituted objects. This is the epistemic world of the comparative science of religion, and it is the world that museums of religions take for granted.

Miller's comments attempt to alert us of the problem, but his attempt at intervention remains trapped within traditional Christian and modern epistemic frameworks. We look on objects as though, in Merleau-Ponty's words, "from above" when in reality we are things immersed in a world of things. Is another way of seeing possible?

Secret Life of Things: The Debate about Animism

Understanding things as sentient—along with the possibility that the dichotomies of spirit versus matter and living versus dead might not be as rigidly separated as we might think—can be both unsettling and liberating. From this point of view, religious objects have "lives," and religious objects, everyday objects, and animals can be thought of as sentient. In the eighteenth century and later, a popular literary trope was the "it narrative," "object narrative," or "circulation narrative." In such works as Charles Johnstone's novel *Chrysal; or, The Adventures of a Golden Guinea* (1760), the anonymous *The Secret History of an Old Shoe* (1734), or Francis Coventry's *The History of Pompey the Little* (1751), we see the predecessors of works such as *The Secret Lives of Dogs*.[34] Richard H. Davis has eloquently traced such lives in his *Lives of Indian Images*, in which he details "the lives of Indian objects as they have been relocated and revalorized over time by various communities of response."[35]

Despite these works, challenging epistemic dichotomies is the exception rather than the rule. The power of the episteme "religion" is well illustrated by the debate concerning animism.[36] During the early years of the twentieth century, in the infancy of the disciplines of religious studies and anthropology, Lucien Lévy-Bruhl and Émile Durkheim famously argued about the notion of animism that had been put forward some forty years earlier by Edward Burnett Tylor.[37] Central to the debate is a division of reality into the transcendent world of the divine and the world of dead objects. Spirit might enter matter, as souls enter humans, but was not of it. Nineteenth- and early twentieth-century debates in the fields of ethnology and comparative religion focused on a curiously similar bifurcation. Thus, "savage" peoples were thought to confuse living beings and objects such as trees, rocks, and various "idols." The theory of animism advanced by Tylor and popularized by James G. Frazer and others claimed that "animism" (along with totemic practices) was a stage in human evolution that was prior to the development of "religion" with its transcendent focus, and that native peoples attributed spiritual capacities and agency to objects as though the objects were animated by spiritual forces.[38] The scholar Preuss coined the term *urdummheit* (primal stupidity) to describe this state. In Frazer's words, "Haziness is the characteristic of the mental vision of the savage. Like the blind man at Bethsaida, he sees men like trees and animals walking in a thick intellectual fog."[39]

Tylor, Frazer, and other scholars were trying to make sense of the data that was piling up from missionaries and early ethnographers alike. But it may well be that "haziness" also characterized the vision of the researchers. Their researches were hampered by transcendentalist and Cartesian biases that had divided matter and spirit and not incidentally resembled the views of Christian iconoclasts. Either these so-called "savage" people were mentally unlike us or they posited an animation of trees, rocks, and idols much as Christians posited human souls animating bodies.

Émile Durkheim and Lucien Lévy-Bruhl working in the next generation with somewhat better data took up the issue again. Although the two men disagreed on a number of issues, both sensed that we moderns were missing something important. According to Lévy-Bruhl, this something was *"participation mystique"*:

> The attitude of the primitive's mind is very different. The natural world he lives in presents itself in quite another aspect to him. All its objects and all its entities are involved in a system of mystic participations and exclusions; it is these which constitute its cohesion and its order.[40]

Critiquing Lévy-Bruhl, Durkheim argued that,

> if the primitive confounds things which we distinguish, he also "distinguishes
> things which we connect together" and he does it "in the form of sharp and
> clear-cut oppositions."[41]

According to Dominique Merllié, who has recently revisited the debate,
Durkheim's uneasiness lay in what he regarded as Lévy-Bruhl's making too great
a division between "us" and "them." But Lévy-Bruhl was quite precise in what
he meant, and it looks as though Durkheim (deliberately, perhaps) misread him.
Lévy-Bruhl is clear:

> But to the primitive mind . . . these objects and these beings become divine only
> when the participation they guarantee has ceased to be direct. The Arunta who
> feels that he is both himself and the ancestor whose churinga was entrusted to
> him at the time of his initiation, knows nothing of ancestor worship. The Bororo
> does not make the parrots, which are Bororo, the objects of a religious cult. . . .
> The ideas which we call really religious are thus a kind of differentiated product
> resulting from a prior form of mental activity.[42]

In other words, for Lévy-Bruhl, the native's "participation" involves no
transcendent dimension, no subject-object dichotomy, and therefore, *by
definition, cannot be religious.*[43]

I have rehearsed this debate because many objects of so-called "primitive"
or "savage" peoples that were the foundation of these inquiries found their way
into early museum collections. Many still reside there and are still framed by our
transcendently biased episteme. Lévy-Bruhl had perceived that our "religion"
assumed no matter could be living without an infusion of transcendent spirit
and that this was not an assumption shared by the Arunta and other peoples
described in the ethnological record. Lévy-Bruhl recognized that if this was
indeed the case, the Arunta were not "religious" and that their epistemic view of
the world was fundamentally different from that of modern Europeans.

New Approaches to Religious Objects

While it is unclear if we can ever grasp things in themselves without some sort
of objectifying referentiality, we can certainly conceive of such approaches and
become alert to the ways our epistemic biases might obscure other ways of being
in and perceiving the world. The debate concerning animism is usually seen as
an attempt to explain how some people could confuse living things with inert

matter, as though animists were either pantheists or believed, like Christians, that spirits or souls were indwelling in objects. But a careful reading of Lévy-Bruhl and Durkheim—who themselves had carefully read the ethnographic record available to them—indicates otherwise. Lévy-Bruhl notes both "participations and exclusions," and Durkheim underscores that while "the primitive confounds things which we distinguish" he nonetheless "distinguishes things which we connect together." Both writers clearly understood that the ethnographic record attested to alternative ways of understanding things.

Scholars have been developing a more nuanced understanding of "things" for some time.[44] An example of this is Mihaly Csikszentmihalyi's essay "Why We Need Things."[45] Csikszentmihalyi begins by noting that "we like to think that because objects are human-made they must be under our control . . . every artifact is the product of human intentionality, but that intentionality itself is conditioned by the existence of previous objects."[46] In essence, Csikszentmihalyi is raising—however gingerly—the question of the agency of objects. Recent work by Bruno Latour, Tim Ingold, Amy Whitehead, Graham Harvey, and Istvan Praet among others have taken up where Lévy-Bruhl and Durkheim left off and now address the question of agency head on. Common to all of these writers is a profound recognition that our modern, scientific, and Cartesian taxonomies blind us to other ways of perceiving and living. Their work can help us to rethink how we approach and display some of the religious objects in museum collections (and perhaps even to rethink what a museum is).

Theodore Adorno once famously noted the relationship between the words "museum" and "mausoleum" and opined that museum objects are "objects to which the observer no longer has a vital relationship and which are in the process of dying."[47] Adorno's comment was perhaps meant more metaphorically than literally, but nonetheless indicates that these objects might be regarded as alive and thus might be thought of as having some sort of agency. But what could this mean?

We might think of the issue of the agency of objects along a spectrum. At one end of the spectrum objects have no agency—they are lifeless. But then we can also think of objects as having a kind of borrowed agency. Thus, people have fashioned objects such as doorknobs, and as we approach a door, we find our hand reaching out to grab the knob as though invited. Another way of thinking of the agency of objects is to note how they can mediate or facilitate social interaction, functioning almost invisibly like nodes in a social networking site. Examining objects such as dolls or religious icons, anthropologists and social psychologists have often pointed to a subjunctive sense of agency whereby, in certain prescribed circumstances, people behave "as if" the icon were a real person.[48] At the far end of the spectrum lies the notion of the objects as persons in themselves, independent from us humans, their creators. When I think of this position I think of the scene in the Walt Disney animated movie *Pinocchio* (1940) during which a wooden puppet is brought to life through the intervention of a fairy.[49] As in the case of Adam, a deus ex machina intervention is needed to magically transform Pinocchio. All of the positions along this spectrum assume the spirit/matter binary cosmology. Agency appears to be a mere stand-in for spirit. Recent research into animism stands as a warning that perhaps the question of agency itself is poorly framed and is dependent on the fundamental taxonomic grid of Western religion and modern science.

The anthropologist Istvan Praet argues in *Animism and the Question of Life* that our modern notion of a universal humanity and our biologically based definition of life and death are recent; ethnographic evidence demonstrates that people in other societies—in the words of Durkheim—"confound things which we distinguish" and "distinguish things which we connect together."[50] Drawing on his own fieldwork among the Chachi (Ecuador) and on ethnographic evidence from a wide range of other "indigenous" peoples, Praet argues that assumptions about life and humanity are not universal. According to the Chachi only things related to me are "alive" and those not related to me are not alive but are "dead." From the Chachi point of view we confuse alive with animate. For the Chachi things can be animate while not living. This includes people. Summarizing his argument, Praet says that

> what characterizes animism is the implicit rejection of an idea that adherents of the Western cosmology have propagated with such great success—that of an effortless humanity. The animistic Humanity is not a classificatory device but a position that has to be maintained and defended perpetually.[51]

Further, humans (meaning *only* the Chachi) are made through continual ritual and behavioral curation, just as icons are made in many religious traditions.[52]

In her study of the Catholic cult of the Virgin of Alcala de loz Gazules in Spain and of the pagan cult of the Glastonbury Goddess in Britain, Amy Whitehead focuses on the role of relationships ("relationality") in understanding agency with regard to what she calls "statue persons."[53] Indeed, statue persons—like relics—stand as a notable challenge to modern attitudes concerning inert matter.[54] Beyond mere "likeness" to a living person, and beyond modern aesthetic metaphors concerning the artist imparting a "spirit" to the sculpture, are traditional procedures of construction and consecration of icons. In some cases, ritual procedures are thought to bring statues to life as persons in communities.[55] "Relationality," says Whitehead,

> is dependent on three things: relationships, performances, and the moment. It is a practice, a *co-inspired form of active, mutual relating* [emphasis in original] that emerges from the unique, personal, even intimate relationships that take place between human and other than human beings rather than a religious label, an ethic or a worldview. Relationality is animist in both theory and encounter. It asserts that moments of active relating contain the possibility of bringing "persons" (exemplified through statue persons specifically) into "liveliness" or being insofar as we are relating with them, not before, not after (which also extends to temporal relating). What happens when we are not engaging statues and other objects is unknown to us. . . . This idea is not "human centered." It asserts that a fair and distributed importance should be afforded objects, artifacts, and other potential *beings* who make up the "living world." Thus this discussion is centered on "personhood," and the ways in which it emerges.[56]

Ironically, then, the relationality we see in religious performances and settings parallels the procedures of museality. Elsewhere, Whitehead elaborates this idea with regard to agency:

> One way of thinking about things—images, objects, clothing, food, spaces, and our bodies—is to regard them as mediating several agents and becoming in the process agents themselves. A thing offers particular affordances, accommodating some uses and not others. It changes the user's relationship to other agents, to the task at hand, and to the thing itself, which mediates these relations. . . . Agency (for want of a better word) or the "liveliness" of objects is co-inspired, co-created, and co-relational. Devotees and objects bring each other into unique forms of ontological being.[57]

From a modern, scientific point of view this will seem like nonsense. Further, it is explicitly *not* a pantheistic notion of everything being alive, nor is it animation of dead objects by spirits. Rather, it points to a set of assumptions according to which anything *might*, in certain circumstances, be accorded "living" status. It "confounds things which we distinguish" and "distinguishes things which we connect together." This aligns with the viewpoint that Praet describes among the Chachi and reminds one of certain Japanese practices (*kuyō*) toward trees and other "material" objects.[58]

Objects and Agency: Latour's Actor-Network Theory and Ingold's Meshwork

So, how can we better attempt to break free of our transcendent-oriented episteme and see differently the things we place in religion museums? Can we imagine a "co-relational" museum? Two promising approaches are offered in Bruno Latour's Actor-Network Theory (ANT) and Tim Ingold's Meshwork theory.

Bruno Latour is a sociologist whose work has been concerned with the history and practice of science. His Actor-Network Theory (French: *acteur-réseau*) is reminiscent of the work of Merleau-Ponty and is a kind of Occam's razor cutting off complex epistemic assumptions of binary oppositions between subject and object, spirit and matter.[59] Latour points out that

> the older philosophical tools of object and subject are wholly inadequate to follow the many descriptions, the many accounts that are pouring out of our scriptoria—be they laboratories, offices, studios or libraries.[60]

Latour's approach—characterized as "irreductionism"—seeks to deconstruct the various cultural biases and their conceptual frameworks that have been naturalized in our societies and thereby to open up the possibility of other ways of understanding our world.[61] In his Tanner Lectures, Latour vividly underscores how our tendency to posit abstractions as convenient labels for materials and processes gets us into trouble. Examining the "discovery" of the first pulsar, he shows how a series of chart-blips and processes are transformed by nominalization and labeling. Thereafter, the physical processes themselves are effaced by the application of the shorthand of the label.[62] An abstract nominalization—an object—is created. Latour argues that "learning means: to reverse the movement that has turned them [processes, discrete observations] into entities."[63]

In a series of books and essays Latour has advanced ANT as a means of performing this reversal. Latour explains what he means by "actor" thus:

> Although ANT shares [a] distrust for such vague all-encompassing sociological terms, it also aims at describing the very nature of societies. But to do so it does not limit itself to human individual actors, but extends the word actor—or actant—to non-human, non-individual entities.[64]

As for actors, Latour says that

> an "actor" in ANT is a semiotic definition—an actant—that is something that acts or to which activity is granted by others. It implies no special motivation of

human individual actors, nor of humans in general. An actant can literally be anything provided it is granted to be the source of an action.[65]

Such actors are the dynamic constituents of a "network" or, in the original French, *réseau*:

The word "réseau" was used from the beginning by Diderot to describe matter and bodies in order to avoid the Cartesian divide between matter and spirit. Thus, the word has had a strong ontological component from the beginning (Anderson 1990). Put too simply, ANT is a change of metaphors to describe essences: instead of surfaces one gets filaments (or rhyzomes in Deleuze's parlance Deleuze/Guattari 1980). More precisely it is a change of topology. Instead of thinking in terms of surfaces—two dimensions—or spheres— three dimensions—one is asked to think in terms of nodes that have as many dimensions as they have connections.[66]

The point of ANT in practice is

the attribution of human, unhuman, nonhuman, inhuman characteristics; the distribution of properties among these entities; the connections established between them; the circulation entailed by these attributions, distributions and connections; the transformation of those attributions, distributions and connections of the many elements that circulate, and of the few ways through which they are sent.[67]

Thus, for Latour, "Actors are not conceived as fixed entities but as flows, as circulating objects undergoing trials, and their stability, continuity, isotopy has to be obtained by other actions and other trials."[68] "ANT is not about traced net-works, but about a network-tracing activity. . . . A network is not a thing, but the recorded movement of a thing."[69] Thinking of this in another way, the metaphors of scales (nation, individual) are replaced with a metaphor of connections.[70] "What is lost is the absolute distinction between representation and things."[71] In short, Latour's irreductionist approach advocates recovering the activities of objects by putting aside the labels and abstract frameworks we have superimposed on them and describing and following their activities and relationships wherever they may lead.

This is precisely the opposite of the approach commonly taken in discussions of religion. As in the case of the British Museum's *Living with Gods* exhibit mentioned at the beginning of this chapter, an exhibition of objects is framed by terms such as "belief," "faith," and "transcendence."[72] By contrast, Latour's "mantra," as he says in one place, is "describe, write, describe, write."[73] By attempting to describe what we encounter without imposing grand frameworks of theories on the descriptions, we stop segregating the world into actors and acted upon, into consciousness and matter, or into subjects and objects. We try to see clearly what is connected to what.

Tim Ingold, formerly the chair of social anthropology at the University of Aberdeen, in Scotland, has articulated a theory he calls "meshwork" that bears similarities to that of Latour.

> To describe the meshwork is to start from the premise that every living being is a line or, better, a bundle of lines. How, then, should we describe the interpenetration of lifelines in the mesh of social life? One possible way would be to think in terms of knots (Ingold 2015: 13–16). A knot is formed when a strand such as of string or yarn is interlaced with itself or another strand and tightened. I suggest that in a world where things are continually coming into being through processes of growth and movement—that is, in a world of life— knotting is the fundamental principle of coherence.[74]

Ingold's close attention to material is something curators and conservators know well. In speaking of materials, he says, "Far from being the inanimate stuff typically envisioned by modern thought, materials in this original sense [mater] are the active constituents of a world-in-formation."[75] He argues that we "take materials seriously, since it is from them that everything is made."[76] "Like all other creatures, human beings do not exist on the 'other side' of materiality but swim in an ocean of materials."[77]

For Ingold,

> the properties of materials, regarded as constituents of an environment, cannot be identified as fixed, essential attributes of things, but are rather processual and relational. They are neither objectively determined nor subjectively imagined but practically experienced. In that sense, every property is a condensed story. To describe the properties of materials is to tell the stories of what happens to them as they flow, mix and mutate.[78]

In other words, one alternative to traditional museum displays is to tell the stories of an object or, if one could, all the stories.

Like Latour, Ingold stresses that we should try carefully to observe and describe things ignoring distinctions such as human or nonhuman that we have imposed on them. Ingold, Latour, and others are sometimes referred to as "neo-animists" because they speak of "agency" of objects. Ingold addresses this directly in an effort to dispel misunderstanding:

> Bringing things to life, then, is a matter not of adding to them a sprinkling of agency but of restoring them to the generative fluxes of the world of materials in

which they came into being and continue to subsist. This view, *that things are in life rather than that life is in things*, is diametrically opposed to the conventional anthropological understanding of animism . . . and harking back to the classic work of Edward Tylor, according to which it entails the attribution of life, spirit or agency to objects that are really inert. It is, however, entirely consistent with the actual ontological commitments of peoples often credited in the literature with an animistic cosmology. In their world there are no objects as such. Things are alive and active not because they are possessed of spirit-whether in or of matter—but because the substances which they comprise continue to be swept up in circulations of the surrounding media that alternately portend their dissolution or—characteristically with animate beings—ensure their regeneration.[79]

Ingold invokes what he calls "correspondence" as a way to characterize his theory, and in speaking of religion he cites the theologian Peter J. Chandler, Jr. who argues that religion is founded in a grammar of participation, not of representation.[80] Ingold continues, saying that religion "has nothing to do with holding beliefs about or concepts of the world and everything to do with corresponding with it."[81] This notion of correspondence is not passive but rather a "doing undergoing." "As already noted, 'of-ness' makes an object of that to which one attends, whereas 'with-ness' brings it alongside as a fellow-traveller."[82] Might it be possible to have a museum not where things are in the process of dying, but rather where we can experience things relationally as living?

Spirits in a Museum or Things Passing through?

On a recent visit to one regional museum in the United States, I encountered a room of Hindu and Buddhist sculptures lined up along the walls with the sparsest of labels: deity name, date, and place. It was as though the sculptures were appliances from an exotic culture—toasters, washing machines, and stoves—all unplugged. Should they, to continue the metaphor, be plugged in? How?[83]

Discussions by Durkheim and Lévy-Bruhl, and more recently Praet's discussion of the Chachi, demonstrate the possibility that the world might be divided up in other than a Cartesian way. Latour, Ingold, Whitehead, and others are trying to make us think outside the Cartesian box, outside of the mind-in-body spirit-in-matter box that characterizes both Christianity and the heritage of the Enlightenment. Latour and Ingold deploy the metaphors of lines to help us see materials through something other than simple subject-object dichotomies—to think of knots, meshes, tangles, and flows. So what, then, are the implications of such views for religious things—or even things more generally—held in museums? Can we imagine not a museum "of religions," but a museum "with religions" (to use Ingold's turn of phrase)?

One way to answer this question is to return to Latour's point about naming. Names—and, by extension, taxonomies or typologies—provide us a shorthand for understanding, classifying manipulating, and representing the flow of the world and its processes. I am reminded of the passage in Genesis, where the various animals are brought before Adam and he names them (Gen. 2:20). It is a kind of *listenwissenschaft* (list science) first found in early Sumerian tablets. When I visit a museum, I often catch myself spending as much time attending to the labels as I do to the things. But such shorthands, as we saw in the discussion of religion in Chapter 1, flatten things and make many things altogether invisible. Like a colored lens they pass only a narrow part of reality and screen out the rest as though it does not even exist. We should be careful to avoid confusing objects—things—with our frameworks for understanding them. This is especially the case in museums, where framing, narrative, and representation are arguably the raison d'etre.

Thinking about this question led me to reconsider a display I visited in 2016 on the Polynesian "god" A'a at the British Museum titled *Containing the Divine: A Sculpture of the Pacific God A'a*.[84] This was a very impressive installation set up in a room just to the right of the entryway to the museum. The sculpture was one of the most famous artifacts in the London Missionary Society Museum (discussed earlier) and is clearly visible in early representations of that museum. It was one of many "gods" offered to the missionary John Williams in 1821 by the inhabitants of Rurutu in the process of their conversion to Christianity. It arrived in Ra'iātea along with other "rejected gods" where it was displayed and described from the pulpit of the church as "a trophy of victory."[85] In line with Williams's policy of preserving and displaying such idols as evidence of the success of missionary efforts—rather than destroying them—it was then shipped back to London and put on display at the London Missionary Society Museum.

The display at the British Museum was a superb example of a context-rich treatment of an object, and it sought to trace the object's movements and actions from the Pacific to London and back again. It included the history of A'a, scientific investigation of the artifact, its historical provenance, the influence of the image on artists such as Henry Moore and Pablo Picasso. In other words, an attempt was made to trace its journey and its various connections, almost as if the curators had been reading Latour or Ingold. But Steven Hooper's essay "Mysteries, Methods, and Meanings: On Looking Closely at A'a" in the accompanying catalog should make us think twice about the title of the exhibit: *Containing the Divine: A Sculpture of the Pacific God A'a.* As Hooper notes, the "name" of the thing was puzzling and contested from the very beginning when it was displayed from the pulpit of the church and described as "A'a, the national god of Rurutu."[86] Indeed, although described as containing a host of smaller "gods" (which have since disappeared), it appears to be neither a "god" not a container for "gods." Careful examination of the carving of its interior and comparison with other Pacific Island artifacts indicates that this was a container for a skull and long bones—or what we might term an ancestral reliquary.

In other words, the label "God" reframes the object in a way that obscures the material clues of its production and use in Rurutu. Despite careful attention to context, the British Museum exhibit still presented A'a through a decidedly Christian, Cartesian, and Western lens, though its function as an example of "primitive" art in modernism is certainly a story worth telling. But it is only a part of the story. Other parts of the story might include its role as a "trophy" in a colonial knowledge regime or its assimilation by missionaries to the Christian category of "idol" or "god."

So how might a museum present things in a "co-relational" fashion? Taking an approach to presenting something like A'a inspired by Latour's ANT and Ingold's meshwork would involve modifying the framing of the exhibit to avoid labeling with big conceptual frameworks and narratives like "religious," "god," or even "ritual" in favor of description tracing an object's material production and circulation, its creation and function as a node or "knot" in flows of people and other material things, including those things standing in front of it in the "exhibit." This might include bespoke tours, intensive contextual story telling of select objects, including their museumification, and coordination between religious communities and museums.

Finally, one might explore the treatment of selected objects based on seeing the museum as a "contact zone" or as a "thirdspace." As mentioned earlier, Clifford used his view of museums as contact zones to help emphasize that museums and the objects in them might function as settings of cultural contact, contestation, and possible learning and exchange. "A'a" can and did serve this role, as the museum engaged and involved the present-day community on Rurutu in the design of the exhibit. This view of museums as frontiers or a boundary zones can be nuanced by combining it with Edward Soja's notion of "thirdspace." For Soja, "firstspace" is the material world we exist in. "Secondspace" is the imagined world, the world of representation, of the imaginaire. Thirdspace is the blended space, "a fully lived space, a simultaneously real and imagined, actual-and-virtual locus of structured individuality and collective experience and agency."[87] Soja describes this space as radically open to "a multiplicity of perspectives that have heretofore been considered by the epistemological referees to be incompatible, uncombinable."[88] A museum of religions encompasses both museums and religions—it exists in a third space where one might trace the "lines" or processes and histories of objects and how they are intertwined with collectors, curators, visitors, and religious communities. It is conceivable that in the third space of a museum of religious objects the objects can bring together multiple "perspectives that have heretofore been considered by the epistemological referees to be incompatible, uncombinable." It is important that we recognize the limitations and blind spots induced by the epistemic horizon of the comparative religion/ world religions typology with its spirit versus matter dichotomy, its heritage of race theory and evolution, and its hegemonic "scientific" grid. Can we imagine a museum "with religion" (Ingold) or a museum emphasizing "relationality" (Whitehead), structured not merely to emphasize similarity but also to highlight differences that could serve as the basis for real engagement and dialogue?

Part Two

Five Museums of World Religions

Introduction

This section of the book examines five museums of religions: the Religionskundliche Sammlung in Marburg, Germany; the State Museum of the History of Religions in St. Petersburg, Russia; Le Musée des Religions du Monde in Nicolet, Québec; the St. Mungo Museum of Religious Life and Art in Glasgow, Scotland; and the Museum of World Religions in Taipei, Taiwan. Of these, the Religionskundliche Sammlung and the State Museum of the History of Religions are early twentieth-century foundations, one inclined to liberal Protestant understandings of the religions, the other inclined to decidedly materialist understandings of the religions. The early history of these two institutions forms an instructive contrast with regard to their approach to religious objects. Yet, in their current disposition, both museums date from the late 1980s. In this regard, all of the museums are representative of late twentieth- and early twenty-first-century understandings of religions. All are indebted to the comparative religion approach that was a product of empire. My aim is not to produce a detailed history of each museum, but to situate each museum with respect to the others and with respect to the development of the enterprise of comparative religion, world religions, and the display of religious objects. These museums curate, create, and present the divine in objects and images. I examine how comparativist principles undergird each museum, how the objects in these collections are framed, and how they might be otherwise deployed. Each museum has a unique history and context and, in each case, we see a dialectic between permanent exhibits and temporary exhibits, objects and ideas where the global is refracted through local and nationalist lenses. Each museum is actually three museums: the permanent collections, temporary exhibitions, and the online virtual "translation" (in case of St. Petersburg the museum web page and distant virtual displays and traveling exhibitions).

The five museums examined in Part Two of this study occupy a spectrum with one end anchored firmly in the research agendas of a university institution, while the other end is just as firmly anchored in the educational and religious agendas of a stand-alone public or private museum. All are indebted to the comparative religion heritage and now approach their task using multiple modes of comparison. All are now structured to examine religion in a global comparative framework, and all see as a key part of their mission the promotion of tolerance in an increasingly globalized world.

The Numinous in Marburg

Rudolf Otto's Religionskundliche Sammlung

Introduction and Brief History

The Religionskundliche Sammlung (Religious Studies Collection) is located on the castle hill above the city of Marburg in Hesse in central Germany. This charming old town is the site of the medieval pilgrimage to the church of St. Elizabeth of Hungary, and it is today the home of Philipps-Universität.[1] Founded by Philip I, Landgrave of Hesse in 1527, it is the oldest Protestant University in the world. Since 1981, the collection, along with the department of religious studies, has been housed in the New Chancery building (Neue Kanzlei), which was built in 1573–75 by the Landgrave of Hesse.[2] To get to the collection the visitor ascends a steep hill where the New Chancery is perched just below the castle.

Max Müller's "Science of Religion" became a tool for seeking the essence of religion, and this search provided a major impetus for the establishment of the Religionskundliche Sammlung in 1927—the first museum of religions expressly based on comparative principles and having a worldwide scope.[3] The theologian Rudolf Otto (1869–1937) conceived of and initiated the museum, and its early history is inextricably linked to liberal Christian understandings of other religions. The museum was moved and substantially reconfigured in 1981, but in keeping with the interests of its founder, it serves as home of the university's Religious Studies Department and as an active educational facility dedicated to the comparative science of religion (*religionswissenschaft*). This comparative science is now conceived in a theologically neutral and historical but, nonetheless, universalist key. Here, I trace the changing curatorial strategies that have led the Marburg museum from its liberal Christian beginnings to a "scientific" comparativism. Despite some efforts at providing contextual information for some of the displays, the choices of grouping, utilization of space, and the placement of displays have the effect of producing "objects" largely shorn of their contexts and relationships. Otto's Religionskundliche Sammlung is in essence an archive of objects and texts for teaching and research about religions.

Rudolf Otto is best known for his book *Das Heilige* ([1917]; the English translation first appeared in 1923 as *The Idea of the Holy*) in which he describes a particular apprehension of holiness that goes beyond the merely ethical.[4] For this special sense, he coined the word "numinous," describing it as having qualities of something "felt as objective and outside the self."[5] For Otto, "this mental state is perfectly *sui generis* and irreducible to any other" and manifests in consciousness as "wholly other."[6] Otto's emphasis on "feeling" is very much in the lineage of romanticism, the thought of the theologian Friedrich Schleiermacher, and German pietism. Otto's work has been immensely influential and was one of the primary influences on the mid-twentieth-century historian of religion Mircea Eliade's work on "the sacred."[7] It has also been the object of many studies. For my purposes, Otto's understanding of religious objects and his efforts in establishing the collection are of primary interest.

Rudolf Otto's interest in non-Christian religions was piqued by encounters during a trip through North Africa, Palestine, British India, China, Japan, and the United States in 1911–12. One of the motivations for the trip was "to prepare an introduction to the world's religions that he was supposed to write for Paul Siebeck."[8] By the time Otto returned to Germany, his plan

> was to include a systematic, collaborative effort to import Asian religions into Europe, especially in German translation, to counter the cultural capital that Britain had accumulated from Orientalist scholarship, notably the Sacred Books of the East—founded, Otto pointed out, by a German.[9]

A visit to a Moroccan synagogue in 1911 apparently inspired the notion of the holy that he would later develop. Stimulated by such experiences Otto tried to elaborate a "methodology of the religious sentiment." Acts of sentiment, ritual behaviors, and visual sensations are sources of "objective" knowledge, an insight, which became central for Rudolf Otto's philosophy.[10] Otto's encounters during his travels prompted him, on his return in 1912, to imagine a collection of the "cultic and ritual means of expression of religions."[11] Otto was interested in how religious objects could "evoke the sense of the numinous." These objects need not be of great aesthetic value but would be instructive in helping educate people about everyday religion.[12] This is not to say that texts were to be ignored, but Otto's was an early recognition of the importance of material religion.

But as Gregory D. Alles has pointed out, Otto's early collecting and his later endeavors admit of an imperialist reading: "I view Otto's Religionswissenschaft as a kind of cultural import business, and one that was a relic, in some sense a post-colonial one, of a more ambitious import-export endeavor that could not survive the force of political circumstances."[13] Alles sees Otto as presenting an analysis of religion as something more than Christianity and supporting it by "importing" objects and texts—especially from South Asia—that illustrated his contention. Otto's comparative analyses in *Mysticism East and West* (1926) and in *India's Religion of Grace and Christianity* (1930) argue that the numinous manifests in two primary ways—wisdom and devotion in India and mysticism and personal piety in the West. He "compared and differentiated" this material in a binary fashion "into which the colonialist imagination divided the religious world, east and west."[14] Although both worlds can be seen to have similar perceptions of the numinous, the Western version is preferred:

> What Otto reveals through his comparative work is crucial: the same fundamental religious experience is present in both east and west. But what he reveals through differentiation is equally crucial: there is always some distinguishing feature that makes the German, Christian West superior.[15]

Alles goes to some lengths to point out that his is not a heavy-handed critique of Otto as colonialist. The caution is worth understanding. Many of the key figures in the development of comparative religion could not have done the work they did or advanced the theories they advanced apart from the colonial context and the material opportunities it presented. Having a realistic view of the contradictions they inhabited, which was the incubator for their theories, will help us better understand their work and its continuing impact on the study of religion today.

Like many other thinkers of his time, such as William James, Otto suggests a progression of types—or evolution of religious action and perception. At their base these are manipulative worldly oriented magical rites and objects designed "to appropriate the prodigious force of the numen for the natural ends of man." In the more advanced Otto posits a "process of development by which the experience is matured and purified, till finally it reaches its consummation in the sublimest and purest states of the life within the Spirit and in the noblest Mysticism."[16]

The publication of *Das Heilige* brought Otto considerable fame. Although appointed to the chair of systematic theology in Marburg in 1917, it was not until 1927 that his ideas for a collection came to any fruition. That year, the

Philipps-Universität would celebrate its 400th anniversary, and Otto was granted 40,000 marks to purchase objects for what was proposed as a "Lehrsammlung für religionsgeschichtlichen und konfessionskundlichen Unterricht" (university collection for the teaching and study of the history of religions and confessions).[17] Otto embarked on a collecting trip during 1927–28, and the first objects were displayed in an exhibit of *Fremde Heiligutümer* (Foreign Sacred Sites and Objects) in the autumn of 1929.[18]

Otto's proposal for a research institute organized around a core collection of texts and artifacts was an attempt to avoid ethnographic, artistic, or antiquities types of presentation. It was to be based on the principal of the equivalence of all religions and thus the comparison of religions.[19] According to Konstanze Runge, curator of the collection, the objects in the collection were to be of instructive, rather than artistic, value and were to be used for teaching scholars and missionaries about everyday religious life.[20]

But there were lengthy delays in the full realization of the museum. Ill-health forced Otto's retirement (though he continued to write and work on the project), and Heinrich Frick took over as director of the Sammlung (1932–52).[21] From 1937 to 1945 he also served as dean of the theology faculty. Frick strove to develop typologies for comparing diverse religious practices and ideas. With Otto's support, Frick proposed

> the foundation of a research institute in the fields of comparative religions. The collection headed by more than ten proposed curators, so they thought, should serve as the core of the research institute. As the home and burial-place of the well-known saint Elizabeth (1207–31), and the meeting place of the two Protestant Reformation leaders, Martin Luther and Ulrich Zwingli (1529), Marburg—and especially the Marburg castle—seemed to be the perfect location. . . . Frick envisioned a kind of an advanced institute of religious studies in the heart of Germany (and Europe as well), which should provide facilities for research fellows from all over the world.[22]

Otto and Frick's lobbying for a religious studies research institute to be sited in the castle ran up against budgetary problems, ideological conflict, and the Second World War.[23] The original idea was to house the collection in the castle; however, the Hessian State archives were there, and thus there was not sufficient room. Despite proposals by Otto and Frick that highlighted "the religious struggle of the German soul" and a generally positive reception by the new Nazi regime, other more overtly "Aryan" projects took precedence.[24] The artifacts were housed in the Art Institute where only limited space for display was available.

A brief look at proposals for the Religionskundliche Sammlung fielded by Otto and Frick is instructive. In the 1931 version of the proposal, the collections were to be divided as follows: "Christianity, Judaism, and Islam, then non-Western religions, followed by religions of antiquity and primitives."[25] The program draft of 1933 omits Judaism, and the proposal of March 1937 (the month of Otto's death) has the following lineup: Germanic religions; Christianity; the Near East, Islam; Indian religions; East Asian religions; primitive religions; and missions and contemporary religious movements. Four supplementary methodological areas were proposed: psychology of religion and pedagogy, religious studies and psychiatry, sociology of religion, and philosophy of religion. Judaism had completely vanished from the proposal.[26] Leaving aside the clearly political omission of Judaism and the primary position of Germanic religions, the lineup was little different from proposals of earlier proponents of the comparative science of religion and to generations of later textbook treatments.[27]

After the war Frick had more success with the US military government, and in 1947 the collection was transferred to the castle.[28] With Frick's death in 1952, Friedrich Heiler (1892–1967) took over leadership.[29] Heiler was a well-known historian of religions and Asianist famous for his comparative typology of prayer and for advocating a view of the church that included non-Christian religions.[30] While a full-fledged religious studies center as envisioned by Otto and Frick was still unrealized, Heiler brought the collection to prominence in 1960 by arranging to host the tenth International Congress of the History of Religions.[31]

In a real sense, Otto's full plan was not to be realized until 1981–82, when the collection was relocated to the sixteenth-century Neue Kanzlei building under the directorship of Martin Kraatz.[32] This massive stone building is a short walk down from the castle proper and remains the home of the Religionskundliche Sammlung to the present.

Martin Kraatz and the Current Museum

Rudolf Otto's idea of a collection that would be at the heart of a research institute for the comparative study of religion (*religionswissenschaft*) only came to full fruition in the last two decades of the twentieth century under the direction of Martin Kraatz. Indeed, Kraatz describes the collection almost as a *kunstkammer* style archive or storage facility:

> Things from some of the religions of humankind were exhibited in two large halls. They were not explained; if at all they were only marked by nothing but

the name of the piece in its original language. Through presenting them in this way, the religions did not lose their strange foreignness for the visitors; instead, they remained as something exotic to them. I more or less planned to give short texts to each exhibit, explaining the name, describing the material, function, and status in the religion it belonged to, and whenever possible, the emotional closeness followers had with the object. For the time being, I had to compensate for the absence of texts by personally guiding visitors through the exhibition halls and trying to bring them closer to a religion foreign to them though oral explanations so that they might recognize it as something as real as their own religious orientation.[33]

According to Peter Bräunlein, who succeeded Kraatz as director of the museum, Kraatz's overall plan has largely been preserved in the present museum layout. In its original configuration, the director, a docent, or an expert with knowledge of a particular tradition guided visitors through the collection. However, this guidance was not always possible, and thus labels have been added.[34]

The Religionskundliche Sammlung is at the heart of a research and teaching network at Philipps-Universität dedicated to the study of religion. In the late 1990s, the department of religious studies was moved to the top floor of the Neue Kanzlei building, as was a dedicated research library.[35] Since 2005, the department offers both BA and MA degrees, and the collection functions as the research lab for students and faculty. Also related are the Zentrum für interdisziplinäre Religionsforschung, a series of research presentations (Religion am Mittwoch), and *The Marburg Journal of Religion*.[36] This was, in other words, a research collection. The configuration of the collection as it stands now is reminiscent more of a curio cabinet or the Pitt Rivers Museum than of Otto's idea of a collection of objects notable for their evocation of the numinous. In the sense in which the full institute emerged after in the last decade of the twentieth century, the current Religionskundliche Sammlung is roughly contemporary to but quite different from the St. Mungo Museum and Le Musée des Religions du Monde (to be treated in subsequent chapters).

The Neue Kanzlei building, of impressive stone construction, consists of four rectangular floors (Figure 3). The floors are connected by a spiral staircase located at the front center of the building. Entry to each floor from the stairwell is through massive vault-like doors. The ground floor houses an exhibit of South Indian Hinduism and the archive—now including the Rudolf Otto archive; the first floor has galleries dedicated to Islam, Judaism, Christianity, and ancient Egyptian and the precolonial Americas, as well as a seminar room; the second floor houses rooms on African traditions, Chinese and Japanese Buddhism,

Figure 3 Entryway to Neue Kanzlei, Religionskundliche Sammlung. Photo by Heike Luu, courtesy of Religionskundliche Sammlung.

South and Southeast Asian Buddhism, and a large room containing artifacts from China, India, and Japan (Hinduism, Daoism, Confucianism, Shinto, and Tenrikyō); and the top floor contains the library and department offices. Two special exhibit rooms were added in 2006 to more easily accommodate the mounting of special exhibitions pioneered by Kraatz and his successor Peter Bräunlein.[37] Approximately 1,000 objects are on display out of some 6,500 in the collection (Figure 4).

Peter Bräunlein has described the relationship between the current layout of the museum and its actual use with visiting groups. Bräunlein notes that the arrangement of the rooms and objects are analogous to the chapters of an introductory handbook of the comparative history of religions and that the museum has found this arrangement useful in accommodating the educational needs of school groups who often have assigned curricula in categories such as "Asian world religions," "Judaism," and so on.[38] Thus, the Religionskundliche Sammlung is a research "library" containing both books and objects, and as a library both books and objects are arranged according to a filing system. This special character means that to get the most out of the museum one needs a guided tour or one must use the detailed website as a stand-in for a docent.

Raumplan der Religionskundlichen Sammlung

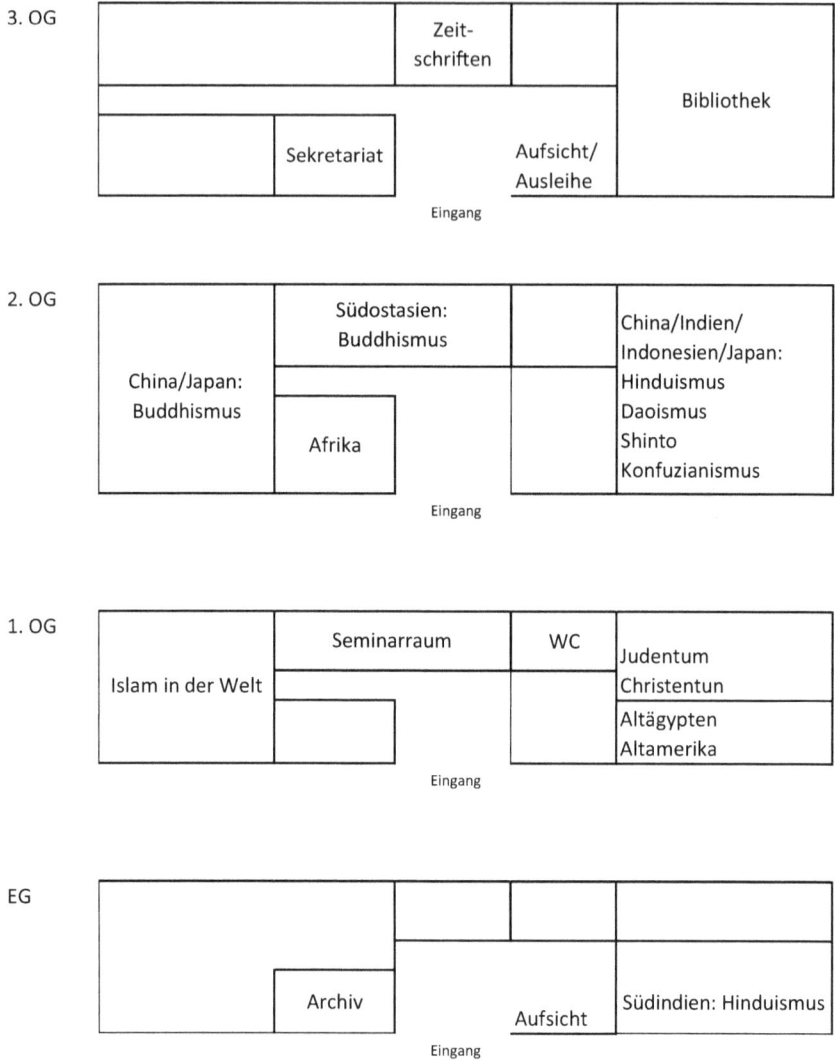

Figure 4 Museum floor plan. Reproduced courtesy of Religionskundliche Sammlung.

It is notable that the Abrahamic religions—Judaism, Islam, and Christianity—located in relatively small spaces on the first floor are typically not the start or end point of tours. Acting on Otto's interest in the equal treatment of religious traditions, such tours simultaneously place these traditions in a comparative framework while downplaying their traditional Western cultural prominence. They are treated as "religions among others."[39] In effect, this "provincializes" them.[40] At the same time, the objects on display have been chosen to highlight the theme of images in the three monotheisms and the key distinctions between the major branches of Christianity.

The second-floor galleries focus on Asia and Africa, with two galleries on Buddhism (one on Buddhism in Southeast Asia [Figure 5] and the other on Buddhism in China and Japan), a small gallery on Africa, and a large gallery containing objects from non-Buddhist traditions of India, China, and Japan (Hindu, Daoist, Confucian, Shinto, and Tenrikyō).

Bräunlein points out that the collection is quite strong in materials related to Buddhist traditions and that images relating to the life of the Buddha make possible the illustration of key Buddhist teachings including the four noble truths and nirvana. The richness of artifacts also facilitates discussions of Buddhist culture in Southeast Asia, China, Japan, and Tibet and of different Buddhist schools (Figure 6). An array of Hindu artifacts focusing on the gods Śiva, Visnu, and Krishna provides a contrast to the monotheisms. Artifacts devoted to ancient Egyptian and precolonial American archeology in a first-floor gallery adjacent to the gallery on Judaism and Christianity can be discussed with the artifacts of Tenrikyō on the second floor to illustrate the notion of "dead religions" and the birth of "new religions."

Figure 5 South Asian Buddhism. Photo by Georg Doerr, courtesy of Religionskundliche Sammlung.

Figure 6 East Asian Buddhism. Photo by author, used with permission of Religionskundliche Sammlung.

The notion of approaching religions from a thematic or cross-cultural view with categories such as "ethnic religions" can be demonstrated in the gallery on the second floor devoted to Africa and Oceania. The same rooms serve for discussions of topics such as divination, masking, initiation, shamanism, magic, healing, and ancestor worship. Finally, there is a small first-floor gallery dedicated to contemporary lived Hinduism which helps to problematize "the distinction between popular and orthodox" within a single religious tradition.[41]

Discussing the contemporary use and outlook of the collection, Konstanze Runge, who served as curator, underscored that the artifacts function as a teaching collection for the department.[42] Otto, Frick, and Heiler saw the collection as a way to "induce a sense of the unity of religions" and to "promote interreligious tolerance, ecumenical endeavor, and mutual understanding."[43] Otto had long championed the idea of a Religiöser Menschheitsbund (religious league of humanity) to foster interreligious dialogue.[44] Runge says that since the initiation of BA and MA programs in 2005 the approach involves a "more open and differentiated understanding of the objects, integrating students, visitors, and colleagues into the process of exploring, researching, and exhibiting material religion."[45]

According to Runge, at present, "more than 80% of our visitors are school children" and the staff has been exploring the use of the museum "in opening up a 'third space' as a communication center on non-confessional but empathetic ground, facilitating discussion about sensitive religion-based issues against the background of well-researched and differentiated knowledge about religions from a neutral perspective."[46] Indeed, since Edith Franke assumed the directorship in 2006, there has been an increase in the mounting of special exhibits which allow "flexibility in responding to current social issues" as well as more contextualization.[47] Runge notes that "in the past ten years the whole process of communicating research findings to a broader public . . . has become the focal point of teaching and research in the Marburg museum."[48]

Museum, Comparison, Classification

Located high on the hill between the main square of the upper town and the castle, the situation of the museum would seem to be ideal, and communicates the centrality of the institution to the university and the city of Marburg. Yet reaching the museum is not easy for less than mobile tourists (it is a steep climb on cobbled streets from the upper town square). Further, despite well-thought-out modern lighting and professional display, this is a sixteenth-century building with massive stone walls and a spiral staircase. The rooms are not large by modern standards and the ceilings are relatively low (in some cases with dark beams), giving the museum a decidedly fortress-like aspect. Entry to each level is through a thick vault-like door that must be unlocked by staff. Perhaps this is not a drawback for a university institution whose mission centers on research and teaching. Most visitors come in school classes by arrangement.

The collection of artifacts currently on display in the museum under the category "religions" is reminiscent of drawers in a filing cabinet or a specimen case. Examining the museum floor plan we can see that under the category religion one finds two organizing subcategories: geographic location and religious tradition. The geographic location category includes Africa, Ancient Egypt, and precolonial America (Maya, etc.), and China/India/Japan (Asia).

The religious "traditions" category includes Islam, Judaism, and Christianity. A further division involves the crosscutting of these two categories: Buddhism in Southeast Asia, Buddhism in China and Japan, and South Indian Hinduism. The geographic gallery India/China/Japan is divided by tradition into Hinduism, Daoism, Shinto, Confucianism, and Tenrikyō—that is, Asia excluding Buddhism.[49]

Thus, despite not having a great deal of space devoted to them, Islam, Christianity, and Judaism constitute the "traditions," while Africa, the Americas, and Asia constitute the "geographic" category, with Buddhism (to which a large amount of space is allocated) and South Indian Hinduism as freestanding mixes of tradition and geographical location. This is not far from the world religions model of Judaism, Islam, Christianity, Buddhism, and Hinduism in contrast to more local and "ethnic" traditions. The religions thus appear to be analogous to class or order. But these harken back to such categories as "universal" and "ethnic" or "religions of the world" and "national religions" first proposed by Chantepie de la Saussaye in 1827. In discussing his experience as general editor of the *Dictionary of Religion*, Jonathan Z. Smith noted that the "'Religions of Traditional Peoples' are largely divided geographically, reinforcing the outdated notion that place rather than history and movement defines them."[50] Further problematic are the religions of "antiquity" or ancient religions versus "new religions," both of which, at least in the *Dictionary of Religion*, are somehow negatively or positively indexed to Christianity.[51]

The Religionskundliche Sammlung presents us a sort of library or encyclopedia of things organized by geographic location and religious tradition. To some extent, and per Otto's intention, things *are* equalized: Tenrikyō is on an equal footing with Shinto and Hinduism. But overall, this is a research collection and reminds one of curio cabinets or natural history museums—with glass cases serving almost as filing drawers, the objects have minimal (or even no) description and are to be taken out and examined as needed. Other taxonomic systems are deployed under the aegis of guided tours, wherein thematic categories such as initiation rites, shamanism, images and iconoclasm, magic, and so on are deployed. At Marburg much depends on the docent.

To some extent, given the genealogy and history of the museum, the changes taken place over time, and the constraints on funding and space, its organization is not surprising. Indeed, when we look at how the museum is being used, there are evident tensions among the agenda of its founders, the constraints of space and funding, the ongoing internal critique of the institutional inheritance, and the growing mission to the public.

Religious Objects in the Religionskundliche Sammlung

Otto was perhaps the first scholar to champion the importance of the material dimension of religion in the context of a teaching and research collection. Toward the end of Chapter 1, I argued that each museum of religion or museum display of religion is in effect a material definition of "religion." The objects inevitably frame each other. Further, I noted that religion museums are a form of cultural discourse in which objects are arranged according to their value in a system of signs designed to produce an ideal object for public display. Museums of religions manage objects and objecthood. They create narrative frames for understanding objects while obscuring and making it difficult to discern the objects as "things." How then are we to answer the following questions: What is the object religion presented to us in the Religionskundliche Sammlung? And what of the things that reside here?

We know that Otto's aim was to select objects evocative of various dimensions of a unitary sui generis "numinous," and that he intended the collection to treat Christianity and Judaism as "religions among others." The objects did not have to be great works of art, and Otto's idea of choosing everyday quotidian objects for their illustrative, rather than artistic, merit is evident in many rooms. The nominalizing power of "religion" and the "numinous" worked to bring objects into conversation that in the field were normally unrelated or even unrelatable. Nevertheless, for the pre-1980s collection, this theologically tinged science of religion simultaneously imposed a flattening taxonomic grid—a kind of pluralist appropriation of "religion" in all of its manifestations ideally disregarding judgments based on class and aesthetic criteria—as well as an hierarchical bias toward Christianity, German Christianity, and mystical approaches to the transcendent.

One important lesson we can glean from the work of Latour and Ingold is to try to put aside prejudices and the interpretive and taxonomic framing and trace all of the "actors." Such framing often dominates how we see, and the framing itself appears as obvious and transparent. Thus, in the British Museum's recent exhibit *Living with Gods* we are told that "seeing *how* people believe, rather than considering *what* they believe [emphasis in original], suggests that humans might be naturally inclined to believe in transcendent worlds and beings."[52] While this instruction to pay attention to what people do as opposed to what they say is laudable, it nevertheless frames religion as "natural" and as "belief" in "transcendent worlds and beings." Transcendence is an assumption of the exhibition, not a deduction from the objects displayed. Indeed, transcendent worlds and beings are not objects. If we wish to follow Latour's suggestions, we should observe not only the objects but also how and where they are located, the display cases, the rooms, the building, and who uses them and how. All, equally, can be and have been "actors." For Ingold,

> Things are alive and active not because they are possessed of spirit—whether in or of matter—but because the substances which they comprise continue to be swept up in circulations of the surrounding media that alternately portend their dissolution or—characteristically with animate beings—ensure their regeneration.[53]

Discussing religion Ingold notes that religion is not about beliefs or concepts but rather involves a kind of "correspondence" with the things of the world, as "things are in life rather than life being in things."[54] How can we make a museum containing religious things into a museum with religious things?

A first step is to try to recognize our epistemic biases, suspend our abstract taxonomies and ideas, avoid reducing the images to "Hindu" or "Jain," and see religion as "made of objects" and what people do with them (bodies, images, actions, placement).[55] What does such a museum look like? Indeed, Otto proposed the first step by insisting on treating Christianity—at least in certain respects—as one among other religions. If the artifacts constitute a definition of religion, what does a particular gallery say? What do the objects want? To put it another way, what would an eight-year-old person see?

Let's have a closer look at one of the larger rooms—the one devoted to non-Buddhist Asian objects on the second floor. Larger objects are freestanding while smaller objects are displayed in glass cases. Two-dimensional images are on the walls. The museum has a number of scale models of shrines and temples. Many items—especially those freestanding—currently have ample explanatory labels positioned nearby. However, many of the items in the cases have minimal labeling or simply acquisition data: "Acquired by Fredrick Heiler."[56]

A visitor with a working knowledge of Asian religions can see that from the entryway an imaginary line bisects the room. To the right are objects and images from South Asia, including a striking *Rāsa-līlā* painting depicting the god Krishna dancing with the cowherd maidens (south wall). To the left are objects and images from East Asia. East Asian objects divide roughly into those from China representing Daoist and Confucian traditions in the left rear and Japanese Shinto and Tenrikyō in the left front. From the door facing the back wall, a Naṭarāja, a *linga*, and *yoni* abut a Chinese ancestral altar over which are hung ancestral portraits. Glass cases containing South Asian images (Hindu and

Figure 7 Asian Gallery. Photo by author, used with permission of Religionskundliche Sammlung.

Jain) are positioned at the right and right center, Daoist images are on the left, and Tenrikyō artifacts in the northwest quadrant of the room (Figure 7).

Although it is evident to someone who knows about religious history that the objects have been grouped roughly according to geographic origin, the room appears to fulfill Otto's desire to put religions on an equal footing. It also has the effect of grouping the "polytheisms" together.[57]

Unlike the other museums in this study that present the visitor with an overt interpretive narrative, the Religionskundliche Sammlung's approach confronts the visitor with very little by way of an overt narrative program (with the exception of purposive tours or special exhibits). Discerning the implied classificatory schema with its comparative religion pedigree—traditions versus geographic location, and so on—requires reflection. In a sense the lack of an overt narrative actually allows us a more direct encounter with the objects themselves than if they were serving a more overt narrative end. Nonetheless, we cannot dismiss the more subtle narrative implied by the disposition of the objects.

Size and color appear to be important; likewise, whether the objects are accessible and can be touched or are in glass cases and therefore can only be approached visually is also important. The two-dimensional artworks are the most colorful items in the room, while many of the sculptures are brown or a dull bronze color. If items in the glass cases were accessible, a person might pick them up, rearrange them by size, or put them near the model temple. Might we see the Śiva statue as related to the ancestral altar and portrait it stands next to? Should the Śiva statue go on the ancestral altar along with the Daoist deity across the room—they are about the same size and the altar looks big enough to accommodate both. Perhaps the model temples would be of interest.

Suspending (as much as one is able) our learned categories and taxonomies, we perhaps would conclude from bare observation and description that all the objects have been chosen because they are somehow related. But what is the basis of that relationship? Observation yields a series of contrasts as follows:

- large items versus small items;
- freestanding versus objects housed in glass cases;
- items accessible to all the senses versus those accessible visually only;
- two-dimensional images versus three-dimensional sculpture;
- beings (humanoid or animal) versus model buildings;
- colorful versus dull brown or bronze;
- metal casting versus wood or clay fabrication.

Gathering small sculptural figurines together in glass cases implies a kind of relatedness. An observer might conclude that the model temples, populated with figurines, and the small images in the glass cases are toys—dolls and dollhouses. What do the images on the wall have to do with objects? There is very little hint of how the objects are to be used—the exceptions being the photographic illustrations of Tenrikyō ritual, Śiva as Natarāja (lord of the dance), the *Rāsa-līlā* painting, or the clearly narrative painting of female Confucian exemplars. The arrangement of the gallery is reminiscent of the arrangement visible in engravings of the London Missionary Society Museum or the Pitt Rivers Museum—a combination of freestanding items and items in glass cases.

What are we supposed to conclude of religion, the numinous, or the holy by looking at these objects? Scholars of religion have often noted that one important dimension of our perception of a special character we label "sacrality" or the "holy" has to do with contextual emplacement and use. The objects in the Religionskundliche Sammlung are like appliances in a storage facility—they are unplugged.[58] Both Michael Pye and Kaatz recognize the problems of such collections. As Pye notes, there is no numinous in Otto's museum.[59] The objects must be used; otherwise, they are simply antiquities or curiosities in glass cases—examples of the exotic "other" which constitute the stuff of empire.[60]

The fact that the objects are "unplugged," or that there is no numinous in Otto's museum, is a reflection of the recent life and use of these objects. What the objects in their current setting do record are the theoretical, collecting, and displaying agendas of the scholars of religion—Otto, Frick, Heiler, Kraatz, Pye, Bräulein, Franke, and others—who have built this museum. The objects display a particular scholarly understanding of religion that emerged in early twentieth-century imperialism and has been modified in accordance with the mid- to late twentieth-century European pluralism.

The objects in the Religionskundliche Sammlung are stored and indexed and only partake of the flow of life when engaged. Otto's initial procurement of objects that he saw as evoking the numinous and the collection's storing of them with little or no interpretive labeling facilitates our apprehending them shorn of imposed ideologies (with the exception of museum ideology). In its current state, the encyclopedic character of the museum organized by geography and tradition is only mitigated by thematically oriented tours and special exhibitions. Religion involves the manipulation of material things, whether they are statues or images or everyday things such as bowls and rugs. The Religionskundliche Sammlung, then, is really a cabinet or archive where objects wait to be taken out and manipulated and brought back into the flow of life by a docent, even if that life is only an academic comparative religion life.

Connections: Tracing the Lives of Religious Things in Special Exhibits

While we may not be able to coax the numinous into Rudolf Otto's collection, we may indeed be able to "plug" these things back into life flows or better indicate how such objects lived their previous lives and functioned before they were collected. Some of this is already done in the form of bespoke tours of the collection and through special exhibits. Indeed, we can discern a range of ways the lives of objects might be traced in the Religionskundliche Sammlung. The spectrum stretches from the already-mentioned bespoke tours, to special exhibits which trace in detail the various "lives" of an object, to special exhibits or even to museum's functioning as "thirdspaces" where curators, scholars of religion, and religious communities can meet for discussion.

While it is evident that the Religionskundliche Sammlung has, in some measure at least, succeeded in Otto's goal of treating Christianity as one among other religions, the structure of the museum means that the collection functions as an archive for teaching in which its full scope can only be realized through personalized tours in which objects are selected, examined, and commented upon. Pye, Bräunlein, and Franke all recognize that the collection can be much more, and to that end have encouraged and developed a program of special exhibits which, in Konstanze Runge's words, open up "a third space" affording a forum for discussion of difficult topics in an informed way on neutral ground. Applying James Clifford's notion of contact zone or Edward W. Soja's notion of "thirdspace" in thinking about a museum of religion perhaps gives us a way to articulate more accurately the kind of space a museum of religions is. To recapitulate, thirdspace is "a fully lived space, a simultaneously real and imagined, actual-and-virtual locus of structured individuality and collective experience and agency."[61] For Soja this space is radically open and able to accommodate "a multiplicity of perspectives that have heretofore been considered by the epistemological referees to be incompatible, uncombinable."[62] Indeed, by bracketing the "epistemological referees" we might recognize the difficulties posed by the normally incompatible positions of a hegemonic comparativism and hegemonic theologies and find ways to use the conjunction of objects from different religious worlds to open up dialogue among curators, visitors, and adherents of different religions.

The dedication in 2006 of two special exhibit spaces and the mounting of special exhibits is an important development which has changed the character of the museum from that of a research collection to more of a public museum. Under the directorships of Peter Bräunlein and especially of Edith Franke, the Religionskundliche Sammlung has increased the number and prominence of special exhibits and outreach to schools. This has allowed the museum to communicate its research findings to a broader public by offering exhibits on current social issues with deeper contextualization.

During my first visit to the museum, I viewed the special exhibit *SinnRäume— Insights into Lived Religiosity in Germany*—produced by students at the university and meant to depict "the materialization of contemporary religion, exploring how religion is practiced at home, how a domestic room becomes a religious space, and how beliefs are materialized."[63] This exhibit was a well-produced exploration of domestic religious practice in Jewish, Catholic, Protestant, Hindu, and Buddhist homes. Thus, it was inherently comparative, and attempted to turn the visitor's attention to the materiality of religious practice. How difficult this

Figure 8 Islam Exhibit. Photo by Georg Doerr, courtesy of Religionskundliche Sammlung.

is to do—note the description, "how beliefs are materialized," and that some unseen dimension, here, belief—is made manifest.

Other special exhibits have included

- *Von Derwisch-Mütze bis Mekka-Cola: Vielfalt islamischer Glaubenspraxis* (From Dervish-Cap to Mecca-Cola: Diversity of Islamic Religious Practice; June 2013–December 2017) (Figure 8).
- *Es gibt keinen Gott! Kirche und Religion in sowjetischen Plakaten* (There is no God! Church and Religion in Soviet Posters; November 2015–June 2016).
- *Äthiopien feiert—Bilder einer Feldforschung* (Ethiopia Celebrates: Pictures from Field Research December; 2011–December 2012).
- *Pilgerfahrt visuell: Hängerollen in der religiösen Alltagspraxis Japans* (Pilgrimage Visual: Hanging Scrolls in the Religious Practice of Everyday Life in Japan; November 2009–June 2011).
- Tibet in Marburg (On the occasion of the awarding of an honorary doctorate to the Dalai Lama; November 2007–August 2009).
- *Gesichter des Islam Begegnungen mit muslimischen Frauen* (Faces of Islam Meetings with Muslim Women; March 2008–May 2008).[64]

The Religionskundliche Sammlung on the Web

When we consider the topic of the museum's web presence, we must underscore that the website is in some sense a separate museum or even a translation of the museum. It is a selection of the objects in the collection now presented and framed as exemplary. Further, it does not actually consist of objects, but of images and discourse. In contrast to the fundamental materiality of the collection itself, the online museum is purely representation.

The website of the Religionskundliche Sammlung follows a standardized, university-wide template. The website is in German with select pages in English. Unlike some of the museums we will examine in the next few chapters, the museum page is integrated into the university and joined to relevant units by links.

The body of the main website contains detailed tradition-specific discussions of key objects for fourteen traditions or geographic areas keyed to objects held in the permanent collection (*Dauerausstellung*): Jainism, Germanic religion, ancient American religion, ancient Egyptian religion, Judaism, Christianity, Islam, religion in Africa, Buddhism, Hinduism, Daoism, Confucianism, Shinto, and Tenrikyō.[65] Clicking on any of the icons brings up further information. For instance, if one clicks on "Buddhism" one is taken to a page with four further icons—Indian Buddhism, East Asian Buddhism, Southeast Asian Buddhism, and Tibetan Buddhism—along with brief explanations of each. Click on one of these and one is taken to a more detailed page of explanation and images.

The Special Exhibitions page (*Sonderausstellungen*) is arranged according to selected special exhibitions along with images of the resulting publications or catalogs.[66] Clicking on any of these brings one to a more detailed page on the exhibit or publication indicated. A further link just below the Special Exhibitions link brings up the floor plan of the museum. Beneath that, clicking on *Besonderer Exponate* ("Special Highlights") brings one to a choice of three objects and accompanying pages, Heilige Kümmernis (bearded female St. Solicitus); Monumentalfigur (Abguss) einer sitzenden Gottheit (monumental figure [casting] of a seated deity); and Kashkul (alms bowl). Links at the right-hand side of the page take one to an overview of the programs and personnel associated with the study of religion at the university, to the Wednesday lecture series, and to the museum and the study of religion. Clicking on links brings up another menu that includes links to museums in Germany and to the museums of religion in Glasgow, St. Petersburg, and Taipei. The Religionskundliche Sammlung does maintain a Facebook page, but it is not linked on the Museum webpage. It is primarily used to announce exhibits and special events.[67]

It is a commonplace that museums can be seen as narratives, and as we shall see, the museums discussed in the following chapters present the visitor with overt and often didactic narratives. The Religionskundliche Sammlung, however, presents the visitor with no explicit narrative. There is an implicit narrative, of course. It is the narrative of Otto, Frick, and Heiler, constrained by the epistemic horizon of the imperial comparative science of religion and its liberal Protestant valorization of the numinous or "holy." This narrative stands in tension with newer late twentieth-century scholarly understandings and critiques of the comparative religion heritage and, ironically, with Otto's own interest in the material objects of religion. Other narratives are present in bespoke tours, tours for school groups assigned topics such as world religions, in special exhibits, and in programming using the collection as a "third space" for discussion and dialogue. I turn now to the other museum founded at almost the same time as the Religionskundliche Sammlung, the State Museum of the History of Religions in St. Petersburg, Russia.

Atheism, Science, and the History of Religions

St. Petersburg's State Museum of the History of Religions

The Religionskundliche Sammlung in Marburg and State Museum of the History of Religions (Государственный Музей Истории Религии Gosudarstvennyy Muzey Istorii Religii) in St. Petersburg were conceived under the influence of diametrically opposed ideologies—liberal Christianity and Marxism. The St. Petersburg museum pursued an agenda that valued and studied religion as a manifestation of human culture and history and, at least in theory, replaced the transcendentalist bias with a materialist bias. Nevertheless, both institutions emerged as a part of the consolidating field of the comparative science of religion. Like the St. Mungo Museum of Religious Life and Art in Glasgow, Scotland, the State Museum of the History of Religions constituted a social intervention. It was a social intervention when conceived and continues to be an intervention in the present. Religious differences, however they may polarize Russians, are now subsumed in a single narrative reflecting "the variety and unity of the spiritual life of humankind," and the agenda to promote tolerance is most evident in school outreach programs titled "Together We Are the Country." The layout of the museum depicting the development of religion from Neolithic times to the present is based on what amounts to a developmental schema of "Archaic and Primitive Beliefs," "Religions of the Ancient World" (the sole treatment of Judaism is here), and treatments of Christianity, Buddhism, Hinduism, and Islam. The schema, the floor plan, and the depth of holdings in Christianity subtly reinforce the centrality of Russian Orthodoxy.

Introduction and Brief History

The State Museum of the History of Religions is an impressive museum. It has strong research and educational outreach programs and a superb interactive website. In contrast to the Marburg museum, the State Museum of the History of Religions in St Petersburg (founded 1932) was one of a number of museums in the former Soviet Union designed to promote atheism and a vision of progress in which scientific socialism eclipses premodern superstition.

In 1918, shortly after the communist revolution, the government decreed the separation of church and state and simultaneously proclaimed freedom of religious belief and freedom *from* religious belief, thus initiating what would be a wide-ranging and long-lasting anti-religious propaganda campaign.[1] Places of worship were emptied or converted into anti-religious museums. Estimates on the number of such museums vary, but eventually they numbered in the hundreds.[2] As Ekaterina Teryukova, the current deputy director of the State Museum of the History of Religion, notes, "It can be argued that through the 1920s and 1930s Russia carried out an exceptional experiment in creating a new type of museum."[3] Perhaps not since the Protestant Reformation has there been such a wholesale reclassification and repurposing of religious objects. Objects once deemed sacred were now deemed important as testimony to the benighted and profane manipulation of the ignorant. According to Crispin Paine,

> this new museology made possible anti-religious museums, a Soviet invention that for the first time assembled religious artefacts and used them to attack both the institutions of religion and religion itself. Initially this was by exposing the crimes and tricks of the clergy; later it was also by promoting the rival claims of science, and by showing how religion developed in all parts of the world along with the Marxist phases of social development, and had become a handmaiden of bourgeois capitalism. In all three campaigns *objects* were central—though the new didactic or "talking museum" approach was universally deployed by anti-religion museums, they all used objects to tell their story.[4]

Distinct from the many other anti-religious museums being established in the Soviet Union at that time, the State Museum of the History of Religions was initiated as an independent institution of the Academy of Sciences on May 13, 1931. In November 1932, it officially opened two temporary exhibits on *The History of the Kazan Cathedral* and *Religion and Atheism in the West* in the former Kazan Cathedral.[5] The choice of site could not have been accidental, as this was one of the two sites (the other in Moscow) dedicated to the Virgin as the protectress of Russia, and its icon was considered the palladium of the state.[6] Anja Lüpken summarizes the purpose of the new museum thus:

> As one stage of development towards the scientific worldview, religions were presented as oppressive systems that had to be overcome. "Religions belong to the museum because they are history, not living (soviet) culture" was the underlying proposition, as can be seen in a handbook of 1965. In this case the process of musealization has been used as a means of forced historiography. During the formation of the Museum there was friction between the Soviet Government and scholars of religion who wanted their subject matter to be treated with neutrality. Finally, the Academy of Science (Академия Наук) insisted on information and education as a major responsibility of the museum. . . . Especially in the case of the Museum of the History of Religions and Atheism, the choice of building represents the replacement of the former order, symbolized by the cathedral, through the new order, which is based on "scientific" principles and has overcome religion.[7]

The approach, at least in the initial years, was nothing less than "the deliberate deployment of sacrilege" in which objects previously held to be sacred are shown to be powerless. "Anti-religion museums took exactly the same approach, exposing the hidden workings of a 'miraculous' icon, and explaining the process of natural mummification. 'Sacred' things are fakes at worst, powerless at best."[8]

Bruce Lincoln has examined a similar phenomenon during which images and churches were desecrated and the bodies of priests and nuns were disinterred and publicly ridiculed in revolutionary Spain. Such demonstrations, argues Lincoln, were intended to expose sacred objects and "miraculous" images as powerless frauds. So too, Lincoln understood such acts as a form of ritual and termed such displays "profanophanies."[9] As in the Spanish cases examined by Lincoln, "Bodies of the saints, for centuries venerated in the monasteries of Kiev and Moscow, were torn from their tombs and publicly exhibited," and scientific explanations were given for their non-putrefaction.[10]

The State Museum can also be understood in terms of James Clifford's understanding of contact zones and as unlikely cousin to the London Missionary Society Museum.[11] In the anti-religion museums a new educated Marxist and scientific elite engaged, debunked, and reinterpreted the beliefs and practices of those they ruled, just as a nineteenth-century Christian colonial elite displayed, debunked, and reinterpreted the beliefs and practices of their colonial subjects.

But what would become the State Museum of the History of Religion was not merely a product of the anti-religious propaganda assault. Rather, it owed a great deal to pan-European developments in the comparative sciences, ethnology, anthropology, and museology at the end of the nineteenth and in the early twentieth century.[12] The initial impetus for the museum came from Lev Sternberg (Lev Iakovlevich Shternberg, 1861–1927) at the Museum of Anthropology and Ethnography (the Kunstkamera).[13] Sternberg was a proponent of a Tylorian evolutionary view of culture and proposed "an independent department for evolution and typology of culture."[14] Sternberg planned a series of exhibitions with the help of Vladimir Bogoraz-Tan (1865–1936), who was a specialist in ethnographic studies of religion. Bogoraz-Tan was an internationally recognized ethnographer and literary figure having done ethnographic work among the Chukchi, and he was a member of the American Museum of Natural History's North Pacific Expedition directed by Franz Boaz (1858–1942). Wishing to present "religious phenomena as they actually were," Bogoraz-Tan conceived of "a comparative typological exposure of ritual objects of various peoples, from high antiquity to modern times."[15] *The Antireligious Exhibition* which opened on April 15, 1930, in the Winter Palace might justly be considered the inaugural exhibition of what would later become the State Museum of the History of Religion sited in the Kazan Cathedral.[16] According to Mikhail Shakhnovich, "Bogoraz-Tan extensively applied a comparative methodology. For example, hung above a statue of Zeus was a painting of Sabaoth that looked like the Greek god, and a three-faced icon of Jesus Christ was placed next to a figure of the three-headed Shiva."[17]

In contrast to the contemporaneous project at Rudolf Otto's Religionskundliche Sammlung in Marburg, here comparativism was inflected by anti-religious Marxist, rather than by Christian, ideology. In place of the numinous or holy is an insistence on the material basis of religion. In both cases we can see a tension between what was considered scientifically objective and prevailing ideological pressures. Bogoraz-Tan stated his objectives clearly: "We should bring our scientific discoveries and artistic layout together into one, organic whole."[18] A poster from 1933 lists exhibits and states that "the MHR shows the historical development of religion from ancient times to the present day, reveals the class role of religion and religious organizations, and describes the development of anti-religious ideas and the mass atheism movement."[19] In contrast to most other considerations of religion, here religion and anti-religion were seen—as they perhaps should be—as related.

Like other early advocates of the comparative study of religion, Bogoraz-Tan and Lev Sternberg were influenced by evolutionary research. Sternberg, in his essay "The Comparative Study of Religion," saw the development from early forms of religion to universal world religions as a matter of social and intellectual development. As Shakhovnich notes, these ideas were combined with Marxist theories aligning a particular stage of development with a particular social, class, and economic level of development.[20] By 1947, a new director, Vladimir D. Bonch-Bruyevich (1873–1955; appointed 1946) was transferred from the Moscow anti-religion museum that had been housed in the Strastnoi Monastery building.[21] Bonch-Bruyevich endeavored to tone down anti-religious ideology in the development of the museum, especially where it was not based on science and did more harm than good. For Bonch-Bruyevich, this did not mean a shirking of one's ideological duties but rather adopting a sensitive approach: "Convincing scientific propaganda must be produced, but it must be done very carefully without ever allowing anyone's religious feelings to be hurt or offended."[22] Indeed, the museum directors early on realized that the mounting of temporary exhibits could mitigate their own exposure to suspicions of ideological deviance. At the same time—and despite the use of explanatory framing and dioramas serving to explain the historical evolution of religion and the rise of anti-religion—the display of religious objects at once made concrete demonstration of religious development while running the real risk of actually evoking piety. Thus, when exhibits left altars and iconostases intact, there were reports of the pious praying in front of the exhibits.[23]

Of course, the museum and its programs were subject to criticism at various points in time. Changes in the title of the museum and its situation with regard to government ministries broadly track the political pressures on the museum's mission. The initial burst of anti-religious policy was moderated under Stalin during the war, but then reasserted under Khrushchev and his successors. Thus, "in 1954 the Museum received a new title: 'The State Museum of the History of Religion and Atheism of the Academy of Sciences of the USSR.' In 1961 it was taken over by the Ministry of Culture of the USSR. In the early 1980s it became the Academic and Methodological Center for the History of Religion and Religious Studies of the Ministry of Culture of the USSR. In 1990, its original title—the State Museum of the History of Religion—was returned to the Museum."[24] The American Methodist academic Mark Elliott visited the museum in 1974 and reported that the exhibits were as follows: Science and Religion, the Origins of Religion, Religion and Atheism in the Ancient World, Religions of the East, the Origins of Christianity, Religion and Atheism in the West, History of Russian Orthodoxy and Russian Atheism, and the Overcoming of Religious Survivals in the Period of the Large-Scale Construction of Communism in the USSR.[25]

Despite what may be viewed by some as an inauspicious beginning and history of the State Museum of the History of Religions, it is very much a part of the comparative study of religion at the end of the nineteenth and the first half of the twentieth century; it preserved much of religious culture that might otherwise have disappeared; it produced and continues to produce world-class research on the study of religion; and its mission is still very much one of education. In contrast to the pursuit of a transcendent "holy" as originally set out in Rudolf Otto's Religionskundliche Sammlung, here the comparative science of religion and its morphological and evolutionary tools were enlisted in the pursuit of the material.

The Present: Permanent Exhibits

The State Museum of the History of Religion moved from the Kazan Cathedral in 2000 and now occupies a large block on Pochtamtskaya Street opposite the old Central Post Office in the core of St. Petersburg.[26] It clearly enjoys substantial resources (and has some 200,000 artifacts). This is an elegant building (though not so elegant as the buildings of the Hermitage)—and was originally a mansion. The rooms are large, and the spaces ample. There is room not only for the permanent exhibits but also for storage, a research library, offices, a large seminar room, a shop, and other amenities. In contrast to every other museum in this study, it has sufficient room to allow a kind of segregation of the various religious traditions (but see below for exceptions). The traditional architecture seems appropriate to the subject matter and its institutional character.

The museum's complement of departments which now form the permanent collection include

- The Origin of Christianity
- The History of Russian Orthodoxy
- The Catholic Church
- Protestantism

New departments, added in 2008, include

- The Pure Land of Buddha Amitabha (the Buddhist Paradise)
- Islam
- Religions of the East: Buddhism, Hinduism, Taoism, Confucianism, Shinto
- The Origin of Religion
- Archaic and Traditional Beliefs
- Religion of the Ancient World

The online "Virtual Museum" (not to be confused with the recently developed "virtual branches") provides a stylized floor plan of the permanent exhibits (the *Virtual Permanent Exhibit*).[27]

One enters the museum at Pochtamtskaya Ulitsa 14 at street level into a lobby with reception, coat check to the right, and a small gift shop to the left. Access to the main floor of exhibits is by the stairs at the left. The plan of the main display floor (Figure 9) (as available on the English website) is roughly "U"-shaped, with a front block from which two wings project back from the street.

On the plan we can see that some of the numbered "rooms" are divided into smaller rooms designated by letters such as "a," "b," "c," and so on. From the perspective of the plan, the Catholicism Department (room 8, sections abcde) and the History of Russian Orthodoxy Department (room 7, abc) occupy the

Figure 9 Floor plan of the State Museum of the History of Religions. Image courtesy of the State Museum of the History of Religions.

front center block of rooms. The left side wing (roughly on the east) is occupied by five rooms devoted to archaic and primitive beliefs (room 1, abcd). At the rear of the wing is the Silver Treasury Department housing mainly Orthodox artifacts (room 2, ab). Moving toward the front of the building we find Religions of the Ancient World: Polytheism (room 3); Religions of the Ancient World: Judaism and The Rise of Monotheism (room 4); Religions of the Ancient World: Concepts of the Soul and Afterlife (room 5); and The Rise of Christianity (room 6). The western and somewhat larger wing of the building is occupied by the Protestantism Department (room 9), and three rooms labeled Religions of the East comprised of Buddhism, China and Japan (including Daoism, Confucianism, Shinto), and Hinduism (room 10, abc). In the center of the wing in a special theater is the Sukhāvatī: The Pure Land of Amitabha (room 11). Finally, occupying the front (street side) of the wing is the Islam Department (room 12, abcd).

Both the Religionskundliche Sammlung and the St. Petersburg Museum of the History of Religions are configured according to long-standing museum practice. Just as museums of art are often arranged in discrete rooms according to century or era, genre or style, so these museums endeavor to put different religions or groups of religions in noncontiguous spaces. By entering a room one leaves one religious world and enters another. Such an arrangement tends to reinforce developmental schema and limit overt engagement between traditions. This is much more evident in the St. Petersburg museum than in the Religionskundliche Sammlung. The Marburg museum, having less space than its Russian counterpart, is forced to put together a variety of Asian religions in a single room. By contrast, the Museum of World Religions in Taipei, Taiwan, and the St. Mungo Museum of Religious Life and Culture in Glasgow, Scotland, take a distinctively different approach, placing objects from different traditions in close proximity. As we will see, religious objects from different traditions placed in close proximity can produce very different effects.

Naturally, as this is a museum of religion in Russia, the rooms and themes contain materials focused on religion across the large territory of Russia. Although many smaller objects are in glass cases, the displays are, on the whole, dynamic and innovative with extensive contextual and explanatory material and integration of sound and video where appropriate. Information is supplied in some of the cases and on walls. In most rooms laminated information cards are supplied, some of which are multilingual. Some of the rooms use large-scale photography or dioramas and many rooms use video or computer technology. Some of the videos in the museum on screens are even playable on the virtual exhibit site.

Moving through the museum is almost like visiting three different kinds of museum: the first, an ethnographic museum; the second, a mainstream museum of art; and the third and much smaller one devoted to children. Dioramas, photographic murals, and information boards dominate the rooms on primitive and archaic religion across Siberia and the Russian Far East, though there are a variety of interesting artifacts including a shaman's costume. The next rooms that are devoted to polytheism and religion in the ancient world are much more artifact driven, with masks, sculpture, models of temples, and so on.

On entering the exhibit on the "Rise of Christianity" (room 6), and then the exhibits treating Catholicism in the Middle Ages (room 8a Figure 10) and the Renaissance (room 8d Figure 11) the displays shift from mostly three dimensional to mostly two dimensional, with paintings—many strikingly colorful— dominating. There are still a variety of artifacts such as small metal objects, statues, monks' robes, and so on. But the overall visual impression is one of large colorful paintings. This persists through the exhibits on Orthodoxy (room 7) and into the treatment of the twentieth century and the "anti-religion" movement.

The treatment shifts once again on entering the rooms labeled Religions of the East (room 10, abc) that explore Buddhism, Chinese and Japanese religions (Figure 12). The exhibit on Buddhism is particularly striking with the whole

Figure 10 Catholicism: Middle Ages. Papacy. Veneration of the Saints. Image courtesy of the State Museum of the History of Religions.

Figure 11 Catholicism: Renaissance. Reformation and Counter-Reformation. Image courtesy of the State Museum of the History of Religions.

Figure 12 Religions of the East: Buddhism, Hinduism, Confucianism, Taoism, and Shinto. Image courtesy of the State Museum of the History of Religions.

Figure 13 Sukhāvatī. Image courtesy of the State Museum of the History of Religions.

room framed by architectural details meant to evoke a temple setting and containing an impressive collection of sculpture and painting from different Buddhist traditions. A separately constructed theater (room 11) contains a full three-dimensional tableau consisting of some 600 pieces of the Pure Land of the Buddha Amitabha (Sukhāvatī) from Buryatia dating from 1904 to 1905 with audio commentary (Figure 13).[28]

The rooms at the front of the wing devoted to Islam (room 12, abcd) are designed with Islamic accents such as latticed windows and traditional geometric designs. The first room on origins and doctrines contains mostly small artifacts, bowls, and so forth. Books—copies of the Koran and Hadith collections—dominate the room that focuses on Islamic culture and the Koran. Another room is devoted to the different branches of Islam and contains a well-designed mixture of two-dimensional imagery, traditional designs, books, small items in cases, robes, and a pair of wooden doors. The last room on Islam is devoted to culture and lifeways and includes glass cases with bowls and other artifacts, robes, and some two-dimensional illustrations.

Finally, in a basement room is a space for programs for young children about "The Very Beginning" of culture and religion decorated to resemble a cavern, and containing animal hides, niches, dolls in fur, wooden trunks, and settees.

Tours aimed at introducing visitors to the whole museum typically begin from the left wing of the building in a prehistoric diorama, moving thence to primitive and archaic religion (with a strong focus on Siberian shamanism—room 1), then into religions of the ancient world (split between polytheism and Judaism and the rise of monotheism—rooms 3 and 4), and then to the room exploring concepts of the soul and afterlife in the ancient world (room 5). On each visit my tour glided over the silver treasury (room 2). At this point one moves into the Rise of Christianity (room 6), and thence into the History of Russian Orthodoxy (room 7) and Catholicism (room 8) occupying two parallel spaces at the front center of the building. From there one enters the west wing and Protestantism (room 9). From here one proceeds in the numbered sequence to the rooms devoted either to Religions of the East (room 10) and the Buddhist Suhkāvatī theater (room 11) arrayed in the rooms at the back of the wing or into Islam (room 12) abutting Catholicism at the front of the wing. The anti-religion rooms are not indicated on the online floor plan but are found in small rooms in proper historical sequence after the Catholic and Orthodox rooms. Judaism is located among the rooms on ancient religions where it serves in the historical sequence to introduce the "rise of monotheism" (room 4). It is not, however, treated elsewhere, leading to the impression that it ceased development in ancient times. Further, virtually all of the artifacts (beautifully displayed) are from rather late Rabbinic Judaism, a selection that creates a sort of anachronism. This is unfortunate, as it replicates a Christian supercessionist prejudice.[29]

The layout of the rooms can thus be read as a historical and evolutionary narrative, and the numbered sequence of the rooms and guided tours following the trajectory from primitives to the "anti-religion" movement in the twentieth century reinforce this narrative. To some extent this trajectory has been suppressed. Indeed, the anti-religious movement of the twentieth century is limited to a small room off of the gallery devoted to seventeenth- through twentieth-century Orthodoxy in Russia, and it is nowhere indicated on the floor plan or elsewhere on the website. It is evident that the diminished role of anti-religious ideology parallels contemporary political developments.

It should be noted that not all tours take this route, and as is the case for the Religionskundliche Sammlung, the State Museum of the History of Religions provides custom tours focused on particular traditions, themes, or artifacts.[30] The museum also provides an extensive variety of outreach services (discussed further).

The State Museum of the History of Religions was originally structured around morphological and evolutionary comparative principles inflected by materialism in line with Marxist-Leninist ideology. In recent times the overtly evolutionary dimension (from primitive religion to anti-religion and the rise of atheism) has been transmuted into a more historical, cultural, and developmental mode, while the ethnographic dimension has been maintained and enhanced and is particularly evident in the research agenda of the museum. Read in its totality, however, the museum's narrative—overt and implied—is structured around a journey from the rise of religion among primitive and indigenous groups on the Asian continent, emerging notions of the soul and afterlife, through ancient polytheism, thence on to the rise of monotheism, and thence to the universal or "world religions" with particular emphasis on Christianity, Islam, and Buddhism. The museum pays particular attention to developments that are distinctively Russian, as one would expect. The displays on Orthodoxy and the silver treasury are particularly impressive. In other words, the basic structure is the historical and evolutionary development of religion focused through thematic treatments.

Research, Special Exhibits, and Education

Ekaterina Teryukova, the deputy director of the museum, describes the museum's current mission as comprised of three elements: "A scientific approach: the study of religion in all its complexity"; "collecting and display"; and "educational activities: exploring the history and cultural traditions of various peoples, while respecting their religious positions, but neither teaching the basics of religions nor imposing any preferences."[31] She also adds a further clarification: "Our research at the museum doesn't aim to explore general theoretical problems of history, sociology, or the philosophy of religion, but to carry out practical studies of museum collections, to support exhibitions and scientific publications."[32]

From the beginning, the State Museum of the History of Religions was simultaneously tasked with research and educational objectives. Academician Alexander Orlov early on opined that "museum" seemed an inadequate title given the research mission of the institution.[33] The current research program is vigorous and world-class. The research mission is carried out in "religion-oriented departments." These are the following:

- Archaic and Traditional Beliefs
- The Religion of the Ancient World and the Origin of Christianity
- The Religions of the East
- Islam
- Orthodoxy: Fine Arts

- Orthodoxy: Decorative and Applied Arts
- Orthodoxy: Graphics
- The Religions of the West
- The Religions of the West: Graphics

Teryukova notes that there are special storage spaces for particular types of objects: precious metals, archival materials and manuscripts, rare books, philately, photographs, and textiles.[34] The museum also functions as a full-fledged research institute and supports a research program for scholars and a research library holding some 192,000 items.[35] The website provides links to research publications, conferences and seminars, and internships.[36] In recent years, for example, the museum has engaged in a joint research project with Academia Sinica in Taiwan. This project focuses on Chinese popular prints collected by V. M. Alekseev in the early twentieth century. The Virtual Museum site has an introduction, and the museum has published an overview of the June 2017 conference on "Folk Images and Late Imperial China."[37]

The ongoing research findings are available in the *Proceedings of the State Museum of History of Religions*, and a listing beginning in 2001 is available online.[38] The results of museum sponsored conferences and seminar are also available on the site by navigating to: Home > Professionals > Scientific Publications > Articles, Reports, Presentations > Conferences, Seminars, Round Tables. There is also a dedicated link for museology.[39]

Along with the permanent exhibitions the museum mounts numerous temporary special exhibitions each year and has extensive educational and outreach programs, locally, regionally, nationally, and internationally. Among notable recent temporary exhibits were "Our feet are standing within thy gates, O Jerusalem: Pilgrimage to the Holy Land" (2008) and "Ethiopian Church" (2011), "Divine Dante" (2015), and "Istambul. The Day of Ashura" (2015), among others. Other themed exhibits include a recent series on Japan, *The Many Faces of Kannon: Images of the Bodhisattva in Russia and Japan*; *Simplicity of Thought and Strength of Soul: Religion in the life of Samurai*; and *Community and Home Rituals in Japan* (2011–16).[40] Comparative projects include such exhibitions as *Water in World Religions* (2009) and *Animals, Peoples, Deities* (2011).[41]

Resources tailored for teachers and outreach are substantial.[42] These include materials on "The History and Culture of Islam," "Family Heirlooms and Jewish Memory," and "Photo Collection of the Russian Bible Society," as well as "Museum for Children" and an "Open University" focused on school-aged children and teens, and a "Media Library" with informative films on selected topics.[43]

The State Museum of the History of Religion has fully embraced innovative thinking and technology in addition to traditional values of collecting, research, and exhibition. Through its Open Storage Project some materials usually held in storage have been made available to museum visitors.[44] For instance, the museum's large holdings on Freemasonry are available through this program. During 2016–18, visitors were able to "access Japanese collections, as well as West European painting and large-scale sculpture."[45]

Deputy Director Ekaterina Teryukova has also highlighted the importance of the educational mission of the museum and its outreach programs, especially those for children. Indeed, she says that "the State Museum of the History of Religion [functions] as a space for dialog," and that its programs are designed "to strengthen the culture of tolerance [for the] special ethnic and religious situation in St Petersburg."[46] To that end the museum has mounted programs such as "The Religious Universe of Petersburg: Faith, Traditions, Culture" and uses guided tours, lectures, concerts, and workshops to promote understanding and tolerance. These efforts are manifest in the inauguration of the Museum Open University for the History of the World Religions in 2008, providing a museum lecture center, and classes of advanced training for schoolteachers in World Religions: History, Culture, Doctrines.[47]

Objects on Screens: The Virtual Museum[48]

In contrast to the Religionskundliche Sammlung and, for that matter, the other museums I describe in this study, the website of the State Museum of the History of Religions is more than a simple index, introduction, and advertising vehicle. While the material objects of the permanent collection form the core of the museum, the website has been made an integral resource for understanding and accessing the many special exhibitions, events, and projects of the museum. Indeed, the website significantly enhances access and understanding of the museum's collections and activities. It is also notable that there are significant differences between the Russian and English language versions of the site, and here using the site in Russian with the aid of Google Translate can help the virtual visitor from abroad to access a wider and more up-to-date variety of events and exhibits.[49]

From the main page in any language one can use the "Menu" tab on the upper left to access various major subdivisions of the page or one can scroll down below the rotating display of "Temporary Exhibits" where we find the following broad subcategories: Visiting; The Permanent Exhibition; Guided Tours; Museum

Children Programs; Temporary Exhibitions; Open University of the History of Religions of the World; The Museum; and To the Researcher.[50] Accessing from the Russian Language page and choosing "English" from the menu at the top right adds two further subdivisions: the Museum's virtual site-based extensions spread across Russia and its "Center for Youth Programs." Within each of these, one can then access, from the drop-down menu on the left side of the page, a variety of subcategories within each major category. For instance, clicking on "the Permanent Exhibition" takes one to a menu of the permanent exhibition as well as a list of more specialized discussions such as "American Indians Shamanism" or "Melanesian Cult of Ancestors."[51]

Clicking on the "Virtual Museum" tab on the upper right of the main page presents a sort of solar system–like chart with bubbles—each clickable—for the following virtual displays:

- Virtual Permanent Exhibitions
- Virtual Temporary Exhibitions
- Virtual Collections
- Virtual Guided Tours
- Outreach Resources
- Media Library
- Video Translation
- Restoration Research Discussions

A particularly interesting development is a series of special "virtual branches": *Buddhism on the Banks of the Neva* (opened in 2015) and *Islam on the Banks of the Neva* (2016). The first of these virtual extensions of the museum was installed on interactive screens at the National Museum of the Buryat Republic and at the largest Buddhist monastery in Russia, the Ivolginsky Datsan Monastery.[52] The museum website also makes some of the content of the virtual programs available at these sites.[53]

The State Museum of the History of Religions supplements its own substantial site by making extensive use of social media including Facebook, Instagram, and Twitter, as well as posting numerous videos on YouTube. The icons for these platforms are found on the upper left of the Museum webpage. Along with the usual information about the museum and announcements of programs, reviews, and "likes" one can find more than sixty videos. The Twitter site is relatively well used with almost 9,000 tweets and over 58,000 followers. The YouTube site hosts almost fifty videos concerned with the museum and with specific objects, works of art, or events connected with the museum.

All five of the museums in this study present objects in permanent collections, in special exhibitions, and various kinds of digital imagery. The State Museum of the History of Religions has melded these into a very sophisticated package. Imagery on the web has become a pervasive part of institutions, businesses, and individual lives. It is clear that the somatic experience of a virtual museum mediated through screens is different from that of a guided tour of a physical space, and the manipulation of 3-D images on a display is different than picking up an object and turning it over in one's hands. But exactly how is it different? Looking back to my comments about Old Sturbridge Village in the Introduction, we can ask, how is the "replica" or simulation different? How does it play on the illusion of "authenticity?" To what end? And what of dioramas? A tour of the State Museum of the History of Religions begins with a diorama display of Neolithic religion. What is the status of these objects? On what data and assumptions are they based? What of replica objects? One of the more remarkable aspects of the State Museum of the History of Religions is its connection with a reproduction workshop especially developed for museum displays. The workshop marked its 100th anniversary in 2019 and is detailed in the page "Museeification the Whole Country."[54] In the absence of the backstory, it is easy to be lulled into seeing these displays and objects as "authentic," just as it is easy to walk around Old Sturbridge Village under the illusion of seeing an eighteenth-century New England village. The founders of the St. Petersburg museum had to negotiate this ambiguity—the display of religious objects in an effort to educate and debunk religious claims presented an opportunity for some visitors to worship the objects. Some visitors defied the museum narrative to pray and make offerings before objects. Some museums have sought to capitalize on such oppositional readings by offering quasi-religious activities such as yoga and Tai Chi in galleries.[55]

A recent study of online Buddhist groups in the virtual environment Second Life directly addresses notions of authenticity, as well as the creation of "desire" in virtual environments that is related to but goes beyond the use of screens for marketing.[56] The study, by Gregory P. Grieve, draws upon work by Gilles Deleuze, who argues that "purely actual objects do not exist" but rather that "the actual and virtual depend upon each other for their existence."[57]

Drawing out the implications of these insights it appears that there is a growing dialectic of the actual and the virtual—of objects and images—through which both are constructed and through which we construct worlds or epistemes.[58] This is in addition to the long-standing dialectic between objects and framing with signs and information boards. In contrast to the relative lack of framing and overarching narrative at the Religionskundliche Sammlung in Marburg, the State

Museum of the History of Religions presents the visitor with framing narratives on many levels and through a variety of media. This is no surprise. The museum was founded with didactic intent—a comparative religion narrative harnessed to an anti-religion materialist ideology. Though it has moved far from the charge of its founders today, the museum presents a largely historical multicultural narrative about education and tolerance, while also carrying on sophisticated high-level research on the history and culture of religions in Russia. Under its current leadership and conditions, it is neutral on religious sensibilities (which its programs do accommodate), and only careful reflection on the floor plan and exhibits reveals its evolutionary comparative religion heritage.

Religion and Local Knowledge

Québec's Le Musée Des Religions du Monde

Situated in a modern purpose-built structure in the town of Nicolet in the heart of Québec, Le Musée des Religions du Monde strives to foreground people rather than objects. At the center of the museum's permanent exhibition are video projections of local teenagers—a Hindu, a Muslim, a Catholic, a Buddhist, and a Jew—telling us their stories and what the practice of their religion means to them. Although the museum has some exceptional objects, most of the objects assembled for the permanent exhibit are everyday objects, and they play a supporting role to the personal and local narratives. The underlying framework of the museum is, not surprisingly, comparative, with the treatment divided into types of activity, including life-cycle rites (birth, marriage, death), prayer, and so on. The visual presence of articulate French-speaking teenagers acts to naturalize diversity and lessen religious and cultural tension. Its localist narrative is combined with educational and ethical agendas that nonetheless tend to marginalize the role of Protestantism in this majority Catholic province of Québec.

The unique approach and layout of the museum cleverly creates separate religious worlds. The visitor to the exhibit enters a series of simulated religious worlds created by the video images of the teenagers and the linked religious objects and artifacts positioned nearby. This strategy works to reinvest these artifacts with some sense of the lived world of religion. The museum's development and unique trajectory have resulted in a strong emphasis on temporary exhibitions on broadly religious and cultural topics of interest to local and regional populations. These exhibitions draw visitors who otherwise would not think of going to a museum of religion.

Nicolet: A Seminary Town

Located in the town of Nicolet, Québec, Le Musée des Religions du Monde is one of the newer and most innovative museums of world religions. Nicolet is a small port town with a population of 7,828 (2011 census) on the south bank of the St. Lawrence River and Lac Saint-Pierre. It sits across the Saint Lawrence from the city of Trois-Rivières (population 134,846 in 2014) and midway between Québec City, some 90 miles to the east, and Montreal, some 85 miles to the west. The area was home to the Abenaki when French colonists and missionaries settled in the late seventeenth and early eighteenth centuries. In the mid-eighteenth century, Acadian settlers expelled by the British moved into the area. But Nicolet was more than just a mix of First Nations people, French Catholics, and British Protestants. Portuguese, Jews, and other ethnic groups also settled in Nicolet, and the first seigneur (or ruling lord) was a Protestant.[1] The town became a major center of religious education, and its location on the St. Lawrence facilitated its importance in the developing industries. The museum owes much to the long presence of major Catholic religious sites and orders.[2]

Nicolet was the site of a significant seminary belonging to the Sisters of the Assumption (Nicolet Seminary; Soeurs de l'Assomption de la Sainte-Vierge) that suffered two catastrophic fires and is now the police training school for Québec province (École nationale de police du Québec).[3] Both Nicolet and Trois-Rivières have cathedrals, and Nicolet was home to both male and female religious orders including the Montfortian Fathers (Company of Mary).[4] Trois-Rivières has what has been and still is a major Catholic pilgrimage shrine—the Basilica of Notre-Dame-du-Cap. This is Canada's national shrine to the Virgin.[5]

The Founding of the Museum

The museum emerged in part thanks to the decline of religious practice in Québec during the last third of the twentieth century. Along with that decline came the dwindling demand for priests and nuns who traditionally staffed the Catholic schools. In a sense, the museum is the descendent of the educational mission of the seminaries.

> The idea of opening a museum with an educational vocation, where the history of Québec and religious traditions are both promoted first came about in September 1981. A year later, the museum's corporation was created and its

first photography exhibit on the region's religious treasures was launched. A propositional report was lodged by the executive committee in November of 1983.[6]

In 1983, the people of the community of Nicolet constituted an executive board and charged a team of specialists (with Father Benoit Lacroix and Jean Simard) to study and evaluate whether a museum of religions might be feasible. The board then, in 1986, hired Michèle Paradis to prepare an initial exhibit of religious items in a temporary location, near the town hall. The exhibit was a success and a search for a permanent home commenced. According to Michèle Paradis, it was first proposed that the chapel of the Petit Séminaire (the institution which later was to house the National Police School) might be suitable, but an unstable ground necessitated the demolition of the chapel.[7] Paradis further notes that

> from the very first day in 1986, it was decided not to just do something easy, like showing religious clothing without a concept behind the exhibition. Thus an expert team was engaged in the production of "Symbol of 4 natures" [translation of "Symboles en 4 temps" referring to the elements earth, air, fire, and water] with Catholics, Presbyterians (a lot were in Nicolet at the beginning of the town), Jews (the first Jew in Québec was in Trois-Rivières, just on the other side of the river!) and First Nation people (Abenakis). Thus, at the very start of the museum, the primary objective was to show and explain similarities and difference between faiths.[8]

The success of the exhibit, held at a temporary location near the town hall, gave momentum to raising money for a permanent home, and as a result, the executive board began a fundraising campaign. Around $700,000 was raised and, with the aid of the city of Nicolet, and the Québec and Canadian governments, $2.5 million was secured to build the museum.[9] Construction began in 1988. Initially, Québec's Culture and Communication Bureau mandated that the institution be an exhibition center rather than a museum, as a full-blown museum with a permanent collection and an acquisition budget would be more costly. In 1989, the Ministry of Culture accredited the institution as an exposition center.[10] But, says Michèle Paradis, "people here wanted to have a museum, so they built like it was going to be a museum, even if the government funding was equivalent of an exhibition center."[11] The museum's genealogy as an exhibition center has had a significant impact on its ongoing configuration and exhibits.

The official opening of the museum in its present location was celebrated in August of 1991. The website characterizes the museum thus: "Being a history, ethnography and religious art museum, it offers temporary exhibits based on the popular and communal significance that is the religious experience."[12] As a result of successive successful exhibits in 2001, the Ministry of Communication and Culture designated the facility "as a collection museum due to its management of important patrimonial collections."[13]

Now designated as a museum, its mission has emerged:

> The Musée des religions du monde is an exhibit and research institution dedicated to the preservation, study and transmission of the Québec, Canadian heritage encompassing several religions while including its Inuit and Amerindian dimensionality. . . . Our mission is also to make the Museum's collections on the major world traditions accessible to both specialized researchers and the general public.[14]

Collection and Funding

First conceived as a museum of the history, ethnography, and religious art of Québec, Le Musée des Religions du Monde has maintained a twin focus on collections and educational outreach. In the words of Jean-François Royal, the current director, the mission of the museum is "education in religious ethnology" and "to conserve that heritage that is significant of what is or has been religious practice in Québec."[15]

> We at the Museum of Religions have accorded a great importance to the ethnological aspect of objects, to the significance of their role in representing religion. For us, the ethnological aspect of an object is primary and essential, since it allows understanding of the different religious phenomena, and it is in this sense that we try to position the Museum.[16]

Thus, Le Musée des Religions du Monde has come to function as a central organizing site for the documentation and care of the religious heritage of Québec and is actively documenting objects held in the surrounding communities and parishes. Some of these are joint research and documentation projects with nearby universities. For example, the museum has partnered with Concordia University to catalog Croix de chemin ("crossroads crosses").[17] The museum also has a substantial collection of religious artifacts and ephemera. Indeed, the collection now comprises over 125,000 objects including popular piety materials such as relics, votives, and over 100,000 prayer cards and school awards.[18] The collection has been built up by donations from the seminary collections, local parishes, individuals, and targeted purchases. During a visit in April 2017, I was given a tour of the storage vault. Among the more striking artifacts of popular piety were collections of relics framed, on red cloth backgrounds, with each relic labeled by a saint's name. Each card had approximately a dozen relics on it. There was also a collection of wooden crosses in bottles—painstakingly constructed by alcoholics in hope of recovery.[19] Commenting on procedures for acquiring objects, the head of expositions, Noémie Deschamps noted that "we have a person who travels to antique shops and auctions for big artifacts; he found us Buddhist artifacts and Muslim artifacts." In the case of donations, an expert committee appraises objects, and donors are provided with receipts.[20]

While approximately one-third of the museum's budget is funded by grants from the Québec government, the museum is nonetheless private and thus two-thirds of the cost must be raised independently or funded through admissions.[21] The museum applies for government grants to help subvent particular projects and exhibitions, and this process aids in finding corporate sponsors and individual donors.[22] Indeed, special exhibitions are the primary draw and are a major source of funding, and the gift shop also contributes considerable income.[23]

Despite this overwhelmingly Québec-centered focus, the core of the museum is organized around the category of world religions. Reflecting recently on the success of the museum, Royal notes that "over 100 exhibitions later, the Museum still aims to present and explain the religious phenomena of the five great world religious traditions: Buddhism, Hinduism, Islam, Judaism, and Christianity."[24] It is interesting that the core of the permanent exhibit is devoted to five "world religions" and these in some way anchor and work in dialogue with the temporary exhibits. As I will discuss later, the innovative permanent exhibit on world religions is expressly designed to, in the words of director Royal, "teach tolerance, to help the visitor understand the religious and social behavior of his neighbor, of he who is different from us. Thus, through our mission, we hope to be able to bring about a little tolerance in the face of difference."[25]

Description and Floor Plan

Le Musée des Religions du Monde is housed in a purpose-built strikingly modern building. The front of the building is marked by broad stairs leading up to the main entrance that is backed by a wall of glass. A sculpture garden is directly adjacent and seems an intentional part of the plan, though it is not, in fact, a part of the museum. Going up the stairs to the entryway, one enters (and exits) through the gift shop in front of the building. Museum offices are located to the far right beyond the cashier. From the shop the permanent exhibit is straight back through a large set of doors and it occupies the center and center left of floor. On the same floor and to rear right is a gallery housing temporary and special exhibitions. Stairs from the gift shop lead to galleries on ground floor, also used for special exhibitions.

The Permanent Exhibit: *Êtes-vous près?* (Are You Close?)

Le Musée des Religions du Monde has been designed to foreground people rather than objects. As mentioned earlier, the heart of the museum's permanent display consists of video projections of local teenagers, each from one of the five world religions. The mostly unexceptional everyday objects displayed in close coordination with the videos play a supporting role to personal and local narratives. The underlying framework of the museum's permanent exhibit is, obviously, a comparative and world religions one, with the treatment divided into types of activity, including life-cycle rites (birth, marriage, death), ritual, prayer, and so on. The visual presence of articulate French-speaking teenagers naturalizes diversity and is overtly designed with the goal of lessening religious and cultural tension. Its localist narrative is focused on central Québec and is combined with educational and ethical agendas that nonetheless tend to elide the role of Protestantism in this majority Catholic province of Québec.

Entering the permanent exhibit—titled *Êtes-vous près?* (Are You Close?)—from the rear of the gift shop brings the visitor into a large space divided into a pair of rooms behind which is a narrow corridor leading back to the entry door. The first space is dominated by a large video screen on one side and by a series of five display cases on the other side. The screen is divided into left and right halves. The right half shows videos of five Québécois teenagers: a Catholic woman, a Jewish man, a Buddhist man (actually in his twenties), a Muslim woman, and Hindu man. Each explains the significance of their religious practice in the context of their Québécois identity, and the discussions are arranged roughly in terms of the life-cycle rites typology. The videos are in French with English subtitles and are professionally done. The left half of the screen displays information to support the topics discussed in the videos. On the opposite side of the room, the display cases have doors with instructions to the visitor to open them. Once opened, the inside of the doors feature images of the teenagers with further explanations. Now open, one can view a range of items inside the cases that focus on clothing, such as prayer shawls, hijab, kippah, tefillin, prayer rugs, mallas, prayer beads, communion dress, Buddhist robes, and small images. The conjunction of the videos and the display cases keyed to the videos is very effective, with the objects giving a strong material basis for the video images. This strategy mitigates museumification and works to reinvest the nearby religious images and objects with some sense of the lived world of religion. The sequence of video interviews and the side-by-side display cases (each in the series stepped back slightly from the next) is overtly comparative and this design has the effect of putting each tradition on an equal footing and normalizing their presence as integral to a multicultural Québec. At the same time, one can choose to open only one door at a time rather than having them all open at once. As a result, the religious worlds may be compared or remain separate. One might view the sequencing and step-backs as some sort of ranking (right to left and stepping back: Catholic, Jew, Muslim, Buddhist, Hindu). I doubt this was intended, but it does roughly correspond to demographics and importance in the body politic of Québec.

Beyond the video installation, one moves into a second large space dominated by what might be described as a giant film strip starting from just above head height and spiraling up toward the ceiling (Figure 14). Each panel of this strip displays images of people performing religious activities or of famous shrines, temples, and so on. Just to the right of entry are large panels/ cases. The most striking of these are two related to "marriage." In one are some fifty-plus Barbie dolls in various white wedding dresses. In the opposite one are twenty-eight dolls in various nuns' habits. On the far side of the room is a

Figure 14 Film-strip display. Image courtesy of Le Musée Des Religions du Monde.

large projection screen. On the other side, one can see a series of large hanging panels that separate the different religions. Between these panels are tall cases containing ritual paraphernalia. The panels then serve to explain key ideas and the items in the cases. For instance, the panel adjacent to the Buddhism case has a discussion "Buddha: the Guide" and also presents a Buddhist "prayer" ("une prére Bouddhiste"—actually a mantra) (Figure 15). This arrangement is repeated for each of the five traditions. In other words, one is simultaneously encouraged to compare while each of the five traditions is provided with a sense of its own space and uniqueness. Notably, the order of the areas is shuffled (Hinduism and Buddhism are reversed) from that of the cases in the previous room. Moving counterclockwise around the room by the projection screen takes one by a large panel discussing pilgrimage ("Mere Steps Away From a God"— the panel has examples from each of the five religions) and thence to a corridor that leads behind the video installation and back to the entry. The corridor is lined with small video displays and display cases with various artifacts. For instance, cases contain items such as a small monstrance, an incense burner, and so on, while videos show ritual activities such as a Hindu man performing a puja. One exits past a panel with a large circle representing the divine and a sort of constellation which explains the title of the display ("how close are you") by discussing the word "religion," and with the words "the closer you are to the circle, which symbolizes the divine, the greater the importance of these

Figure 15 Prayer display. Image courtesy of Le Musée Des Religions du Monde.

rituals."[26] The imposition of the comparative religion grid has the simultaneous effect of making the ritual practices of different religious traditions appear to be similar while effacing their differences. In line with the liberal Protestant origins of comparative religion all activity is indexed to "the divine."

Special Exhibits and Outreach

Le Musée des Religions du Monde, like the seminaries that once were the heart of Nicolet, serves as an educational institution in central Québec and provides extensive and tailor-made programming for all levels and even for individual needs. A sample of these can be viewed by accessing the Educational Programs tab on the website.[27] Museum staff members also visit local schools, and Deschamps notes that doing this mitigates the cost of transporting children to the museum, although bringing children to the museum is more effective.[28]

The museum was initially accredited as an exposition center by the Canadian government, and this remains a primary focus of the institution. When I first visited the museum in 2014, the basement gallery housed the exposition *I Still Remember 1984* dedicated to Pope Jean Paul II's visit to Canada.[29] The most impressive object was the "Pope-mobile" built in Canada and used by the pope during his visit. The basement gallery was, for all intents and purposes, a temporary shrine to the pope.

The Head of Expositions Noémie Deschamps noted that the majority of visitors are drawn to the museum to see particular exhibitions, not to see the museum's permanent display about world religions. What's more, what she termed "blockbuster" exhibits are where much of the museum's revenue is made.[30] Le Musée des Religions du Monde mounts, on average, six to eight exhibitions per year (typically one "blockbuster"; two exhibits by artists; and three to five exhibits that are drawn from their collection) and show approximately 200 artifacts per year.[31] Every fifth year, Tibetan monks from Québec City construct a sand mandala. In short, the exhibitions either are overtly about "religion" or involve the more "spiritual" end of the arts. Some of these exhibits go on tour and some have been cooperative ventures with other museums.[32]

Michèle Paradis, who was instrumental in the founding of the museum, notes that the staff of the museum are not specialists, but generalists, and thus the museum consults specialists in preparing exhibitions. For instance, the museum worked with Andréanne Pâquet (an anthropologist) and Frédéric Castel (a specialist in Islam) to prepare an exhibition about veiling in religions.[33]

The list of special exhibitions is impressive and includes[34]

- *Damn You Alcohol!* (June 8, 2018, through October 14, 2019) is designed to "evoke the ambivalent relationship surrounding the consumption of alcohol from a social and religious point of view over time in Québec."
- *In Hockey We Trust* (June 9, 2017, through October 8, 2018) "Is hockey a religion?" "You've heard it: hockey is a religion in Québec. But is it true? In this exhibition, we try to answer this question by letting you play in the museum." The exhibit makes comparisons, including the pairing of hockey cards with spiritual cards and ritual objects with hockey shirts.
- *Trait d'esprit* (*Witticisms* April 14 through October 15, 2017) was a display of religious caricatures and cartoons.
- *L'art du dimanche* (*Popular Religious Art* September 23, 2016, through March 12, 2017) treats popular or even "outsider" religious art in Québec.
- A thirty-year retrospective exhibit, *Museum: 30 Years of Objects and Emotions* (June 10, 2016, through March 12, 2017), was "a display of 30 exceptional artifacts from its collection" advocating "the importance of cultural institutions for our society," and "30 years of promoting public awareness regarding differences, tolerance and open-mindedness." As a result, "You will be moved to reconsider how you view museums!"[35]
- *Tu ne tueras point* (*Thou Shalt Not Kill!* May 15, 2015, through September 7, 2016). The exhibit was part of the commemoration of the centennial of the First World War. It included a remarkable recreation of a trench network and posters of the period including anti-war posters.
- *Les enfants font la fête* (*Kids Celebrate* November 18, 2015, through April 17, 2016) "be it India's *Diwali*, the New Year in China, the Jewish celebration Hanukkah, Toonik Tyme in Iqaluit or Canada Day—what better way to appreciate the diversity of celebrations in Canada than through Kids Celebrate!"
- *Religions in the Eyes of a Tourist* (photo exhibit January 30, 2015, through April 19, 2015) "Throughout his travels, Serge Tousignant has pictured religions worldwide. Discover his travel diary and learn about the religious traditions of Madagascar, India, China, Guatemala, Tunisia, Chili, Argentina . . . beautifully captured."
- *Darshan. Mirrors of the Soul* (nd) Photographs of Marcel Poulin here inflected through the Hindu notion of Darshan (auspicious gaze). "These photos were taken in natural light by Marcel Poulin, during his travels through the Orient. They show people from different places, different

cultures and religions. The photographer brings these gazes from the other side of the world to life, allowing them to travel all the way to Canada to be seen by eyes from here."

The museum staff conducts research to find out how people hear about the exhibitions and to discover which sorts of exhibitions bring people to the museum. For instance, a 2011 exhibit, *Life before Death*, featuring photographs by Beata Lakotta and Walter Schels of people with terminal diseases, alive and then dead, attracted many visitors and helped to put the museum on the tourist map. According to Deschamps, the exhibit had a huge impact because it addressed questions about dealing with death and thus reached an audience that beyond those interested in "religion" per se.[36] The hockey exhibit was designed to bring in men—and people who are not interested in religious practices—to show them they have superstitions, rituals, and practices that are comparable to those held by religious people. An exhibition on swearing in Québec, *Tabarnak: A Look at Swearing in Québec*, was specifically designed to attract teenagers.[37] At the time of my most recent visit (April 2017), the museum was planning for an exhibition of paper sculpture by Claude Lafortune based on the story of Noah's ark.[38]

Visitors and the Dialectic of Special Exhibits and Permanent Exhibits

As a museum of religions, Le Musée des Religions du Monde occupies an ambivalent space in central Québec. Nicolet is a small town, but it is proximate to a much larger city and traditional Catholic pilgrimage site. It was home to major Catholic institutions, but these are now largely gone, and the reputation of the Catholic Church as a whole has been damaged by recent scandals. Thus, the museum has two quite disparate audiences—pious Catholics and those who have grown up secular or who have become anti-religious. The museum has tried to collaborate with the sanctuary of the shrine at the Basilica of Notre-Dame-du-Cap in Trois-Rivières, but, according to Deschamps, beyond logistics, pious pilgrims tend to be put off by the permanent exhibit on the five religions. Thus, the challenge for the museum is that the word "religion" either frightens people or else they think only of "big Catholic objects."[39] This difficulty has prompted discussions about changing the name of the museum or changing the marketing around the name Le Musée des Religions du Monde.

Speaking strategically, Deschamps says that the museum wants to continue with big exhibitions that attract a broad range of visitors. "We want to promote tolerance and humanity," she says, "and show people how they have spirituality in all parts of their lives." The problem is how to be more popular so as to "take down the wall between us and the first time visitor." Once the museum gets people in the door they come back again: 50 percent of visitors return.[40]

So, who visits Le Musée des Religions du Monde? Most visitors come from Montreal and central Québec with smaller numbers from elsewhere and from abroad. Women and people between forty and sixty years with university degrees are considered a target audience, as are scholars and students. Fully one-third of visitors come in school groups. This is no surprise, given that in Québec province the five religions, First Nations, and the teaching of ethics and tolerance form an integral part of the school curriculum.[41] Recently developed tourist attractions, such as promotion of cycling routes in central Québec, have added to visits.[42]

The museum has several means to track visitors, including a guest book and questionnaires. Questions include name, age, gender, and where the visitor found out about the museum. At the end of every exhibition the museum tries to track who visited and what they thought of the exhibits. During the summer tourist season the gift shop gives a 10 percent discount for completing a questionnaire. The tourism office also uses questionnaires, and feedback from student groups contributes to this data collected by the museum staff.[43]

On the Web: Virtual Reserve and Guides (Website)

The website of Le Musée des Religions du Monde is well designed, colorful, and easy to navigate. At the top of the page, along with the masthead, are the "Home," "Who Are We," "Contact," and language tabs (French or English). Just below are "Exhibitions and Events," "Schedule, Access and Pricing," "Educational Programs," and "The Store." The page below is dominated by brightly colored blocks—"Our Exhibitions," "Our Store," "Partners of the Museum," "Why Become a Member," "Itinerant Exhibitions," "Photo Galleries," "Schedule, Access and Pricing," "Become a Volunteer," and "Donate"—each of which when clicked opens on a sub-page with further links. The background wallpaper of the page is a photo looking upward at the "film-strip" display in the permanent exhibit, and this wallpaper is repeated as background in each of the pages. The donations page is set up not only for monetary donations but also to provide detailed instructions for the donation of objects for the collection. Scrolling further down the home page brings us to "Exhibitions and Events." Below this is the "Museum News" section, with links to Facebook, Twitter, and RSS feeds. Finally, at the foot of the main page are links for all of the main page sections, the museum address and contact information, and a link to the TripAdvisor site.

Though nicely designed, some sections of the web page are information rich, while others are very sparse. In some cases, information is only available in French. This is not a major drawback but is more indicative of how the website is intended to be used—that is primarily as an index of what is currently on offer for tourists and school groups. The link to "Educational Programs" found at the head and foot of the home page is not included in the clickable colored block part of the page. Clicking on this link takes one to a menu of offerings designed to complement primary and secondary school curricula in Québec. There is also information on "À la carte" or bespoke tours. The page in English contains a link to download a flyer on the educational offerings (in French). However, the French version of the page ("Programmes éducatifs") contains further information, including a sign up for an email feed and distinct downloadable brochures for teachers of primary and secondary grades. The nicely designed two-page brochure details activities developed to complement school curricula. For example, the museum offers students a chance to try their hand at creating sand mandalas using traditional techniques: "Mandala de sable Expérimentez cette technique artistique de méditation bouddhiste."[44]

The "Educational Programs" tab has a sub-page titled "Our Collections" in English and "Nos collections" in French. While the two versions share some material there are significant differences. The English version of the page has clickable images of key objects in the collection (a Koran stand, a Tibetan Thanka, a Prayer Wheel, etc.).[45] Below are brief study guides in PDF format prepared for the "Great Religions": Buddhism, Christianity (Catholic), Hinduism, Islam, and Judaism, as well as documents on the name of Allah and a comparative document on mourning in the five religions. The parallel page in French has more resources. Instead of images of key objects with little by way of information on them, the page in French has a link taking one to a substantial page about collections which itself has several sub-pages.[46]

The "Collections" page contains an introduction to the museum and some seventeen sub-pages of images, each bringing up details and further information. The first of these pages has a sampling of the huge collection of votive cards held by the museum. Further pages include images from across the world including Chinese funerary sculpture and painting, puppets, crèches, and many other items. Indeed, this constitutes an exceptional resource for students, teachers, and researchers.[47] There are also links to partner museums, through a shared website, including Le Musée québecois de l'agriculture et de l'alimentation and Musée des Abénakis. Another tab (Récherche) brings up a form allowing searches of the collection. There is an informative page about the various sources of the collection ("à propos").[48]

Returning to the top page in "Nos collections," we are presented with much more substantial information on "les cinq grandes religions du monde."[49] For instance, there are separate documents on various forms of Christianity, including Orthodoxy, Methodism, Seventh Day Adventists, Lutherans, and so forth. There is also additional material on Hinduism and on Islam, as well as documents on explicitly comparative topics such as mourning customs (Deuils); Father Christmas (Père-Noël); the Way of the Cross (Le chemin de silences/Le chemin de croix); religious games and toys (Jeux et jouets religieux); demonology (La dèmonologie); festivals, and the four elemental symbols (Symbols en 4 temps).

The Facebook and Twitter platforms available by clicking on the familiar icons provide much beyond the typical postings and visitor reviews.[50] The Facebook page in particular hosts a sizable number of videos, many of them chronicling exhibits, including the sand mandala exhibit. It is also notable that under the "Events" tab there are ongoing meditation and yoga workshops at the museum—a phenomenon that is becoming more common even at mainstream art museums.[51]

Narratives and Objects

Le Musée des Religions du Monde strongly connects religious narratives and meanings of objects. Objects remain enmeshed in the broader world religions and comparative religions narratives that in turn are used to promote mutual understanding and tolerance. The narrative of the permanent exhibit is brilliantly presented but is very much framed as the mid-twentieth-century comparative religion/world religions narrative—a narrative designed to cast religions in terms of similarities in order to promote multicultural tolerance. Not surprisingly, more devout visitors steer clear of the permanent exhibit and its explicit comparison of religious practice (life-cycle rites, pilgrimage, prayer, etc.). Nevertheless, Le Musée des Religions du Monde does not have the dialogical edginess that one finds at the St. Mungo Museum of Religious Life and Art. The comparative framework at the Nicolet museum is effective in its work of draining the exhibit of its danger and domesticating objects that might at first seem strange. In a sense, Le Musée des Religions du Monde has a built-in tension or, perhaps, a better term might be "dynamic." The museum creates a dialectic relationship between the permanent exhibit on the five world religions and the ongoing special exhibitions. While the world religions exhibit occupies a domesticated space in the body politic of Québec—never more evident than in its support of institutional primary and secondary school curricula—the special exhibitions present challenges to visitors not only by stretching the definition of religion to other "world religions" but also by reorienting the notion of religion to see it in the flow of everyday life, sport, and in the arts. It is evident that it is the blockbuster exhibitions that draw visitors to the museum, not the world religions permanent exhibit.

Many who visit Le Musée des Religions du Monde clearly appreciate the world religions typology and the kinship among religions it seeks to promote. The choice of this typology was intended as a fitting follow-on to the religious institutions of Nicolet, and it is fully integrated with primary and secondary curricula. But the resistance to visiting the museum shown among pious Catholics visiting the national shrine to the Virgin a mere 10 miles distant makes evident that the comparative religion model is well understood by some as an inadmissible form of comparison which seeks to promote tolerance at the expense of a key difference. Further, the permanent exhibit—despite its innovative video and object simulation—reinforces the notion "great religions" that goes back to James Freeman Clarke. Although the museum has hosted shows on First Nations and Abenaki traditions, I longed to see a First Nations teenager take a place in the permanent exhibit.

A Dialogical Museum

The Sacred Gaze and the St. Mungo Museum of Religious Life and Art

The St. Mungo Museum of Religious Life and Art in Glasgow forms an interesting contrast to Le Musée Des Religions du Monde in Québec. The St. Mungo Museum, sited in the precincts of the Glasgow Cathedral (now the High Kirk of Glasgow), is a relatively small museum expressly designed as a social intervention promoting tolerance and understanding in a city long marked by Catholic and Protestant sectarianism.[1] In the words of Mark O'Neill, who helped to design the museum: "The power of religion to move and motivate people means that St. Mungo is more than an attempt to create an interesting exhibition. It is an intervention in society, a contribution towards creating greater tolerance and mutual respect among those of different faiths and of none."[2] The core exhibit space is on the first floor (British). It includes "Religious Art" and a display of "Religious Life" organized on comparative principles around life-cycle rites. The "Scottish Gallery" (third floor) is devoted to the diversity of Scottish religious life and history and has recently been updated to reflect the experiences of new immigrants to Glasgow.

In contrast to the museum in Québec, the St. Mungo Museum contains some stunning objects (a large bronze image of Śiva, some exquisite Buddhist images, fine Christian stained glass, etc.), and the compact display space produces a kind of intimacy among the statues, images, and paintings that directly engages the visitor. As a result, the objects share an intimate visual space and are inevitably in dialogue. In the words of David Morgan, the visitor finds that the "sacred gaze" of the images is unavoidable.[3] The phenomenological impact of the objects is reflected in visitors' deep discomfort or transformative engagement, responses recorded in the tens of thousands of "talk-back" or comment cards.[4] The contrast to Le Musée des Religions du Monde is striking. There the rather quotidian images and objects of different traditions have a weaker impact on the viewer than the objects at St. Mungo, but they are connected for the visitor by being linked into a simulacrum of a living relational network created by the videos of the five teenagers. At the St. Mungo Museum, a small number of impressive and strategically placed objects engage one another and the visitor in a relational network. It is tempting to visualize how a museum might integrate the approaches of Le Musée des Religions du Monde and the St. Mungo Museum.

A Small Museum at the Heart of Glasgow

The St. Mungo Museum is located in a fine modern Scottish baronial-style building in the cathedral precinct of Glasgow, Scotland. A visit there on one of the relatively rare sunny Glasgow days is a memorable experience. The stone glows creamy yellow in the high latitude light. Immediately across the street is Provend's Lordship, the oldest building in the city. The magnificent cathedral, now properly the High Kirk of Glasgow, survived the reformation relatively unscathed (it was protected by the guild members). Over it looms the Glasgow Necropolis with its prominent statue of John Knox surveying the cathedral and the city from the prow of the hill. Nestled within the wall of the museum is a small Zen rock garden, the only one in Scotland, and a clootie tree, representing Celtic traditions.

Contemporary Glasgow is Scotland's largest city and the third largest city in the UK. Situated on the River Clyde, in the western Scottish lowlands, the city numbers some 600,000. A church was reputedly founded by Glasgow's patron Saint Kentigern—commonly known as Saint Mungo—who was consecrated bishop in the year 540. The museum is named in his honor. With regard to religion, the modern city is dominated by Protestants, and especially by Presbyterians of the Church of Scotland (the Kirk, dating from the Reformation), and by Roman Catholics. Catholicism was the dominant pre-reformation tradition, and its presence remains strongest in the west of Scotland and the Highlands. The Catholic Church was strengthened by further Catholic immigration from nearby Ireland and the continent (Poland) as Glasgow's growing shipbuilding, mining, and heavy industry attracted workers in the nineteenth century. As a result, sectarian tension between Catholics and Protestants and "marches" in Glasgow are second only to those found in Belfast.

In addition, Glasgow's nineteenth-century function as the "Second City" of the British Empire drew a significant influx of immigrants from South Asia and, after the Second World War, a further influx of immigrants from Pakistan and the rest of South Asia. These immigrants brought Muslim, Buddhist, Hindu, and Sikh religious practices to the city. Meanwhile, mainstream Christian church attendance fell off drastically, and over 36 percent of Glaswegians indicated "no religion" on the 2011 census.[5] The numbers, however, can be misleading. Sectarian tension can still run high, especially during "marching season" and at matches between Glasgow's rival football teams, the Rangers (Protestant) and the Celtics (Catholic). What's more, the "no religion" census response does not capture the burgeoning spread of alternative "spiritualities" which many people do not define as being "religious" (i.e., as going to a mainstream traditional church). As Woodhead and Heelas have shown for nearby Cumbria, England, paganism, and traditions originating in South and East Asia such as Buddhism, yoga, acupuncture, Taiji, and so on have extensive followings.[6] The Scottish Lowlands and Glasgow itself also are home to alternative religions. For instance, the Kagyu Samye Ling Tibetan monastery, located in Galloway, is reputed to be the largest Buddhist monastery in the UK and is a major tourist attraction.[7]

The St. Mungo Museum, then, is situated both physically and ideologically in these various currents. Originally conceived and supported by Glasgow's Friends of the Cathedral, the building that now houses the St. Mungo Museum was to be a visitor center for the cathedral. Financial problems led the Glasgow City Council to reconsider, and it was decided that a museum of religious life and art would be a tourist attraction and would complement other Glasgow museums, and help accomplish other strategic priorities. Although the city population today is largely "secular," marches and sectarian tensions persist.[8] Glasgow's immigrant community—much of it from South Asia—sometimes finds itself challenged by growing Islamaphobia and anti-immigrant feeling, though the city has a deserved reputation as welcoming to immigrants and asylum seekers from all over the world. Thus, it was thought that the museum could serve to promote tolerance and to educate the community "for all of whom religion was part of their cultural background, even though many were no longer believers."[9]

The Museum Design

Entry to the St. Mungo Museum is either directly from Castle Street or from the cathedral close, past the Zen rock garden titled *Where We Are* (1993) by Yasutaro Tanaka. It is the oldest such garden in the UK. Curiously, for those immersed in Scottish lore, the garden also evokes sites such as the Callanish

Standing Stones on the Isle of Lewis as well as many other standing stone sites.[10] Tucked into a corner just at the edge of the garden next to a wall is a "clootie" tree, the rags tied to its branches indicating traditional beliefs about healing wells.[11] The entry (ground) floor houses reception, a donation box (admission is free in all Glasgow museums), the bookstore, cafeteria, and a lecture hall.

Ascending the stairs to the first floor one passes through a small lobby and turning left one enters a light and airy room with a high ceiling. Immediately as one enters is a glass case containing a striking ancient Greek vase, a bowl, and a few other artifacts. The light cream-colored room is the Religious Art Gallery, and it is framed on two sides by stained glass windows salvaged from churches. Set about fifteen feet in front of the windows, a series of Buddhist sculptures are installed, including two of the Buddha touching the earth (indicative of the story of the Buddha's defeat of Mara and enlightenment) and one of the bodhisattva Avalokiteśvara.[12] Turning around to face the other side of the room, we see two more stained glass windows framing, in the middle of the room, a Muslim prayer rug and an work representing the "Attributes of Divine Perfection" by Ahmed Moustafa—a rendering of the names of god. At the far end of the room a wall holds a Christian-themed painting of the crucifixion. When I first visited the museum in 2012, this wall held Salvador Dali's *Christ of St. John of the Cross.* When this painting returned to the Kelvingrove Museum it was replaced with another depiction of the crucifixion. Just to the right of the painting is a foot-wide slot allowing a glimpse into a small room, and to the left a doorway into that room. Here, framed by another stained glass window and a glass case containing a pietà, is a large bronze statue of the Hindu lord of the universe—Naṭarāja—the lord dancing the destruction of the universe at the end of the eon.[13]

Exiting this room into the Religious Art Gallery and turning to the left one enters the Religious Life Gallery. This gallery, organized around life-cycle rites, forms a contrast to the bright open space of the Religious Art Gallery. The Religious Life Gallery is long and rectangular lined with display cases; a long double-sided display case fills the center of the room (Figure 16). The cases and walls are painted black, and one is greeted by a case containing a life-size skeleton adorned with flowers. The cases lining the walls present life-cycle rites in various religious traditions—birth, coming of age, sex, and marriage, death and the afterlife, and so on—while the cases in the middle of the room are devoted to particular traditions (Judaism, Islam, Buddhism, etc.) and themes (war and peace, religion as a profession, missions and missionaries, divine rule). The cases are well lit, and are supplied with ample descriptive material, photographic illustrations, and, in many instances, audio. Returning to the

Figure 16 Religious Life Gallery. Image courtesy of Glasgow Life.

Religious Art Gallery a stairway to the right of "Attributes of Divine Perfection" leads up to the temporary exhibits space on the second floor.

The third-floor landing features a large window with a splendid view of the cathedral and the Glasgow Necropolis (the Victorian cemetery overlooking the cathedral and the museum). Until 2018, the Scottish Gallery on the third floor was devoted to the diversity of mostly contemporary Scottish religious life and history. The gallery is supplied with several discrete wooden stations or displays, each with images and artifacts representing one of the major religious communities in Glasgow (Hindu, Jewish, Sikh, Catholic, Protestant). The walls have glass display cases with further information about religious communities in Glasgow and major events concerning them. At the center of the room telephone handsets provide audio commentary. Off of this room is an area for school group activities.

Since 2018, the Scottish Gallery has also housed an exhibit devoted to "New Scots" immigrants. This exhibition was designed as a part of the Refugee Festival Scotland[14] (Figure 17). The new display extends the gallery's previous examination of the various religious and ethnic groups in Glasgow with a focus on immigrants and refugees who have come to Scotland as a result of war and upheaval in the former Yugoslavia and in Syria. The exhibition now explores notions of "home" for asylum seekers. According to Sabir Zazai, chief executive of Scottish Refugee Council,

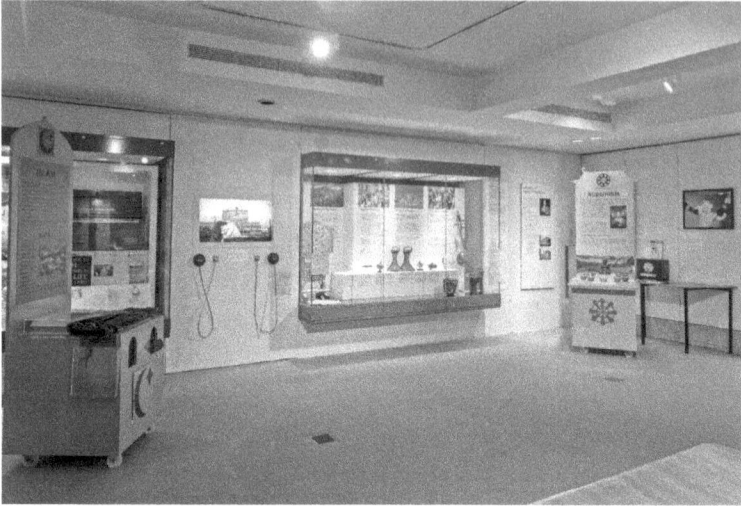

Figure 17 New Scots and Scottish Religions Gallery. Image courtesy of Glasgow Life.

> The story of people seeking refugee protection and rebuilding their lives in a place of safety is part of the story of Glasgow itself. This exhibition gives old and New Scots a chance to learn a little more about each other in a very personal and powerful way. Just like Refugee Festival Scotland, it gives people from different backgrounds the chance to get to know each other better, to find out a little about each other's cultures and to discover the things we have in common.[15]

The display includes objects donated by members of the community. A film about the New Scots accompanies the exhibit.[16]

Planning a Museum of Religious Life

The new exhibition expands the meanings of Scottish religious life but is congruent with the museum's founding mission. Mark O'Neill, the senior curator of history in Glasgow museums at that time, was the project manager.[17] Conceived at a time when ideas about multiculturalism were ascendant in British society, and cognizant of a heritage of sectarian tensions and ethnic and religious prejudice against those seen as foreign (particularly migrants from South Asia who are a prominent part of Glasgow's population), the planners located one source of tension in cultural and religious "ignorance."[18] There was no fuzziness about the mission of the museum and its goals. O'Neill expressly says, "St Mungo's is not an objective museum. It exists explicitly to promote a set of values: respect for the diversity of human beliefs" and further that "the aim of the museum could perhaps more accurately be stated as being 'to promote mutual understanding and mutual respect amongst people of all faiths which respect universal human rights.'"[19] Reflecting on the aims of the museum, O'Neill, referring directly to the mission of the museum which was inscribed over the entryway, said,

> Like all museums St Mungo represents a set of social values, an ideal of how society should be, though it is unusual in having its objective stated in the foyer: "Our aim is to promote mutual understanding and mutual respect amongst people of all faiths and none."[20]

O'Neill and his team found that the change in initial direction from a welcome center for the cathedral to a museum meant that the planning process and timeline were somewhat truncated.[21] Nonetheless, bringing communities into the planning process was deemed crucial to its success. According to O'Neill,

> If the aim was to communicate something of the meaning of the objects, we had to reverse the usual process in museums of draining them [the objects] of their dangerous meanings to render them safely aesthetic, historical or anthropological. In the case of religion, "meaning" has an emotional or spiritual dimension that can be described much more powerfully by those who experience it than those who have simply studied it. Some sort of consultation or collaboration with believers was therefore required.[22]

Thus, exhibit planning and design engaged local communities. Comment was invited on exhibit mock-ups, design, and annotation.[23] Community members provided oral testimony that was then used as written and oral commentary in the displays.[24] Input from a Muslim representative prompted a change from an original plan showing six religions in the same display case in the Religious Life Gallery to the current configuration with different religions side by side in separate display cases.[25] Consultations continued even after the museum opened. Thus, the statue of Śiva was placed on a pedestal to prevent visitors from "look[ing] down on the god."[26]

This process of community engagement and input has not, typically, been the norm in the design of museum displays and represents a relatively new movement that has slowly been gaining ground among curators. As I noted in Chapter 1, in 2002–05 the Luce Foundation funded a series of workshops at the Ackland Gallery of Art in Chapel Hill, North Carolina, to explore such new approaches to museum displays of religious objects. The Ackland has a superb collection of South Asian religious sculpture as well as a rich collection of other religious artifacts. The museum was proposing doubling its floor space, and the series of workshops brought together museum professionals, scholars, and members of religious communities to devise a handbook for the display of religious objects in museums.[27] Part of the difficulty involves the divergence between museums as caretakers of objects and religious communities for whom the objects in museums are usually seen as alienated and "dead." As Anja Lüpken notes, "If (religious) groups are allowed to design museum space or conduct rituals there . . . museums become their space. They are no longer just visitors or 'exhibition objects' but they become a part of the museum—and the museum becomes theirs. The boundaries between temples and museums become blurred."[28] Community response was similarly a concern during the early development of the State Museum of the History of Religion in St. Petersburg when the display of icons presented the opportunity for believers to perform an "oppositional reading" which would transform an "educational" anti-religious exhibition into a sacred space.

Other considerations were important in the planning process. Although designers were interested in creating interaction among objects and altering design in response to community involvement, the power of religious objects also meant that the designers needed to create boundaries. According to the architect David Page, "The driving notion was to give each object its own space and place. We could not treat these objects as if they had been found in an archaeological dig, these were objects of faith and we had to create for each a metaphorical respect by carving out its own space."[29] Harry Dunlop, who along with Mark O'Neill helped to develop the museum, noted that a good deal of forethought was devoted to avoiding situations that might provoke complaint: "In the Art Gallery we realized having all faiths together could be quite threatening for Christians, but we tried to give each object a ritual space. In the Religious Life gallery all the faiths have equal space, and the cases on the afterlife were determined by the number of grave goods we had."[30] Despite these efforts, the limited exhibition space, particularly in the Religious Art Gallery, renders interaction inevitable. This interaction is a unique advantage of the St. Mungo Museum as well as a danger.[31]

The St. Mungo Museum was designed to promote tolerance and was dependent upon an enlightened multicultural outlook. As O'Neill later noted,

> Over 120 different faiths are represented, spread across 5000 years of human history. The texts interpreting the objects express external (curatorial) and internal (believer) perspectives, and the architecture was designed to evoke a contemplative atmosphere.[32]

The museum opened on April 1, 1993, and initial reactions were positive. The following day, a review of the museum appeared in the *Herald* newspaper:

> There is no other such museum in Britain, or anywhere else in the world as far as we know, and its appeal is likely to be very wide indeed, whether you are Christian, Buddhist, Hindu, Jew, Sikh, Muslim or indeed have no religion. The St Mungo Museum explores in three beautifully designed galleries the many and varied aspects of religious life throughout the world, and one looks more specifically at that of the West of Scotland.[33]

In an interview about the new museum appearing in the *London Times* found Mark O'Neill claiming, "Our aim is to promote mutual respect and understanding of different religions. We are trying to get rid of prejudice, on the grounds that it is mostly based on ignorance."[34]

But O'Neill, reflecting on the opening of the museums from the perspective of some years later, recalls that there were initially few reviews and an overall attitude of puzzlement. The planners had tried to anticipate and mitigate if not preempt controversy, and the museum was mostly celebratory of religious life though it did include "a small number of examples of the human destructiveness justified on the grounds of religion, including the Holocaust, sectarian strife in Northern Ireland and female genital mutilation."[35] Indeed, O'Neill has stressed that the principle of tolerance, fundamental to multiculturalism and the museum's design, has its limits:

> In a museum of world religions we decided that being "neutral" in the name of tolerance seemed like an evasion. Despite the apparent triumph of moral and cultural relativism, there are limits to tolerance and for us this includes persecution of minorities, religious discrimination—and feminine genital mutilation.[36]

O'Neill noted that "the staff guessed wrong in most cases" as they tried to anticipate areas of controversy.[37] We get a sense of the controversies from this report in *The Christian Science Monitor*:

> It has also already been the focus of controversy: criticism for inaccuracies by the Moderator of the General Assembly of the Church of Scotland; a feminist protest about a photograph displayed in a section dealing with coming-of-age ceremonies of a young Egyptian woman undergoing a barbaric circumcision ritual; a protest from a Muslim man objecting to the sale of alcohol in the museum cafe; vandalism inflicted on a large bronze of the Hindu Shiva as Nataraja (Lord of the Dance); and objections by the David Livingstone Centre to a caption they felt suggested the renowned missionary was a colonialist.[38]

According to Mark O'Neill, when asked, the person who vandalized the Śiva statue replied that he had done it for Christ.[39] Nevertheless, things quieted down fairly quickly, and the museum has become a notable tourist attraction in Glasgow. The museum has approximately 200,000 visits a year, about half of which are tourists visiting Glasgow and a significant portion of visits are by school groups.[40]

Visitor Reactions

The complex reactions to the St. Mungo Museum arose perhaps less from its mission of tolerance than from the designer's desire that the museum itself would push its visitors to make meaning, even religious meaning. As O'Neil puts it,

> The museum also sought to take the metaphorical idea of the museum as a site of ritual more literally and to provide cultural resources which people could use to create meaning and for some, to achieve a sense of transcendence.[41]

As Lüpken pointed out, encouraging museum visitors to use the museum "as a site of ritual" means that the management, placement, and interaction of objects— especially objects that the designers sought *not* to drain of "their dangerous meanings" or "to render them safely aesthetic, historical or anthropological"— would be crucial.

For instance, in discussing the plan of the Religious Life Gallery—a long darkly painted room with side-by-side exhibits of rites of passage in different traditions—curator Harry Dunlop commented that "the gallery attempts to communicate what people believe and share in common (such as Rites of Passage) and what is unique and special in each cultural tradition."[42] But conveying both similarity and difference with the full understanding of the diversity of visitors is no easy feat. The side-by-side arrangement of traditions—though separated in individual cases—was in part the result of objections from the community to having different traditions in the same display cases. Comparison would only be tolerated only if distinct and physical separation could be maintained.

Despite deliberate attempts "to give each object its own space and place" the Religious Art Gallery provoked some real discomfort. As O'Neill notes, the gallery

> created startling juxtapositions, with Salvador Dali' s Christ of St John of the Cross in the same room as an ancestral screen from the Kalibari people of Nigeria, a seventeenth-century Turkish prayer rug and an Australian Aboriginal

dreamtime painting. The room was shaped by the architects so that, even though the objects were of greatly differing scales and visual qualities, all were seen to be treated with equal respect.[43]

But to treat each with "equal respect" is, for some visitors, a clear disrespect. The negative perception of scientific comparison and a kind of flattening cannot be easily avoided. Anticipating this difficulty, the planners deployed "talkback boards" in part as an effort to head off anger or vandalism. As Harry Dunlop says,

> We included a talkback board in the Gallery of Religious Life which invites visitors to add their own opinion to the displays. Since most people have an opinion on at least some aspect of religion, these have proved extremely successful. Visitors love having a good read and an argument with each other.[44]

By 2004, nearly 40,000 talkback comments had been transcribed and cataloged by the museum staff. Jemima Fraser analyzed a representative sample of these comments in her 2004 doctoral thesis. Many comments reflect the successful achievement of the Glasgow City Council's objective that the museum promotes tolerance and respect: "The museum helps to confirm that we are all part of one big family—the message is one of tolerance and love."[45] Fraser's work demonstrates that many visitors are indeed being encouraged to construct a new vision of religious identity in Glasgow.

But the visitors do not always agree with the designer's egalitarian and tolerant message. One person wrote, for example, "I think the room with the Dali paintings should only have Christian objects in it and the other room the Buddha and other statues. It creates a chaotic impression and disturbs appreciation of the painting." Another comment, echoed elsewhere, is that "it would be better to separate out all religions."[46] While these sentiments were a minority, they were not insignificant. Richard Sandell's careful attempt to tease out ambiguities and resistive readings by visitors to the Anne Frank House and the St. Mungo Museum further reinforce Fraser's findings and indicate just how difficult it is to anticipate and manage visitor reactions.[47] In its design and in its encouragement of talkback, the St. Mungo Museum has been at the forefront of exploring the museum as inclusive of its community and engaged in a process of significant dialogue with those who "use" the museum in various ways. This commitment to community and dialogue is evident in the configuration of both permanent and temporary exhibits and in the museum's public programming and outreach activities.

Special Exhibits and Outreach

The St. Mungo Museum mounts a variety of programs, lectures, films, educational workshops, and events dedicated to cultural and religious understanding and dialogue. Their aims are to promote mutual understanding, fight prejudice, and integrate minorities. Susanne Claussen, a scholar studying museums, underlines the political dimension of this: "Glasgow as a 'multi-faith'-city—this is not only a historic declaration but also a political statement: a clear commitment to religious plurality."[48]

The commitment to educating visitors concerning the pluralistic nature of Glasgow's religious heritage is executed through a wide variety of programming. For example, in 2014–15, the museum hosted a series of public lectures titled Seeing God, which included talks by scholars of Islam, Judaism, Christianity, Buddhism, and Japanese traditions. Special exhibits also emphasize this mission. Installed in the second-floor gallery, they are accompanied by a host of activities, including lectures, tours, films, and events for children. Current examples include one-day programs aimed primarily at children on *Pilgrimage Souvenirs* and *Mandala Stones*. One recent special exhibit was titled *Heavenly Creatures: Angels in Faith History and Popular Culture*.[49] The exhibit included a range of items from stunning stained glass by Burne-Jones to kitsch and religious ephemera cleverly designed to appeal to children and adults. It even included a box of angel dress-up items that children (or adults) could try on. As I noted in a review, "The exhibit goes beyond the objects and involves a penumbra of thirty-seven gallery talks, screenings, scholarly lectures, and events (how to make paper angels, a twilight tour of the angels in the nearby Glasgow Necropolis, etc.) that leverages a much larger and deeper impact far beyond the immediate size of the exhibit."[50]

St. Mungo on the Web

Unlike the simulacra of a living relational network of people and objects provided by the videos and website of Le Musée Des Religions du Monde, the St. Mungo Museum website contributes little to its mission. The museum's chief innovation lies in the interactions it fosters among objects and between objects and visitors. Following cuts in local council spending and trends in consolidation, the St. Mungo Museum appears on the web as a part of Glasgow Life's comprehensive website. The Glasgow Life website includes official programming in "Arts and Music," "Museums," "Sport," "Libraries," "Communities" for all of Glasgow.[51] All of the city's museums can be found under the "Museums" tab. As a result it is very easy to begin on the St. Mungo website and inadvertently find oneself on the page of a different Glasgow museum. The unified website provides a single central information clearing house for major events in Glasgow within a single unified format. Graphics images and information are well chosen but are kept at a very sparse and simple level. In contrast to the website of St. Petersburg's State Museum of the History of Religions, the Glasgow website functions as little more than a bulletin board—a place to check what is currently "on."

Like other museums in this study, the St. Mungo Museum makes use of Facebook, Twitter, and YouTube. The links are placed in the upper left of the museum webpage. There is a Facebook page dedicated to the museum, and one on Twitter as well. These are primarily used to publicize events. The Facebook page also hosts a few videos, such as "Religious Dress in the Flesh" and "Legacies of Slavery in Glasgow."[52] The YouTube link takes one to a site used by all of the Glasgow museums, making it difficult to find videos specific to the St. Mungo Museum. In all, the website is an opportunity lost, especially given the innovative nature of the museum itself.

Objects and Semiotics: "Sacred Gaze" and Dialogics

The task the designers of the St. Mungo Museum set for themselves, to treat objects equally and to "create for each a metaphorical respect by carving out its own space" (architect David Page), while not "draining them of their dangerous meanings to render them safely aesthetic, historical or anthropological" (Mark O'Neill), is a difficult one. None of the other museums in this study actually attempts this. Part of the difficulty is illustrated by the notion of equal treatment which in itself relies on the notion of comparison discussed in Chapter 1 (and with regard to the Religionskundliche Sammlung in Chapter 3): that religious objects are somehow comparable can be a threat to the unique status claims of their supporters. The community feedback elicited during the planning of the Religious Life Gallery made this problem evident. Community members demanded that the different traditions be installed in separate cases. Similar issues were expressed in the "talkback cards" to the effect that Christian images and artifacts should have a separate room and not be placed with artifacts and images from other traditions. O'Neill's wish not to "drain" objects of their power and his desire to let them retain some of their indigenous power has created an interestingly anomalous and powerful museum.

The multicultural assumptions of a pluralistic society are, in many cases, directly the opposite of the claims of the various traditions. The museums I am examining are products of a multicultural and pluralistic, democratic, scientific, and therefore, comparative ideology. It is one that many people in the modern world aspire to and wish to live in. But such an ideology is not universally accepted, and some religious traditions are theocratic and expressly reject such pluralism. We need to keep in mind that pluralism is itself hegemonic on one issue: it brooks no claim to exclusive sovereignty.

The three permanent exhibit spaces in the St. Mungo Museum (five if we count the small room containing the Śiva image off of the main Religious Art exhibit and the Rock Garden as separate spaces) and the space on the second floor for temporary exhibits are segregated architecturally and function more or less independently. It is almost as if these were separate museums. But within each of these spaces the museum is deliberately political in its choice of "equal treatment" and a kind of in-your-face comparison. What does the Buddha tell me about Dali's Christ? Indeed, in the three main galleries the images are for all intents and purposes enjambed.

The St. Mungo Museum contains a number of very powerfully executed and stunning objects (a large bronze image of Śiva, some exquisite Buddhist images, fine Christian stained glass, etc.) and the compact display space—especially in the Religious Art Gallery—belies the light and airy setting and produces a kind of intimacy among the statues, images, and paintings.[53] David Morgan describes what he calls the "sacred gaze" to indicate the way images can have an uncanny power. So too, Amy Whitehead has described the uncanny power of "statue-persons."[54] Indeed, it is as though the gaze of the images and the museum visitor interlock. The phenomenological impact of the objects is reflected in visitors' deep discomfort or transformative engagement (as represented in studies of their comment or "talkback" cards).

The contrast to Le Musée des Religions du Monde is striking. There, the images and objects of different traditions are also proximate to one another. Nevertheless, they do not overtly interact as in the St. Mungo Museum. Instead, in Le Musée des Religions du Monde the objects are linked into a simulation of a living relational network centered on the videos of the five teenagers. At St. Mungo—especially in the Religious Art exhibit but also to a lesser extent in the Religious Life and Scottish galleries—a small number of impressive and strategically placed objects engage one another and draw the visitor into a relational network. It is tempting to visualize how a museum might integrate the approaches of Le Musée des Religions du Monde and the St. Mungo Museum.

The continuing attraction of the St. Mungo Museum is that it favors encounter and inevitably prompts dialogue. The other museums in this study, notably the Religionskundliche Sammlung, have moved deliberately to open up what Soja has called a "thirdspace" in their special programming and outreach. Such a move has its risks but opens up a real space for understanding, if not for agreement. The scholar of South Asian religions, Diana Eck of Harvard's Divinity School, notes that interreligious dialogue is not a matter of friendly discussions whose aim is to promote harmony. Rather, dialogue includes perception of difference, disagreement, and dispute:

> Dialogue is the discipline of thought that enables us to gain clarity about our own situatedness, our own forms of questioning our own position—whether methodological, political, religious, secular, even antireligious—so that our own subjectivity, our own language, and our own categories are not privileged and universalized unwittingly in our work.[55]

The St. Mungo Museum, like other museums in this study, assumes the ideology of comparative religion and presents itself as a neutral reflection of a multicultural and pluralistic Glasgow and West Scotland community in the late twentieth and early twenty-first century. The St. Mungo Museum was deliberately conceived as a social intervention. As Timothy Luke has pointed out, "Museums help to forge reality, and then they organize the collective rites of this unstable reality's reception that will write authoritative accounts of the past, present, and future in their displays. By doing this, museums serve as ontologues, telling us what reality really is."[56] But, as I have argued elsewhere,

> At its worst, efforts to promote the values of pluralism and multiculturalism— though well intentioned—can result in a flattening of difference in the service of majorities, elites, and the market. It can, in effect, be a form of ethnicity management that glosses over real points of dispute rather than seeking to clarify and negotiate them. We should not lose sight of the fact that democratic pluralism is a hegemonic ideology that is in direct conflict with the hegemonic values of theocracy. Tolerance, in short, is a category of the dominant and it explicitly excludes intolerance.[57]

Despite the comparativist template of the Religious Life Gallery designed around life-cycle rites and largely purged of sectarianism, the signal innovation of the St. Mungo Museum is its effort *not to flatten or completely museumify* the objects in its collection, but to foreground a dialogical mode of presentation and visitor "talkback."[58] This is particularly evident in the Religious Art Gallery. The St. Mungo Museum is an experiment in giving a voice both to the "things" in its collection and to the communities that have considered those things important. Nevertheless, it has yet to come into its own as a kind of "thirdspace" for community dialogue.

A Religious Museum

The Museum of World Religions in Taipei

Mediation between faith communities and secular society and providing museums of religions as spaces for interreligious dialogue and education have emerged as important goals of museums of world religions. The newest such museum, the Museum of World Religions in Taipei (Shijie zongjiao bowuguan), advances a mission overtly opposed to secularism and dedicated to promoting education about religions and interreligious dialogue. It does this, however, through a mixture of comparative religions methodology and traditional Chinese, and especially Chinese Buddhist frameworks.

The Museum of World Religions was conceived by the Buddhist monk, the Venerable Hsin Tao, and its exhibitions were designed in collaboration with the Center for the Study of World Religions (CSWR) at the Harvard Divinity School.

The Venerable Hsin Tao (pinyin: Xintao 心道, his Buddhist name means, roughly, "Heart of the Way") was born in Burma in 1948 to a Chinese family from Yunnan. After a stint in the army of the Republic of China in his teens that led him from Burma to Taiwan, Hsin Tao became interested in religion. The famous Buddhist master Hsing Yun (pinyin: Xingyun 星雲) ordained him in 1973 at the Foguangshan monastery. During the late 1970s and early 1980s, Hsin Tao withdrew to the mountains to practice various forms of meditation and asceticism. Finally settling on a peninsula in Northeast Taiwan, Hsin Tao founded the Ling Jiou Mountain Monastery (pinyin: Lingjiushan wusheng daochang 靈鷲山無生道場) in 1983. It is named for the famous Vulture Peak (Mt. Gṛdhrakūṭa) of Buddhist lore where the Buddha is said to have preached many of his sermons. During the last decade of the twentieth century, Hsin Tao has founded a variety of institutions and charitable organizations, culminating in the founding of the Museum of World Religions in Taipei.[1]

Officially opened on November 9–11, 2002, the Museum of World Religions is housed in a modern multistory glass-clad building—"Beyond Plaza"—on the busy Jungshan road in the Yonghe district of New Taipei, Taiwan. This is just south and across the river from the old Wanhua section of Taipei.[2] Along with the museum, the building houses shops and offices. The museum itself was designed by the famous architectural firm Ralph Appelbaum Associates, who have also designed numerous other museums including the Holocaust Memorial Museum in Washington, DC, the Hayden Planetarium, and the National Museum of Scotland.[3] Applebaum himself was intimately involved in the project and recounted his involvement in the planning in an essay in the *New York Times*.[4]

According to the "Founder" page of the museum website, Hsin Tao describes the mission of the museum thus: "The MWR [Museum of World Religions] promotes an interreligious and intercultural movement we call 'life education.' The unity-in-diversity exemplified by the interaction of the three religions of China forms the base of our tradition, stimulates a model of creativity, and contributes to the harmonious evolution of the world."[5] According to the main page of the website, "The Museum of World Religions belongs to all faiths. Its founding is inspiring and encouraging interfaith dialogue so that we all work together to create peace and understanding in the world we share."[6] The museum website further articulates why such an institution is needed:

> The traditional education system . . . fails to provide a good conduit for religious belief. In response to these various problems, Master Hsin Tao's dream of the World Religions Museum is to pioneer a correct form of religious education, to satisfy the public's spiritual needs, and to provide a leisure place that serves both education and enjoyment. He hopes to raise the standards of Taiwan's artistic and cultural life, as well as to establish a tourist destination of international reputation for Taiwan.[7]

The stated agenda, moreover, asserts the essential identity, or unity, of religions. Indeed, the entire museum assumes the ultimate underlying unity of religious traditions and is structured on a ritual process. The quotation on the page introducing "The Hall of Life's Journey" from the Sikh Guru Gobind Singh sums up the underlying message: "The same Reality is the creator and preserver of all; Know no distinctions between them, The monastery and the mosque are the same; So is the Hindu worship and the Muslim prayer. Humans are all one!"[8] Hsin Tao's approach to this mission was obviously inflected by Chinese notion of the harmony of Buddhism, Daoism, and the teachings of Confucius, but also by his acquaintance with comparative religions and contemporary perennialism. Professor Lawrence E. Sullivan of the Harvard Divinity School's CSWR served as the concept and content developer. Along with Alison Edwards, head of the CSWR's Religion and the Arts Initiative, an international group of graduate students worked together with religious leaders on the team that designed the museum. Sullivan, who is now Professor Emeritus of Theology and Anthropology at the University of Notre Dame, earned a PhD in History of Religions at the University of Chicago. He is a well-known historian of religions and expert on ritual process and healing. Among his many publications is *Religions of the World: An Introduction to Culture and Meaning* that I examined in Chapter 1. According to Edwards, "For me, the mission of the museum—which is not about representing religions from outside, but from within the traditions or cultures to allow for diversity and dialogue—was first realized through the process of our work together."[9]

A Journey through the Collection

A brief introduction to the Museum of World Religions is helpful in understanding its layout and structuring principles. The museum's floor plan and virtual tour features provide an excellent overview of the presentation of the world's religions. What is immediately noticeable is the very open floor plan. The main exhibits are spread over two floors. One enters on floor seven. Eight permanent exhibits are devoted to Buddhism, Daoism, Christianity, Islam, Hinduism, Sikhism, Judaism, and Shinto. There is also an exhibit focusing on Taiwanese Popular Religion as well as two exhibitions (originally meant to be rotating) treating Ancient Religions (Egyptian) and Indigenous Religions (Maya). Floor six presents life-cycle rituals across a variety of religious traditions. The spherical Avatamsaka World theatre—whose name derives from a famous Buddhist scripture—occupies a two-floor atrium-like space at one end of the building. Although visitors can browse the museum according to their own interests, the museum has been structured in such a way as to coax visitors through a particular religious and educational journey. Maria Reis Habito, a scholar of Chinese Buddhism who has worked closely with the museum, wrote an interesting analysis of the permanent galleries shortly after the museum opened. She compares the structuring of the permanent exhibit to the sequencing of a religious ritual, dividing the museum into fourteen steps: "The museum experience is an orderly succession of times magnified and mapped onto a series of spaces that invite the visitor's interaction. The aim is to offer the visitor an experience that, like a ritual, is satisfying and transformative and yet remains an experience proper to an institute of learning."[10]

Flags, multicolored banners, the symbols of different religions, and the museum name and logo announce the street level entryway to the Museum of World Religions. Walking into the small lobby one immediately notices the curved dark blue ceiling with various points of light. My guide indicated that this represented the notion of Indra's Net and Buddhist ideas concerning the interpenetration of all reality.[11]

The image of Indra's Net is based on the doctrine of interpenetration in the *Avatamsaka Sutra* (Chinese translation: *Huayanjing*).[12] In the scripture, the Buddha explains the nature of reality thus,

If untold buddha-lands are reduced to atoms,
In one atom are untold lands,
And as in one,
So in each.
The atoms to which these buddha-lands are reduced in an instant are unspeakable,
And so are the atoms of continuous reduction moment to moment
Going on for untold eons;
These atoms contain lands unspeakably many,
And the atoms in these lands are even harder to tell of.[13]

All of these atoms are likened to jewels fastened to knots in a vast net. Francis H Cook's classic study of the text contains one of the clearest explanations of the metaphor of Indra's Net:

Far away in the heavenly abode of the great god Indra, there is a wonderful net which has been hung by some cunning artificer in such a manner that it stretches out infinitely in all directions. In accordance with the extravagant tastes of deities, the artificer has hung a single glittering jewel in each "eye" of the net, and since the net itself is infinite in dimension, the jewels are infinite in number. There hang the jewels, glittering "like" stars in the first magnitude, a wonderful sight to behold. If we now arbitrarily select one of these jewels for inspection and look closely at it, we will discover that in its polished surface there are reflected *all* [emphasis in original] the other jewels in the net, infinite in number. Not only that, but each of the jewels reflected in this one jewel is also reflecting all the other jewels, so that there is an infinite reflecting process occurring.[14]

Applied in the design of the museum, and thus referring to various religions, the metaphor is an argument that all religions are in some way "one" and that all religions, despite their seeming differences, are actually reflections of each other and of ultimate reality. The teaching of Indra's Net is a core theme in the Museum of World Religions.

Just to the side of this entry hall is an elevator that goes to the museum proper. The actual museum occupies the sixth and seventh floors, and the actual entry and starting point of the journey is on the seventh floor. Pricing of admission as of late 2018 was 150 NT (about US$5) for the permanent exhibits, 100 NT for special exhibits, and 100 NT for "Love Land," the special educational space for children's programs. There is preferential pricing for students, seniors, and so on.[15]

Stepping out of the elevator one can proceed ahead to the main galleries or to the right to "Love Wonderland" (the children's area). While parts of the museum can be browsed in a variety of ways, the architects and curators have designed the museum exhibitions to be viewed in sequence, and the various spaces are designed as total environments with attention to visual, auditory, and tactile sensation. Over the entryway large gold letters proclaim: "The doors to goodness, wisdom, and compassion are opened by keys of the heart." This is a free interpretation of the accompanying Chinese inscription which might be more literally rendered thus: "The 100,000 entry ways to the Teaching all return to the heart." The saying is a traditional one attributed to the fifth Chan (Japanese "Zen") patriarch Daoshin.[16] As is the case in St. Petersburg's State Museum of the History of Religions, Nicolet's Le Musée des Religions du Monde, and Marburg's Religionskundliche Sammlung, the different languages often carry somewhat different messages. In this case, a saying meant to refer to different types of Buddhism is intended to take on more universalist implications in the free English rendering. The reinterpretation is signaled in the English language guidebook as "expanded in meaning to include peoples of all religions."[17]

Walking ahead and to the left the first display is a "Water Curtain" in which visitors may put their hands in a gesture of purification. The guidebook explains the significance of water in Hindu, Christian, Sikh, Buddhist, and Shinto settings.[18] The implication is that the visitor, like a person performing a religious rite, begins with an appropriate gesture of purification and separation from the mundane world. The structuring of the museum to conform to the ritual process typology (at its simplest, separation-transition-incorporation) that is a common tool of comparative religion was an intentional part of the museum design. Proceeding along the preferred path, visitors circumambulate the seventh floor, walking clockwise, the correct direction in Buddhism for honoring a Buddhist image, dignitary, or monument. The design is not accidental, nor is the placement

Figure 18 Pilgrim's Way. Image courtesy of Museum of World Religions.

of a model of the great Buddhist stūpa at Borobudur, Indonesia, at the very center of the central gallery on this floor.[19]

One next walks along a long corridor called the "Pilgrim's Way" (Figure 18). Along the left wall are near life-size images of pilgrims from different religious traditions so that one appears to be walking with them. A soundtrack produces questions in various languages—a kind of murmuring—and on the right side questions such as "Who am I" are projected onto pillars both in Chinese and in English.[20] The floor is also part of the package—light strips of stone are interspersed with darker stone—rough and smooth in texture—and the intervals between the strips vary. A black wall stands at the end of the corridor. It is surfaced with a heat and touch sensitive material where the "pilgrims" can leave a handprint that then slowly vanishes. An accompanying plaque discusses the meaning of hands and particularly of religious action and attitude. The guidebook says that the handprints "represent the visitor's blessing for the Museum of World Religions."[21] The entire corridor—water, pilgrim way, and handprint wall—is well designed for children.

Turning away from the wall to the right one enters the "Golden Lobby" where, according to the guidebook, "a visit to the museum starts formally."[22] The dominant color is gold: two golden mosaic walls, two large gold pillars. The ceiling is a dark blue hemisphere with tiny points of light representing the heavens at the time of the birth of the founder Hsin Tao.[23] The floor, also in the dominant golden color, is described as a "cosmography":

> Representing the three dimensions of the cosmos—Heaven, Earth, and humankind . . . . The labyrinthine pattern of the Cosmography resembles the maze on the floor of the Chartres Cathedral, France, which has been slightly altered to include colors and animal images symbolizing the world's major religions, and adjusted to lie in harmony with the four main compass points on which the MWR lies.[24]

The guidebook also explains, "In Western traditions, even the process of walking through the maze represents a kind of search for truth."[25] Emblazoned on the pillars is the motto, "Love is our shared truth—Peace is our eternal hope." Those unfamiliar with Chinese traditions will likely miss the heaven-earth-humanity triad, which has a long history in Confucian thinking, as well as the orientation to the four quarters and the blue heaven gold earth color scheme—also traditional and heavily laden with imperial symbolism. Those familiar with Daoist ritual will also recognize the affinity with the altar setup in a *jiao* or rite of offering or cosmic renewal. There too one finds a hemispheric ceiling hanging with the constellations and a cosmic diagram that is ritually traced out on the floor by the steps of a Daoist priest.[26] One surprise is that in this case the diagram itself is largely comprised of Western symbols. The classical cosmograms derived from the *Yijing* or *Book of Changes* are not evident here.[27]

Thus, the visitor is encouraged to see the journey through the museum that will follow as an analogue to the walking of this maze and the accomplishment of a religious orientation. Adjacent to the Golden Lobby, the next stop on a tour is called "Origins." Here a twelve-minute film called "Creations" focuses on creation myths in world religions and in science (the "big bang"). The film is in Mandarin with English subtitles. As Lüpken notes, although the film is beautiful, it makes assumptions that the viewer possesses sophisticated hermeneutical tools, and local visitors to the museum have found it difficult to understand. As a result, in 2006 a second film was added. This film, titled "People," takes a multicultural approach and ends with a praise of ethnic, cultural, and religious diversity.[28]

After the film, visitors are invited to exit by the stairway at the front of the theater where they descend to the sixth floor and the "Hall of Life's Journey" (Figure 19). The hall "is subdivided into five areas: birth, coming of age, mid-life, old age, and death and the afterlife."[29] It is obvious that the hall was inspired by the comparative framework of "rites of passage" as developed by the

Figure 19 Hall of Life's Journey. Image courtesy of Museum of World Religions.

twentieth-century European ethnographer Arnold van Gennep and popularized by the anthropologist Victor Turner. Each of the five stations in this exhibit includes informative panels discussing the stage of life and a glass case with artifacts in front of which is a touchscreen. On the opposite side of the room is a large projection screen, and between the touchscreen and the projection screen are circular tables with small ritual items. The height of the displays mimics the progression of a life—the table is low at the station concerned with birth, reaches a high point at the midlife display, and then lowers again by death and the afterlife station, thus forcing the viewer's body to perform a metaphoric version of life's journey. At each station music and objects have been chosen to provide an appropriate accompaniment to the images projected on the screen. For example, the "Coming of Age" display case includes a communion dress and a Japanese festival kimono for a children's celebration. Other items in the display include a tefillin used in Jewish Bar Mitzvah ceremonies and a Chinese contract with the goddess of the dipper stars traditionally believed to be the guardian of children.[30] Even the wood of the benches has been chosen to align with the stage of life under discussion. Cedar is used in the midlife displays, and small text panels link it to various items, such as Christian dowry boxes.[31] The careful coordination of image, material objects, sound, and text is designed to reinforce the notion that such stages are universal.

Two additional rooms flank the Hall of Life's Journey. On one side is a small theater showing a film, "Awakenings," while on the other side is a "Meditation Gallery." The Awakenings room is dominated by a large screen in front of which are rows of benches. Here people both famous (Jane Goodall, for instance) and local "talk about transforming events in their own lives that led to spiritual awakenings and new directions."[32] The Awakenings room includes small recording booths as well in which visitors can record their own awakening experiences. Some of these stories are then incorporated into the display.

The Meditation Gallery is a dimly lit room with three screens and a raised wood platform for seated meditation. Images from six religions—Judaism, Christianity, Islam, Daoism, Hinduism, and Buddhism—are projected onto the screens. Each image is intended to conform to the category "meditation." Thus, for Judaism we see recitation, for Christianity a rosary, for Islam recitation, for Daoism a person performing Tai Chi, and for Buddhism a person practicing Zazen. The room also has explanations of the various meditation methods mounted on the wall. According to the guidebook,

> As religious practice, meditation can be divided into two main types, active and passive. The former affirms the qualities, strengths or moral values of an individual's existence. The latter emphasizes a complete renunciation and transcendence of existential thought. The meditation process should begin with an initial stage of purification and harmonization. The meditator should then seek renunciation and transcendence of ego, leading to personal transformation. Finally this realization should be integrated into everyday life. In this way meditation can help a person become compassionate in their relationship with the rest of the world.[33]

It is notable that this discussion imposes a very particular and, one could argue, a very modern and Western interpretation on these quite varied religious practices. Even leaving aside the notion that the Islamic recitation of the *shahadah* (the profession of faith in Allah and his prophet Muhammed) is somehow equivalent to the practice of Zazen or the use of the rosary in Catholicism, the typological distinction between active and passive forms, individual and society, transcendence and existential thought all conspire to homogenize quite disparate forms of practice to binary categories of active and passive, worldly and transcendent, individual and society. The flattening effect of the comparative method as well as the choice of religions is evident.

Just beyond the end of the Hall of Life's Journey one enters the Avatamsaka World—a golden sphere inside of which is a high-tech theater. Visitors are seated on circular benches and the film is projected onto the dome of the theater. The acoustics of the theater were designed so even whispering can be heard throughout, and the original thought was to have a demonstration of the idea of interdependence as presented in the *Avatamsaka Sutra*.[34] This, however, was dropped in favor of a twelve-minute film "containing reflections of humanity's shared history."[35] Along with images of happy people, Hindu and Buddhist deities, and so on, one is also presented with images of suffering and war—and this is the only place in the museum where negative images occur.[36] The film is designed to encourage people to create a world of peace.

> The design concept for this space comes from the *Avatamsaka sutra*: One is all and all is one. . . . It is hoped that through this film visitors can share their sacred and mysterious experiences of the Cosmos and enter into the spirit of the Avatamsaka World.[37]

The displays and films are impressively executed and designed to induce a sense of an underlying commonality of spiritual quest despite the apparent diversity of people and religions.

Exiting the Avatamsaka World visitors are now once again on the seventh floor and can enter the last major segment of the permanent exhibit, the Great Hall of World Religions. The hall covers most of the seventh floor and contains ten display cases along the two long walls (Figure 20). To orient the visitor, there is a general information board about "World Religions" in Chinese and English that creates context and frames the major display cases on the floor. It says,

> The Museum of World Religions honors the world's faiths, past and present, and highlights some of those that have the largest number of adherents. All religious traditions are of equal merit and value; the ten shown here typify the rest. You will see what these faiths have in common, and will learn their beliefs and histories.[38]

The top and bottom of the display consists of a list of some seventy different religions (e.g., Yoruba, Tenrikyō, Christian Science, etc.). The center of the board has a beautiful collage-like image representing the religions. A Buddha is at the very center, a Hindu deity to the lower right, Shinto images to the lower left, a

Figure 20 Great Hall of World Religions. Image courtesy of Museum of World Religions.

Daoist Worthy at the upper right, an Egyptian statue of Horus at the upper left, and an inscription in Arabic across the bottom. Each of the major religions in the display is represented on this image. Despite protestations of equal value, a semiotic read of this image can suggest that the placements are not random. Further, it is not explained how these ten "typify the rest." Again, the list of major religions is little different from early lists of "ten great religions," though at least in this case, we are informed that the choice has something to do with the number of adherents.

The visitor begins in a corridor with a display of a Buddha made by the contemporary glass artist Jiang Sheng (蔣昇). Walking to the left one first encounters two small displays devoted to Zoroastrianism. Continuing around the corner to the left on this side of the room are displays for Buddhism, Islam, ancient Egyptian religion, Judaism, and Christianity. Walking to the other side of the room one finds displays devoted to Daoism, Shinto, ancient Mayan religion, Sikhism, and Hinduism. At the far end of the room from the Avatamsaka Theatre that the visitor has just exited is an exhibition devoted to Taiwanese religion. The exhibits on Egyptian and Mayan religion were conceived to be temporary exhibits but have been in place since the museum's founding.[39] They represent no longer extant and indigenous religions respectively.[40]

Moving onward to the exhibit cases each station consists of a long glass-fronted display. The background walls are black. In front of the cases are descriptive panels placed at waist height and keyed to the items in the case (most of the description is only in Chinese, but laminated cards near the exhibits provide brief descriptions in other languages). At the center of these descriptive panels is a touch screen with further information and imagery and recorded sound. To the left of the display cases is a poster introducing the religious tradition in Chinese and English. The floor in front of the display has set in it a symbol representing the tradition. Most of the information is carried by the display panels—the items in the display cases are accompanied by minimal information. The displays contain some striking and exquisite artifacts chosen to illustrate key ideas and practices. The displays manage to include numerous objects without feeling overcrowded. Maria Reis Habito, a scholar of Chinese Buddhism who has served with Hsin Tao's organization, writing shortly after the opening of the museum, notes that

> eight common themes are explored for each tradition: (1) existing religion and its subdivisions; (2) history and development; (3) geographical distribution; (4) doctrines; (5) rituals, rites, and calendar; (6) organization; (7) types of architecture; and (8) influences and future development, especially in Taiwan.[41]

Rather than detailing each exhibit, I focus here on representative examples, including the cases devoted to Buddhism, Judaism, Christianity, Taoism, and the Religious Life of the Taiwanese.

The Buddhism case is dominated by a variety of Buddhist statues, two-dimensional images, and other artifacts such as traditional Tibetan canonical books, miniature stūpas, beads, and ritual implements. At the very center of the display is an exquisite near life-size statue of Meitreya—the future Buddha—in the "royal ease" posture. To the right, among many other images and artifacts is a stone carving of the impression of the Buddha's feet dating from the second century CE. To the left is fragment of a bas-relief of the Buddha's birth dating from the third century CE.

The case devoted to Judaism is situated on the same side of the hall as the Buddhism display. On one side is the display on Egyptian religion. On the other is the display on Christianity. The introductory panel, as with the other displays, is on the left and includes a Star of David and explanatory text in Chinese and English. The accompanying image is a menorah. The explanatory panels (in Chinese) treat subjects such as "The Torah" and "The Synagogue." At the center of the display is a prayer shawl. The display also includes a Sefer Torah (a handwritten Torah), a beautiful Shiviti or Synagogue Plaque, a menorah, and a Megillah or Esther Scroll used at Purim celebrations.

The next display is devoted to Christianity. The main panel presents basic information about Jesus and the church, and the display case has items from Catholic, Orthodox, and Protestant branches of Christianity, but discussions of sectarianism are notably absent. Indeed, a similar lack of sectarian differences is notable in the Islam and Buddhism displays. Clearly, a decision was made to emphasize what the religions—both inter and intra—have in common. Descriptive panels discuss the evangelical missions, the saints, and so forth. Visually, the display case is dominated by a large painting of Jesus as good shepherd (carrying a lamb on his shoulder) and displaying the stigmata on his body. Beneath this painting is a carving of Jesus and the apostles representing the charge to spread the Gospel. To the left is a crucifix and another painting of St. Peter. On the right are orthodox icons including one depicting the Virgin and Christ Child.

The display concerning Daoism has a number of interesting features. The main panel talks of Daoism's origins being traced to Laozi, but in line with contemporary scholarship, it also describes the development of Daoism as a religious tradition in the second century CE that branched into various "schools." The display boards in front of the main case take up topics such as the word "Dao" and the Daoist pantheon. The medallion on the floor in front of the display has at its center a "pearl" of yang surrounded by the eight trigrams from the *Yijing*, astrological animals, and so on. Prominent at the center of the display is a robe worn by Daoist priests, a large wooden carving of the Daoist divinity the Queen Mother of the West (Xi Wang Mu), and some musical instruments as used in the Daoist *Zhai* and *Jiao* rituals. To the left are carvings of the popular "eight immortals" and to the right is an exquisite painting of the Daoist pantheon.

A display on "The Religious Life of the Taiwanese" occupies the wall of the gallery opposite the Avatamsaka Theatre. This placement sets it apart from all of the other display cases. In addition to the information panel on the left of the display case, there is a video panel on the right that includes video of Daoist rituals. The panels in front of the case carry no information. Rather, small information placards are placed inside the case describing particular objects. Chinese characters, written on the lower part of the glass in gold, proclaim virtues such as "revere heaven" (*jing tian* 敬 天). The main display case has, at its center, a large vermillion placard inscribed with the title of the Jade emperor next to which is a large wooden statue of the deity the "Dark Warrior" (Xuan Wu 玄武), a deity popular in Taiwanese folk traditions. On the right is an elaborate incense burner (incense is a traditional means of communicating with the gods). The case also contains a sampling of other deities popular in Taiwan, including small images of the Lord of Hell's two henchmen, Fan and Xie, who are related to rites for the dead. Surprisingly, I saw no representations of "Confucian" traditions.

In its original configuration, the central part of the room had only benches. The space seemed useless and a change was made to exhibit miniature models of famous religious buildings replete with cameras showing the interiors. The models are quite impressive. At the end of the room closest to the Avatamsaka Theatre is Chartres Cathedral. Moving clockwise we find the Ise Shrine in Japan; the Luce Chapel in Taichung, Taiwan (named in honor of the nineteenth-century American missionary); the Golden Temple in Amritsar, India; Kandariya Mahadev Temple at Khajuraho, India; the Assumption Cathedral at the Trinity St. Sergius monastery in Russia; the Altneuschl (Old-New Synagogue) in Prague; the Dome of the Rock in Jerusalem; and finally, Foguang Buddhist Temple in Shanxi, China. At the center of the floor is a large model of the great Buddhist stūpa at Borobudur in central Java. Given the museum's theme inspired by the *Avatamsaka Sutra*, this central placement seems quite appropriate. A major section of the scripture depicts the spiritual quest of the young seeker Suddhana. The story is rendered in reliefs throughout the stūpa.[42] Each of the models is supplied with a placard and description in Chinese and English. Some of them have video displays showing interiors. The display of religious buildings is quite impressive and serves to anchor the entire gallery. At the same time, as in some other museums, nowhere do different traditions and deities occupy contiguous spaces—all traditions and objects are safely sequestered in their display cases.

The final stages of the permanent exhibit are the "Wall of Gratitude" and "Blessings." Heading back across the length of the seventh floor toward the Avatamsaka Theatre and the elevator, one walks past the "Wall of Gratitude" on which one sees the names and handprints of supporters of the museum. Finally, the visit to the museum is completed with a blessing—visitors press their hands on two handprints on the wall and a screen above produces a blessing or benediction (mirroring the entering blessing and completing the ritual process).

The Museum of World Religions offers a variety of other services for visitors, not the least of which is "Love Wonderland" or "Kid's Land," originally launched in 2005. This is an extensive space on the seventh floor specifically designed for games, educational events, and parties for small children. Redesigned and updated for fifteenth anniversary of the museum, it has become "Planets of Love" (愛的星球).

"Planets of Love" provides different "planets" where young children learn about different forms of love. They learn to perceive themselves in the Emotional Planet; to love nature in the Natural Planet; and to love their families and communities in the Love Planet. In addition, a "Gas Station" within the "Planets of Love" let children to deliver and share love.[43] Somewhat older children can take advantage of the "Computer Games Room" as well as a "Broadcast Studio," both on the sixth floor. The games offered in this room—in contrast to what is on offer in most gaming culture—are devoted to inculcating respect for life, while the Broadcast Studio is dedicated to showing religious films and music on multimedia computers.[44] The sixth floor also provides a small library as well as classrooms, a café, and a sizable gallery for special exhibits. The seventh floor houses an excellent restaurant and the obligatory gift shop.

Special Exhibits

The Museum of World Religions regularly mounts special exhibits in the two large sixth-floor galleries. The English language web page tab on "Exhibitions" is divided into three sub-pages: one devoted to the permanent exhibition, one for "current exhibitions," and one for "past exhibitions." The Chinese page includes "Kids World" as a separate category under permanent exhibits.

At the time of writing, two special exhibitions were on offer. The first, *A Deep River Runs Far—Theravada Culture Exhibition*, features objects drawn from the museum's collection, including Buddha images and texts collected and donated by the Buddhist Master Yuan Kuang who spent many years preaching Buddhism in the Philippines. According to the web page for the exhibit, "After research and curation, this exhibition, launched on the 17th anniversary of the museum, consists of over 50 Buddha statues, statues of gods and goddesses, objects, and scriptures. Dynamic spread maps and situational devices are integrated to introduce the historical background, Buddhist meditation, and religious life of Theravada." It is notable that despite the relative lack of historical discussion in the permanent exhibit, the page discussing this exhibit emphasizes the historical spread of what many scholars now refer to as Nikāya or Mainstream Buddhism across South and Southeast Asia.[45]

The second current exhibition is *Embroidered Buddha—The First Korean National Treasure Embroidery Artist Han Sang Soo*, and presents in embroidery the Korean Buddhist tradition in which the Buddha's return to Lingjiu Mountain to expound Buddhist teachings is reenacted in a "Yeongsan-jae ritual" or "Vulture Peak ritual."[46]

Under *Past Exhibitions* are listed forty-eight shows stretching back to 2002, with roughly three special exhibitions per year. A little more than half of these have dealt with Asian topics and an ongoing series of exhibitions concerns sacred buildings. The earliest special exhibit predictably focused on Buddhism. It featured listed artifacts "selected by Dalai Lama, including the *tangka* he uses during contemplation, Buddhas, Buddhist musical instrument and monk's robe." Also in the exhibit were "thirty-three precious antiques from Drepung Loseling Monastery, and seventeen collections from MWR."[47]

In keeping with the museum's focus on world religions, many of the special exhibits over the last seventeen years have spanned Western and Asian topics and have often focused on promoting tolerance and mutual understanding. These exhibits have included, for instance, *Painting a Story* taking its cue from the painting *Adoration of Shepherds*. This exhibition has "a detailed discussion on religious painting of Christian art, from symbols in bible and religious paintings to paintings in different periods."[48] Other examples included an exhibit on the Mexican Day of the Dead; another titled *Tolerance, Understanding, Coexistence—Oman's Message of Islam*; another on *Chongqing Dazu Rock Carvings*; and six exhibits on sacred buildings.[49] Special exhibits and events surrounding them are also chronicled in the museum's quarterly periodical, *Zongbo jikan* 宗博季刊 (available in Chinese only).[50]

Outreach and Educational Mission

The "100,000 Dharma Doors" and the "Jeweled Net" are the guiding principles for the continuing development of the Museum of World Religions' collection, exhibitions, educational programs, and research. The efforts of the museum's education section have been focused on providing religious, cultural, and art education to schools at all levels. In consonance with its founding ideal, on December 5, 2009, the museum officially established its "Life Education Center." The center's "life education navigators" assist the museum's education programs by engaging in such activities as discussions, research, interpretation, and publishing.[51]

The Museum of World Religions and Related Institutions

The Museum of World Religions is only one of the Reverend Hsin Tao's efforts at spreading an inclusive sense of religious harmony. Hsin Tao's core foundation is the Lingjiou Buddhist Monastery.[52] The monastery is located on Taiwan's northeast coast and includes the Three Yanas Buddhist College, three libraries (one of which is at the Museum of World Religions), a research center focused on "Zen, Huayan, Guanyin, and the Water-Earth Repentance Ceremony" and on providing "a theoretical basis for promoting interfaith dialogues and the ideals of the Global Family for Love and Peace."[53] The monastery also operates the Institute for Enlightened Life that "opens Buddhist and secular courses on the model of a community university with the aim of broadening learners' mind and enriching learners' knowledge. It is hoped that learners can learn to respect every life and religion through these courses" as well as a dedicated University of World Religions. According to the website, the university is based

> on what Hans Kung, President of the Foundation for a Global Ethic, had said, if there is no peace among different religions, then there will be no peace among different races, and if there are no interfaith dialogues, then there will be no peace among different religions. The Museum of World Religions is dedicated to promoting equal dialogues among different religions and cultures in the world.[54]

To this end the organization publishes a journal, *New Century Religious Studies* (*Xin shiji zongjiao yanjiu*).[55]

Finally, there is the Global Family for Love and Peace, a foundation affiliated with the United Nations Department of Public Information and with the United

Nations Economic and Social Council. The mission of the foundation is stated thus:

> Transforming the power of love into action through intercultural and interfaith dialogues, conflict resolution, activities related to the United Nations Culture of Peace and the International Day of Peace, peace education, and war orphan programs.[56]

Building in an overt way on the metaphor of Indra's Net and the Buddhist notion of the "100,000 Entryways to the Teaching," the Museum of World Religions serves as a primary but not the sole gateway into a program of promoting peace and understanding through the use of the "world religions" model.

Museum of World Religions on the Web and on Social Media

The Museum of World Religions and its related organizations such as the Lingjiou Mountain Monastery and the Global Family for Love and Peace demonstrate a sophisticated understanding of the use of the web as an adjunct to and extension of brick and mortar institutions. As is the case at Le Musée des Religions du Monde, a section of the Museum of World Religions' primary website presents a selection of objects under the "Collections" tab. The objects available are key objects in the seventh-floor displays and some, such as the "Rice Barrel Lantern" (*Dou Deng* 斗燈) used in Daoist ritual, are available in 3-D format.[57] The objects can be sorted by tradition, although, again, the English page brings up fewer items than the Chinese page. Neither Le Musée des Religions du Monde nor the Museum of World Religions has attempted anything as sophisticated as the virtual programming of the State Museum of the History of Religions in St. Petersburg.

It should come as no surprise that the Museum of World Religions (as well as its allied organizations) has a presence on social media. At the bottom of the museum main page one finds a variety of links including those for Transportation, Links, Facebook, YouTube, and an RSS feed. Under the "Links" tab, one can find the Lingjiou Mountain Buddhist Society, the Republic of China Tourism Bureau, Beliefnet, the Parliament of the World's Religions, and the North American Interfaith Network. The Facebook page appears to be used primarily to post upcoming events and pictures of visitors and visitor reviews. The YouTube site has seventy-eight subscribers and hosts videos on some of the museum's special exhibits (Christian art, Voudun, Islamic culture, etc.) as well as one on the establishment of the museum.[58]

The World Religions Narrative, Objects, and Observations

The Museum of World Religions pursues decidedly laudable goals. Its message that "one is all and all is one" expressing the idea that there is "wisdom and character common to all religion and all life" draws its inspiration from Buddhist metaphors derived from the *Avatamsaka Sutra*, from the Chinese notion of the "the Three Teachings are fundamentally single" and from what we might understand as a broadly modern and perennialist vision of all religions reflecting a single underlying truth—despite their diverse forms. Whatever its global ambitions, the museum is, after all, a product of an East Asian Buddhist milieu. The Avatamsaka World is indicative of the Buddhist goal of the museum and the summit of a mild Buddhist form of comparative religion (*panjiao*). This strategy has a long history in Buddhist thought. Buddhists in South and East Asia practiced a kind of comparative religion that ranked Buddhist teachings based on when and to what audience the Buddha gave a particular teaching. Called "dividing the teachings " (Chinese, *panjiao*), it was extended by the medieval Japanese cleric Kūkai in his *Aims of the Three Teachings* (*Sango shiiki*) to appropriate Confucian and Daoist teachings as well as what the esoteric master deemed less advanced varieties of Buddhist teaching. This was a concept of world religions avant la lettre.[59] The museum's founder Hsin Tao made this comparative strategy explicit. He claims,

> The MWR promotes an interreligious and intercultural movement we call "life education." The unity-in-diversity exemplified by the interaction of the three religions of China forms the base of our tradition, stimulates a model of creativity, and contributes to the harmonious evolution of the world.[60]

Despite—or perhaps because of—this invocation of underlying unity, "interaction" within the permanent displays of the museum is not evident— everything in the museum has been structured to promote a vision of "unity in diversity." To use a musical metaphor, the museum promotes a kind of "singing in a choir." In the Taiwanese Museum of World Religions, as in the Religious Life Gallery at the St. Mungo Museum in Glasgow and the State Museum of the History of Religions in St. Petersburg, objects are arranged so that they do not give the appearance of interacting. Only at the center of the main floor of the Museum of World Religions are objects from different traditions in close proximity, but these objects are models of famous sacred buildings. They are not icons or deity images and thus do not engage one another. The arrangement of the building itself exemplifies the guiding principle of the museum. As in the traditional Chinese Buddhist form of comparative religion, competing religions are accommodated within a hierarchy with the overall framework of the "Avatamsaka World" that pierces both floors of the museum as though meant to be a physical demonstration of the Buddhist teaching of interpenetration. "One is all and all is One." By virtue of its being the underlying ideology of the museum, this "oneness" places itself as first among equals.

One lacuna that puzzled me more as I studied the museum is the almost total absence of Confucius in a culture that has canonized his teachings. Aside from the debates over whether "Confucianism" is a religion or a philosophy, this absence seems a glaring omission.[61] Perhaps an exhibit might choose a few objects to foreground the journey of "Confucianism" in the politics and religion of the nineteenth and twentieth centuries. Certainly Taipei has many cultural resources that would lend themselves to the inclusion of Confucian thought and practice (e.g., the Taipei Confucian Temple).[62]

Various activities sponsored by the museum and its allied organizations are designed to encourage engagement and dialogue, for example, with the Buddhist-Muslim Dialogue Series sponsored by the Global Family for Love and Peace, and various of the museum educational programs.[63] But the permanent exhibits—especially the Great Hall of World Religions—drain objects of their danger to visitors and of their interaction with one another. As discussed in Chapter 1, this multiculturalist approach tries to promote harmony but can end up silencing much-needed debate about difference. The absence of any mention of sectarian divisions is indicative of this harmony-oriented approach. Ensconced in their individual displays as though separate chapters in a world religions textbook, the Great Hall exhibit seems to do exactly the opposite of what Master Hsin Tao has been working to achieve—genuine dialogue. In its current state, the permanent exhibits at the Museum of World Religions imprison the many exquisite objects in a Western and, to some extent, Buddhist comparative religion narrative. Indra's Net reflects only harmony, and the objects are robbed of potentially discordant voices. Selecting one or two objects a year to tell their life stories and trace their journeys (à la Ingold or Davis) and giving them the sort of treatment that the British Museum gives to certain objects (the "God" A'a, for instance, discussed in Chapter 1) would do much to probe fault lines both within and between religious traditions and might remedy this sterile textbook treatment.

Conclusion

Rethinking Museums of Religions

Having spent the last several years exploring, examining, and enjoying these five impressive museums and talking and corresponding with the professionals who manage them, I have come away with an admiration for what they have accomplished and are accomplishing. Each one of these museums is a thoughtful intervention: an attempt to educate people and make the world a more tolerant and less conflict-ridden place.

At the beginning of this study, I traced the genealogy of the world religions taxonomy to the rise of the comparative science of religion in the nineteenth century and to its development and deployment in the service of imperialism. I also posed the following questions: How can religions be compared? To what ends? Why compare religions at all? From the very beginning, the world religions model has divided the world of religion into spirit and matter, and it has divided religions into those with texts such as "ours" (Western), or "theirs" (Eastern), and all the rest (savage, primitive, indigenous). Comparative religion as a discipline is deeply flawed, and though I have great respect for the founders of the discipline, we must not—wittingly or unwittingly—allow their biases to blind us. We must build on their insights and avoid repeating their mistakes.

It should be obvious that each of the museums I discuss here, along with each exhibit, constitutes a *material definition* of "religion." Religion as found in Nicolet is not the same religion as found in Glasgow or Taipei. Religion includes Africa in Marburg, St. Petersburg, and Glasgow. But one must look very hard to find Africa in Nicolet and Taipei where the world religions paradigm is strongest. Given limited space and local interests, a museum using the world religions model must choose what to leave out, whether five religions are included or ten.

Even if we leave aside comparative religion's imperialist and racist genealogy with its history of superiority, appropriation, and subjugation, we must still reckon with the epistemic horizon of the enterprise. Comparative religion couples a Cartesian disdain for the material world with Christian values that proclaim the ascendancy of the transcendent, the holy, the sacred, or the numinous as the sui generis and irreducible focus of religion. Based on such premises any approach to matter—to objects in museums—is already compromised and overdetermined. Corralling religious objects within the epistemic horizons of transcendence and the hegemonic "scientific" grids of comparative religion—such as life-cycle rites or ritual process—produces a lowest common denominator sameness that effaces difference and, I would argue, renders real engagement and understanding difficult. Pointing out that all cultures find ways to punctuate life transitions and events is illuminating insofar as it shows us that apparently dissimilar cultures and practices can have something in common. But to stop at the comforting feeling of similarity encourages a shallow sense of multicultural pluralism. The challenge is what to do from this point of departure.

A similar danger attends presenting religion in terms of sweeping generalizations. Consider once again the statement for the British Museum's *Living with Gods* exhibit:

> Seeing *how* people believe [emphasis in original], rather than considering *what* they believe, suggests that humans might be naturally inclined to believe in transcendent worlds and beings. Stories, objects, images, prayers, meditation and rituals can provide ways for people to cope with anxieties about the world, and help form strong social bonds. This in turn helps to make our lives well ordered and understandable.[1]

Where do we go from here? Yes, "belief" can help form strong social bonds. But does it not also serve to tear those bonds apart? And what exactly is belief or faith?

Similarity, as presented by the comparative science of religion or world religions model, can short-circuit deeper inquiry. Comparison, then, "is, at base, never identity. Comparison requires the postulation of difference as the grounds of its being interesting . . . and a methodological manipulation of difference, a playing across the 'gap' in the service of some useful end."[2] The useful ends for each of these museums are multiple. Increasingly, they involve the promotion of tolerance, but to promote tolerance successfully requires not only a sense of how we are alike but—more importantly—a sense of how and where we differ.

To a greater or lesser extent, the objects in these museums of world religions are imprisoned in an interpretive network. These museums are actually producing "religion" for many of the people who visit them. In some cases they produce a religion in tune with visitors' expectations. In other cases, as Sandell has pointed out, visitors resist the interpretations they are presented with. This resistance is especially strong when visitors holding hegemonic religious beliefs are confronted with the hegemonically pluralist approach of comparative religion. In an effort to head off conflict, museums more often than not attempt to segregate religions, drain them of danger, and place their objects in glass cells. Ironically, a discipline whose express purpose is comparison finds it necessary to avoid making comparison too obvious. To their credit, the St. Mungo Museum and the Religionskundliche Sammlung have made efforts to resist this tendency.

Although the State Museum of the History of Religions and the Religionskundliche Sammlung were founded during the first third of the twentieth century, their contemporary configurations actually date from the 1980s. From this point of view, all five museums are late twentieth-century foundations, and all five might be seen as responses to an increasingly globalized world. All five took their cues from the discipline of comparative religion and from understandings of multiculturalism, but now increasingly they see their roles as educational outreach, providing a "thirdspace" (Soja) for negotiating religious conflict.

Rudolf Otto's idea for a museum whose objects would help to communicate a sense of the numinous that he saw as common to all religions was the inspiration behind the Religionskundliche Sammlung. Of the five museums considered in this study the Marburg museum is the one most thoroughly integrated into the academic enterprise. Its collection is not presented to entertain the casual visitor but is more like an enormous filing cabinet requiring an expert guide to fetch select objects and construct a narrative from them. It is arrayed as an archive—a collection organized by religious tradition and geographic origin. From the point of view of the objects, the museum stands as a physical definition of religion as constructed first by a distinctively German pietistic but nonetheless imperialist scholarship, then by a late twentieth-century critical-historical scholarship. Now, in the twenty-first century, the collection and the scholarship it is integrated with is increasingly being harnessed to create what curator Konstanze Runge termed "a third space," an empathetic but non-confessional space for "discussion about sensitive religion-based issues" carried out "against the background of well-researched and differentiated knowledge about religions from a neutral perspective."[3] This is particularly evident in the impressive series of special exhibitions mounted by the museum in the last ten years.

The theme of education for tolerance is also a major concern of the State Museum of the History of Religions in St. Petersburg. Founded on the comparative science of religion, the museum is now the most historically oriented of the museums in this study, though it still bears traces of its early evolutionary bent. The State Museum of the History of Religions has always been conceived of as a social intervention, first in an attempt to dethrone transcendental ideas and to inculcate the anti-religious attitude of Marxist-Leninist materialism, now in promoting a sense of the nation's diverse religious and ethnic history. It has extensive displays and educational programming concerning Islam, as well as Buddhism and other Asian religions that constitute the heritage of the Russian population—traditions that are often marginalized in comparison with Orthodoxy and Catholicism. The museum is also a major research institution and its two roles—education and research—are well integrated.

According to director Jean-François Royal, the mission of Le Musée des Religions du Monde is to "teach tolerance, to help the visitor understand the religious and social behavior of his neighbor, of he who is different from us. Thus, through our mission, we hope to be able to bring about a little tolerance in the face of difference."[4] This museum is a fitting tribute to the institutions—the Catholic seminaries—that preceded the museum in the Nicolet area. The museum pursues its educational goals through wide-ranging and impressive special exhibitions and through its production of programs integrated with the primary and secondary school curricula in Québec province. Although many visitors come to the museum for the special exhibits, inevitably they encounter the permanent exhibit on five world religions. The museum's permanent exhibit is organized around comparative religion and world religions typologies.

According to Mark O'Neill, who helped to design the St. Mungo Museum of Religious Life and Art in Glasgow, the St. Mungo Museum was "more than an attempt to create an interesting exhibition. It is an intervention in society, a contribution towards creating greater tolerance and mutual respect among those of different faiths and of none."[5] The St. Mungo Museum's innovative displays and joint planning with community members represent a strikingly open and community-oriented approach to museums of religion. It continues to promote dialogue through recent additions to the Scottish gallery treating Syrian immigrants to Glasgow.

The Museum of World Religions in Taipei is dedicated to education and dialogue. Hsin Tao's efforts have been to situate the museum as a platform for education about religious harmony and as a major node in a group of institutions such as the Global Family for Love and Peace. Building on the Buddhist metaphor of Indra's Net, "the Museum of World Religions is dedicated to promoting equal dialogues among different religions and cultures in the world."[6] Like the permanent exhibit of Le Musée des Religions du Monde and the Religious Life Gallery at the St. Mungo Museum, the Museum of World Religions' "Hall of Life's Journey" is structured according to the life-cycle rites typology and its

"Great Hall of World Religions" conforms to comparative religions typologies that stretch back over a century.

In this regard, it is interesting to consider the way these museums are organized. The State Museum of the History of Religion, the permanent exhibit at Le Musée des Religions du Monde, and the Museum of World Religions in Taipei are programmatic to varying degrees. This programmatic style is most notable in the Taipei museum where the design itself produces a ritual process through which the visitor passes. It is possible to "browse" these museums and to enjoy focused bespoke tours, but they were designed with an overall progression in mind. So too, the Religious Life Gallery at the St. Mungo Museum, based on the thematic grid of life-cycle rites, coaxes the visitor to follow the ritual journey from birth to death and afterlife. Such is not the case in Marburg's Religionskundliche Sammlung where the museum's filing cabinet design necessitates informed tours or leaves the uninformed visitor to bemused browsing.

In the permanent exhibits of these five museums, the different religious traditions are carefully separated and despite—or because of—the comparative grid do not interact. This segregation is surprising, given that all five museums are focused on education, tolerance, and interreligious dialogue. Only the Religious Art Gallery of the St. Mungo Museum achieves something different. Although the designers intended to carve out separate ritual spaces for objects of different religious traditions, the relatively small gallery results in encounters among visitors and images from different traditions. In all the other cases, including the Religious Life Gallery at the St. Mungo Museum, the objects have been carefully segregated, drained of danger, and rendered safe. But if these institutions are serious about dialogue and about creating what Edward Soja has termed a "thirdspace" where dialogue can happen among "a multiplicity of perspectives that have heretofore been considered by the epistemological referees to be incompatible, uncombinable," then these museums should carefully consider the St. Mungo model.[7]

A selective focus on differences—on areas of contestation—can provide a starting point for dialogue. Such dialogues might be focused through intensive discussions of a single object. If the goal of a museum is to open a space for dialogue, perhaps it would be best to emphasize both what different traditions share and where they disagree. Eck's caution, cited earlier, bears repeating:,

> Dialogue is the discipline of thought that enables us to gain clarity about our own situatedness, our own forms of questioning our own position—whether methodological, political, religious, secular, even antireligious—so that our own subjectivity, our own language, and our own categories are not privileged and universalized unwittingly in our work.[8]

Inspired by the work of Bruno Latour, Tim Ingold, and other writers seeking to alert us to the hegemonic and blinding effects of our Cartesian episteme and its reduction of material particularity to the abstract and universal, I have tried to discuss the five museums in a way that avoids as much as possible speculative and global categories. This "irreductionism" (to use Latour's term) seeks to keep the focus as much as possible on things and objects—on the material being displayed—and to trace connections with all the actors, be they animate or inanimate. From the perspective of Latour or "new animist" thinkers, the comparative religion approach severs religion from the flow and matter of life. We are challenged, then, to imagine how a museum of religion might bring objects back into the flow of life or what Whitehead has called "relationality."

Some Recommendations

Focusing on similarity within the confines of an abstract comparative grid has its advantages, but the suppression of conflict, both within and among traditions, is likely to be counterproductive. The following are some suggestions for alternative strategies for museums of religions. I make these suggestions fully aware of the many pressures curators must face and that some suggestions may be impracticable in some contexts.

- Wherever possible resist using the "world religions" typology. It is inherently confusing and biased toward "great traditions."
- Attend to the production and use of objects; avoid reducing them to signs of "transcendence," the "sacred," or the "numinous."
- Compare overtly and deeply with a stated goal. For instance, how is the Catholic Confirmation different from the Hindu *upanayana*? What can we say from this comparison about attitudes toward maturity, religious responsibility, and so on?
- Restore selected objects to the flow of life or use. This restoration might involve in-depth treatment of the "life story" of an object (including its museumification). The British Museum's A'a exhibition is a good example. Another possibility is to put the object in use for a limited time as a demonstration, perhaps with the help of local communities. Allow objects or duplicates to be handled. Museums should plug some of the objects in.
- Use similarity as a starting point to explore difference. Such exploration of difference can take place in an academic format or in the form of community dialogue using the museum as a "thirdspace."

Throughout this book I have found myself wondering what Rudolf Otto would say if he could have toured these museums with me. Although I find problematic his colonialist collecting, his German nationalist leanings, and his sense that Christianity was the pinnacle of religious evolution, Otto clearly saw that material objects were central to religion and that they could be the basis for interreligious dialogue. I venture to say that he would likely want to see the objects in these collections be brought more fully into the flow of life.

Notes

Preface

1 "Old Sturbridge Village," https://www.osv.org/ (accessed January 18, 2019).

2 Amanda M. Hughes and Carolyn H. Wood, *A Place for Meaning: Art, Faith, and Museum Culture* (Chapel Hill: University of North Carolina Press, 2010).

3 Victoria S. Harrison, A. Bergqvist, and G. Kemp, eds., *Philosophy and Museums: Essays on the Philosophy of Museums* (Cambridge: Cambridge University Press, 2016).

4 Bruce M. Sullivan, ed., *Sacred Objects in Secular Spaces: Exhibiting Asian Religions in Museums* (London: Bloomsbury Academic, 2015).

5 For instance, the Glencairn Museum in Pennsylvania has a collection of objects with worldwide scope, including objects from Asian religious traditions and the ancient Near East. But its primary focus is on Christianity, Judaism, and Islam. "Glencairn Museum," https://glencairnmuseum.org/ (accessed January 18, 2019). Also see Ed Gyllenhaal, "Religion at Glencairn Museum: Past, Present, and Future," in *Religion in Museums: Global and Multidisciplinary Perspectives*, edited by Gretchen Buggeln, Crispin Paine, and S. Brent Plate (London: Bloomsbury Academic, 2017), 239–46. There is also an interview with Crispin Paine in the "Glencairn Museum News" of March 30, 2017 (accessed January 18, 2019). https://glencairnmuseum.org/newslet ter/2017/3/27/religious-objects-in-museums-an-interview-with-crispin-paine. Other such museums have been built or are in planning. A branch of the Museum of World Religions in Taipei has long been in the planning stages for Birmingham, UK. The "Concept Paper" dated 2010 (accessed January 18, 2019) is found in http: //home.btconnect.com/ghfa/concept.htm but there has been little activity since 2014. Some of the formerly anti-religion museums in former Soviet republics are also developing religion museums. The Grodno State Museum of the History of Religion in Belarus is focused primarily on Christianity, Judaism, and Islam. The Pyramid of Peace and Reconciliation in Astana, Kazakhstan, is an event center built to host the Congress of Leaders of World and Traditional Religions. The Congress focused on Judaism, Islam, Christianity, Buddhism, Hinduism, Daoism, and other traditions and the building continues to host displays related to these traditions. The website is at http://astana-piramida.kz/en/. Another former anti-religion museum is now named the Azerbaijan State Museum of the History of Religion with displays representing Buddhism, Judaism, Christianity, and Islam. Its website is at

https://kataloq.gomap.az/en/all-poi/culture/museum/8fb99ef4d56611e0ad490022 6424597d (accessed February 18, 2019). There is also the Chaitanya Jyoti ("Flame of Consciousness") museum founded in 2000 by the Indian guru Sai Baba in commemoration of his seventy-fifth birthday. The museum celebrates various Hindu gods and religious prophets from other religious traditions as preparing the world for the advent of Sai Baba. I have not had a chance to visit this museum. The website has very limited information: http://chaitanyajyotimuseum.com/chaitanya-jyoti-mu seum-visiting/ (accessed July 29, 2019). As far as I have been able to determine the museum is structured according to a distinctively Hindu avatar ideology and is not based on Western comparative religion principles. For a brief discussion of the museum, see Mark Maclean, "Chaitanya Jyoti, the Sai Baba Museum," *Material Religion*, 1, no. 2 (2005): 300–1.

6 See, for instance, "World Religions and Spirituality," https://wrldrels.org/ (accessed January 18, 2019), "GCSE Religious Studies A: World Religions," https://www.ocr. org.uk/qualifications/gcse/religious-studies-a-world-religions-j620-j120-from-2012/ (accessed January 18, 2019), "Ashmolean Museum: Learning Resources World Religions," https://www.ashmolean.org/learning-resources-world-religions (accessed January 18, 2019).

Chapter 1

1 For an appraisal of these roles see Crispin Paine, *Religious Objects in Museums: Private Lives and Public Duties* (London: Bloomsbury, 2013).

2 For an incisive discussion of the Protestantism and the material see Peter Pels, "The Modern Fear of Matter: Reflections on the Protestantism of Victorian Science," *Material Religion*, 4, no. 3 (2008): 264–83, doi: 10.2752/175183408X376656.

3 Jonathan Z. Smith, *Imagining Religion: From Babylon to Jamestown* (Chicago and London: The University of Chicago Press, 1982), xi. See also Jonathan Z. Smith, "Religion, Religions, Religious," in *Critical Terms for Religious Studies*, edited by Mark C. Taylor (Chicago: University of Chicago Press, 1998), 269–84. For thoughtful responses to Smith see *A Magic Still Dwells: Comparative Religion in the Postmodern Age*, edited by Kimberley C. Patton and Benjamin C. Ray (Berkeley: University of California Press, 2000). Ivan Strenski's recent generally appreciative critique of Smith's work is "The Magic and Drudgery in J. Z. Smith's Theory of Comparison," in *Contemporary Views on Comparative Religion in Celebration of Tim Jensen's 65th Birthday*, edited by Peter Antes, Armin W. Geertz, and Michael Rothstein (Yorkshire: Equinox Publishing Company, 2016), 7–16. For a more recent statement of this critique of religion see Timothy Fitzgerald, *The Ideology of Religious Studies* (New York and Oxford: Oxford University Press, 2000).

4 "religion, n." OED Online. June 2019. Oxford University Press, https://www-oed-com.colby.idm.oclc.org/view/Entry/161944?redirectedFrom=religion& (accessed August 1, 2019).

5 Ibid.

6 Max Müller, "The Science of Religion: Lecture One," from *Lectures on the Science of Religion* (1870), in *The Essential Max Müller on Language, Mythology, and Religion*, edited by Jon R. Stone (New York: Palgrave Macmillan, 2002), 117.

7 As cited on the Museum of World Religions webpage introducing "The Hall of Life's Journey," https://www.mwr.org.tw/mwr_en/xcpmtexhi/cont?xsmsid=0I0 52391577771211747&sid=0I057612803752905496 (accessed October 1, 2018).

8 Fitzgerald, *The Ideology of Religious Studies*, 31. Perennial philosophy has its roots in romanticism and views the various religions and forms of spirituality as reflections of a single underlying truth. The term was popularized by Aldous Huxley in his book *The Perennial Philosophy* (New York and London: Harper & Brothers, 1945). For a range of perennialist positions see *The Underlying Religion: An Introduction to Perennial Philosophy*, edited by Martin Lings and Clinton Minnaar (Bloomington: World Wisdom, 2007). For a critique of the relationship between perennialism and mysticism, see Richard King, *Orientalism and Religion: Post-Colonial Theory, India and "The Mystic East"* (London and New York: Routledge, 1999), esp. 120ff., 135–86.

9 Burton Feldman and Robert D. Richardson, Jr., eds., *The Rise of Modern Mythology 1680-1860* (Bloomington: Indiana University Press, 1972), 19.

10 Henry Fielding, *The History of Tom Jones, a Foundling* (Baltimore: Penguin Books, Inc., 1966), 129.

11 George Eliot, *Middlemarch, A Study of Provincial Life* (Cleveland: Burroughs Brothers Company, 1888).

12 Ernst Troeltsch, "The Place of Christianity among the World Religions," in *Christian Thought: Its History and Application*, edited by Baron F. von Hugel (London: University of London Press, 1923), 26.

13 For the debate on religion as sui generis and irreducible, see *Religion and Reductionism: Essays on Eliade, Segal, and the Challenge of the Social Sciences for the Study of Religion*, edited by T. A. Idinopulos and E. A. Yonan (Leiden: E. J. Brill, 1994).

14 Robert Ford Campany has written an articulate defense of the category. See his "On the Very Idea of Religions (In the Modern West and in Early Medieval China)," *History of Religions*, 42, no. 4 (May 2003): 287–319.

15 T. Griffith Foulk, "The Ch'an *Tsung* in Medieval China: School, Lineage, or What?" *Pacific World*, n.s., 8 (1992): 20.

16 For discussion of the terms "Hinduism" and "Buddhism" as synthetic terms and the result of colonial encounter and knowledge production, see King, *Orientalism*

and Religion, especially chapter five, "The Modern Myth of 'Hinduism,'" and chapter seven, "Orientalism and the Discovery of 'Buddhism.'" For "Confucianism" as a product of Western sinology, see Anna Sun, *Confucianism as a World Religion: Contested Histories and Contemporary Realities* (Princeton and Oxford: Princeton University Press, 2013), and especially Shiyin Liu, "Deciphering James Legge's Confucianism" (PhD thesis, University of Glasgow, 2019).

17 Fitzgerald, *The Ideology of Religious Studies*, 33, referring to Eric J. Sharpe, *Comparative Religion: A History* (London: Duckworth, 1975; second revised edition, 1986).

18 Ibid., 33.

19 For a concise discussion of the problems presented by this bias and some possible ameliorations, see Fitzgerald, *The Ideology of Religious Studies*, 17–19.

20 In the UK, religious studies is part of the secondary curriculum and there are A-level subject tests in religious studies. Although there are currently no religious studies subject tests in the United States, religious studies and world religions are taught in some public secondary schools. See the Guidelines published by the American Academy of Religion and other material at the Religious Freedom Center website, https://www.religiousfreedomcenter.org/grounding/aar-guidelines/ (accessed August 14, 2019).

21 As cited from the First Amendment Center website, http://www.firstamendment schools.org/freedoms/faq.aspx?id=12823 (accessed September 25, 2018).

22 The number of textbooks produced for introductory courses since 1950 probably run into the hundreds in English alone. Among the long running ones are: David S. Noss and Blake Gangaard, *A History of the World's Religions*, 13th ed. (New York: Routledge, 2016; originally *Man's Religions* by John B. Noss, 1956); Huston Smith, *The World's Religions* (New York: Harper Collins, 2008, reissue of 1991 edition); Willard Oxtoby et al., *A Concise Introduction to World Religions*, 3rd ed. (Oxford: Oxford University Press, 2015).

23 Jack Miles et al., eds., *The Norton Anthology of World Religions*, 2 vols. (New York: W. W. Norton & Company, 2014).

24 Lawrence E. Sullivan, et al., *Religions of the World: An Introduction to Culture and Meaning* (Minneapolis: Fortress Press, 2012).

25 Ibid., 31–32.

26 Ibid., xxii–xxiii.

27 See https://www.amazon.com/Religions-World-Introduction-Culture-Meaning/ dp/0800698797 (accessed July 15, 2019). For the idea of beliefs as part of cultural systems of meanings, see Clifford Geertz, *The Interpretation of Cultures* (New York: Basic Books, 1973). For a critique of Geertz's theory of ritual and the construction of meaning as contradictory and circular, see Catherine Bell, *Ritual Theory, Ritual Practice* (New York: Oxford University Press, 1992), 19–37, 57–61.

28 Arnold van Gennep, *The Rites of Passage*, translated by Monika B. Vizedom and Gabrielle L. Caffee (Chicago: The University of Chicago Press, 1960). Authors also draw on Victor W. Turner's reboot of van Gennep, *The Ritual Process: Structure and Anti-Structure* (Harmondsworth: Penguin Books, 1969).

29 The problematic nature of the world religions typology is now well known, at least in scholarly circles, and yet, despite half a century of trenchant critique, any search of a bookstore (or of Amazon) for "world religions" titles yields an apparently bottomless supply of such books. But you will have to know of Tomoko Masuzawa's *The Invention of World Religions* (Chicago and London: University of Chicago Press, 2005) or *After World Religions: Reconstructing Religious Studies*, edited by Christopher R. Cotter and David G. Robertson (London and New York: Routledge, 2016) and place an order to find either one.

30 Immanuel Kant, "Fourth Essay: Service and Pseudo-service under the Sovereignty of the Good Principle, or Religion and Pfaffentum," in *Religion within the Limits of Bare Reason* (2017), 86. The version consulted was accessed on December 30, 2018, https://www.earlymoderntexts.com/assets/pdfs/kant1793.pdf.

31 Johann Wolfgang von Goethe, *The Metamorphosis of Plants*, translated by Douglas Miller (Cambridge, MA: MIT Press, 2009).

32 Ibid., 105.

33 See Pierre D. Chantepie de la Saussaye, *Manual of the Science of Religion* (London: Longmans, Green, 1891), 54. The fourth edition of Tiele's work is now available online. See Cornelis Petrus Tiele, *Outline of the History of Religion to the Spread of Universal Religion*, translated by J. Estlin Carpenter (London: Trübner & Company, 1888). Available at Archive.org, https://archive.org/details/outlinesofthehi00tielu oft/page/n26.

34 Ibid., 3.

35 Arie L. Molendijk, *The Emergence of the Science of Religion in the Netherlands* (Leiden: E.J. Brill, 2005), 31.

36 Quoted in Sharpe, *Comparative Religion*, 44. Despite claims to be independent of theological bias, it is clear that Müller conceived of this science in liberal Protestant terms and presented it as an important tool for missionizing. For a discussion, see Fitzgerald, *The Ideology of Religious Studies*, 35–36. For an excellent treatment of Müller, see "Friedrich Max Müller: The Annunciation of a New Science," in Marjorie Wheeler-Barclay's *The Science of Religion in Britain: 1860-1915* (Charlottesville and London: University of Virginia Press, 2010), 37–70. Also see Masuzawa, *The Invention of World Religions*, 207–56, and John R. Davis and Angus Nicholls, "Friedrich Max Müller: The Career and Intellectual Trajectory of a German Philologist in Victorian Britain," *Publications of the English Goethe Society*, 85, no. 2–3 (2016): 67–97.

37 See Fitzgerald, *Ideology of Religious Studies*, especially "Comparative Religion: the Founding Fathers and the Theological Legacy," 33–53.

38 See, for example, Gerardus van der Leeuw, *Religion in Essence and Manifestation: A Study in Phenomenology*, 2 vols. (New York: Harper and Row, 1963).

39 For a detailed discussion of Goethe's approach and its importance for Mircea Eliade, see Jonathan Z. Smith, "Acknowledgments: Morphology and History in Mircea Eliade's 'Patterns in Comparative Religion' (1949–1999) 'Part 1: The Work and Its Contexts' and 'Part 2: The Texture of the Work,'" *History of Religions*, 39, no. 4 (2000): 315–51.

40 Ibid., 316.

41 Mircea Eliade, *Patterns in Comparative Religion*, translated by Rosemary Sheed (Cleveland and New York: The World Publishing Company, 1970). For a recent reappraisal of Eliade's work, see Christian K. Wedemeyer and Wendy Doniger, eds., *Hermeneutics, Politics, and the History of Religions: The Contested Legacies of Joachim Wach and Mircea Eliade* (Oxford and New York: Oxford University Press, 2010), especially "Part II: Mircea Eliade: Literature and Politics," and "Part III: Mircea Eliade: Politics and Literature."

42 Eliade, "Approximations: The Structure and Morphology of the Sacred," in *Patterns in Comparative Religion*, 3.

43 Max Weber, *The Methodology of the Social Sciences*, translated and edited by Edward A. Shils and Henry A. Finch (Glencoe: The Free Press, 1949), 90. The emphasis is in the original. For a discussion of Weber's method with regard to religion, see Paweł Załęski, "Ideal Types in Max Weber's Sociology of Religion: Some Theoretical Inspirations for A Study of the Religious Field," *Polish Sociological Review*, no. 171 (2010): 319–25.

44 For a cogent account of Max Weber's methodology, see the *Stanford Encyclopedia of Philosophy*, Max Weber (5.2: Ideal Type), https://plato.stanford.edu/entries/weber/#IdeTyp (accessed December 30, 2018).

45 Jonathan Z. Smith, "Adde Parvum Parvo Magnus Acervus Erit," *History of Religions*, 11, no. 1 (August 1971): 68–70.

46 Ibid., 71.

47 To be clear, Smith is not referring here to ethnographic "thick description," but rather to unsystematic cross-cultural comparisons. For the classic account of "thick description," see Clifford Geertz, "Thick Description: Toward and Interpretive Theory of Culture," in *The Interpretation of Cultures*, 3–30.

48 Smith, "Adde Parvum," 76–77.

49 Ibid., 80. The piling up of contextless data (James Frazer's *The Golden Bough* immediately comes to mind) has, rightly, been dubbed *listenwissenschaft* ("list science"). Frazer's opus eventually ran to twelve volumes (1906–15). It can be browsed more conveniently through *The New Golden Bough: A New Abridgment of the Classic Work*, edited by Theodore H. Gaster (New York: Mentor New American Library, 1964). For a discussion of Frazer's method, see Jonathan Z. Smith, "In

Comparison a Magic Dwells," in *Imagining Religion: From Babylon to Jonestown* (Chicago and London: University of Chicago Press, 1982), 21, and his "When the Bough Breaks," *History of Religion*, 12, no. 4 (1973): 342–71.

50 Smith, "Adde Parvum," 83–85. To add to the confusion scholars have used a variety of labels for their endeavors. Eliade's method, for example, is often mistakenly called "phenomenological" while it is in fact morphological.

51 Ibid., 86.

52 See my discussion of the Pitt Rivers Museum in Forebears: The London Missionary Society Museum, the Pitt Rivers Museum, and the Horniman Museum.

53 Smith, "Adde Parvum," 86. The result is well illustrated by E. B. Tylor's *Primitive Culture* (1871) which, as Smith points out, was "a rather confused attempt to apply the Linnaean category of species to cultural phenomena" likening a bow and arrow to a species. Claude Levi-Strauss pointed perceptively to the flaw in such an analogy: "The historical validity of the naturalist's reconstructions is guaranteed, in the final analysis, by the biological link of reproduction. An ax, on the contrary, does not generate another ax." Claude Levi-Strauss, *Structural Anthropology* (New York: Basic Books, 1963), 4–5.

54 None of these institutions can be reduced to a single style of comparison. We see, rather, loose use of the terms evolution, development, morphology, and ethnography both in museum documents and in some of the secondary literature. This fluidity is especially visible when we look at the changing institutions over time. It is important to understand that while we can distinguish these types of comparison they are often blended. For example, morphology can be used in an unbiased ahistorical fashion but it was, in many instances, used to justify evolutionary sequences and "progress" or "backwardness."

55 Chidester, *Empire of Religion: Imperialism and Comparative Religion* (Chicago and London: University of Chicago Press, 2014), 4.

56 Ibid., 27.

57 John P. Burris, *Exhibiting Religion: Colonialism and Spectacle at International Expositions 1851-1893* (Charlottesville and London: University Press of Virginia, 2001), 65.

58 Ibid.

59 Masuzawa, *The Invention of World Religions*, 309–28.

60 Ibid., 2. Jonathan Z. Smith notes that "a World Religion is a religion like ours; but it is, above all, a tradition which has achieved sufficient power and numbers to enter our history, either to form it, interact with it, or to thwart it." See "A Matter of Class: Taxonomies of Religion," *The Harvard Theological Review*, 89, no. 4 (October 1996): 396–97. The comment originally appeared in Smith, *Map is Not Territory* (Leiden: E. J. Brill, 1978), 295. Smith's discussion of world religions anticipates the later, more detailed treatment by Masuzawa.

61 Müller, cited in Stone, ed., *The Essential Max Müller*, 346.

62 Masuzawa, *The Invention of World Religions*, 4.

63 For an attempt to rethink the comparative issue, see especially Paul Hedges, "Comparative Religion and the Religious Studies Toolkit" and Michael Bergunder, "Comparison in the Maelstrom of Historicity: A Postcolonial Perspective on Comparative Religion," in *Interreligious Comparisons in Religious Studies and Theology: Comparison Revisited*, edited by Andreas Nehring and Perry Schmidt-Leukel (London: Bloomsbury Academic, 2016), 17–33; 34–52.

64 Chidester, *Empire of Religion*, 46–47.

65 Steven Connor, "Myth and Meta-myth in Max Müller and Walter Pater," in *The Sun Is God: Painting, Literature, and Mythology in the Nineteenth Century*, edited by J. B. Bullen (Oxford: Clarendon Press, 1988), 221.

66 As cited in Chidester, *Empire of Religion*, 62. In his revised lectures of 1882, Müller modified the translation to "classify and understand." Chidester, *Empire of Religion*, 85.

67 Chidester, *Empire of Religion*, 46.

68 Ibid., 5; 64.

69 Germain Bazin, *The Museum Age*, translated by Jane van Nuis Cahill (New York: Universe Books, 1967).

70 Krzysztof Pomian, *Collectors and Curiosities: Paris and Venice, 1500-1800* (Cambridge: Polity Press, 1990), 77, as cited in Tony Bennett, *The Birth of the Museum: History, Theory, Politics* (London and New York: Routledge, 1995), 40. For discussions of cabinets of curiosities, see Oliver Impey and Arthur MacGregor, eds., *The Origins of Museums: The Cabinet of Curiosities in Sixteenth and Seventeenth-Century Europe* (Oxford: Clarendon, 1985; reprint Ashmolean Museum, 2018). Also see Steven Lubar, "Cabinets of Curiosity: What They Were, Why They Disappeared, and Why They're so Popular Now," https://digital.soas.ac.uk/lms/geography/ (accessed November 12, 2018).

71 For a detailed and perceptive look at the role of museums in making regimes of power and knowledge visible, see Bennett, *The Birth of the Museum*, especially "An Order of Things and Peoples," 95–98. Bennett draws on Michel Foucault's notion of the "episteme" which I discuss in Chapter 2.

72 Peter H. Hoffenberg, *Empire on Display: English, Indian, and Australian Exhibitions from the Crystal Palace to the Great War* (Berkeley: University of California Press, 2001), xiv.

73 Burris, *Exhibiting Religion*, xv.

74 *Colonial and Indian Exhibition, 1886: Official Catalogue* (London: William Clowes and Sons, Limited, 1886), 52.

75 Ibid., 266.

76 Burris, *Exhibiting Religion*, 124.

77 Ibid., 125.

78 Richard Hughes Seager, *The World's Parliament of Religions: The East/West Encounter, Chicago 1893* (Bloomington: Indiana University Press, 1995). Also see Eric J. Ziolkowski, ed., *A Museum of Faiths: Histories and Legacies of the 1893 World's Parliament of Religions* (Atlanta: Scholars Press, 1993).

79 For an analysis, see King, *Orientalism and Religion*, 93–94; 135–42.

80 Clarke (1810–88), theologian, abolitionist, and member of the transcendentalist movement drew upon the emerging "science of ethnology" to make his argument. James Freeman Clarke, *Ten Great Religions: An Essay in Comparative Theology* (Boston and New York: Houghton Mifflin Co., 1871), 15. The first six essays were originally published in the *Atlantic Monthly* in 1868.

81 Burris, *Exhibiting Religion*, 125. Indeed, "native" displays were not set up by representatives of the peoples involved, as were displays on Japan and other groups, but by anthropologists. See *Exhibiting Religion*, 109.

82 For a pity description of the midway "hierarchy," see Burris, *Exhibiting Religion*, 117.

83 William E. Cameron, *History of the World's Columbian Exposition* (Chicago: Columbian History, 1893), 313–14, as quoted in Burris, *Exhibiting Religion*, 137.

84 William Pietz, "The Problem of the Fetish, I," *RES: Anthropology and Aesthetics*, no. 9 (Spring 1985): 5.

85 Ibid., 7.

86 Ibid. For a full discussion, see Pietz's further installments in "The Problem of the Fetish, II: The Origin of the Fetish," *RES: Anthropology and Aesthetics*, no. 13 (Spring 1987): 23–45; and "The Problem of the Fetish, IIIa: Bosman's Guinea and the Enlightenment Theory of Fetishism," *RES: Anthropology and Aesthetics*, no. 16 (Autumn 1988): 105–24. Bruno Latour has concocted a hilarious send-up of a discussion between a Christian and an African concerning the fetish and the crucifix. See "Fetish-Factish," in *Key Terms in Material Religion*, edited by S. Brent Plate (London: Bloomsbury Academic, 2015), 87–94.

87 Chidester, *Empire of Religion*, 47.

88 The meetings of the International Association for the History of Religions continue to this day with the next meeting in 2020 in Dunedin, New Zealand. For the conference proceedings including those of the 1900 Paris meeting, see their website, http://www.iahrweb.org/proceedings.php (accessed July 15, 2019).

89 Homepage of the Council for a Parliament of the World's Religions, http://www.parliamentofreligions.org/index.cfm?n=1 (accessed November 8, 2014).

90 On the use of policy to manage diversity, see Reza Hasmath, ed., *Managing Ethnic Diversity: Meanings and Practices from an International Perspective* (Surry: Ashgate, 2011).

91 A radical critique argues that "the ideal form of ideology of this global capitalism is multiculturalism, the attitude which, from a kind of empty global position, treats each local culture the way the colonizer treats colonized people—as 'natives' whose mores are to be carefully studied and 'respected.'" Slavoj Žižek, "Multiculturalism or the Cultural Logic of Multinational Capitalism?" *New Left Review*, I/225, 44 (September–October 1997), 28–51.

92 There were, of course, a number of others in France, Germany, Belgium, and so on that could be used for this purpose, including the British Museum or institutions like Musée Guimet. These institutions were organized according to a variety of regimes, including ethnography, antiquities, and art. For the history of Musée Guimet, see https://www.guimet.fr/francais/a-propos-du-musee/histoire-du-musee-guimet/.

93 The documentary archive of the London Missionary Society is available online through SOAS at https://digital.soas.ac.uk/lms (accessed January 14, 2019).

94 The London Missionary Society was an interdenominational society founded in 1795.

95 Chris Wingfield, "'Scarcely more than a Christian Trophy Case'? The Global Collections of the London Missionary Society Museum (1814–1910)," *Journal of the History of Collections*, 29, no. 1 (2017): 111–12.

96 Cited in Ibid., 113.

97 A quantitative analysis of the 1826 catalog reveals that "manufactures" and other natural history curiosities well outnumbered religious items. Ibid., 114–15.

98 Ibid., 122.

99 Ibid., 123.

100 Cited in Rosemary Seton, "Reconstructing the Museum of the London Missionary Society," *Material Religion*, 8, no. 1 (2012): 101. The original appeared in the *Juvenile Missionary Magazine of the London Missionary Society* (1860): 12.

101 See Seton, "Reconstructing," on visitors, 100.

102 Wingfield, "Scarcely more than a Christian Trophy Case"? 124.

103 Ibid.

104 Michael O'Hanlon's *The Pitt Rivers Museum: A World Within* (London: Scala Arts and Heritage 2014) is an indispensable introduction to this most unusual museum. "No 'Boxroom of the Forgotten': The Museum's Displays over Time," chapter two of O'Hanlon's book chronicles how the museum has changed as well as why it still resembles a curiosity cabinet. The museum maintains a superb website, both for visitors and for researchers at https://www.prm.ox.ac.uk/ (accessed December 31, 2018).

105 William Ryan Chapman, "Arranging Ethnology: A.H.L.F. Pitt Rivers and the Typological Tradition," in *Objects and Others: Essays on Museums and Material Culture*, edited by George W. Stocking, Jr. (Madison: The University of Wisconsin Press, 1985), 25.

106 Ibid., 26.

107 Augustus Pitt Rivers, "The Evolution of Culture," in *The Evolution of Culture and Other Essays*, edited by J. L. Myers (Oxford: Clarendon Press, 1906).

108 Ibid., p. 37.

109 A brief history of the Horniman Museum is available on its website at https://www.horniman.ac.uk/about/museum-history (accessed December 31, 2018). There is a thoughtful account of the treatment of religious objects in the Horniman by Neysela da Silva, "Religious Displays: An Observational Study with a Focus on the Horniman Museum," *Material Religion*, 6, no. 2 (2010): 166–91.

110 *Guide to the Collections in the Horniman Museum and Library, Forest Hill, London, S.E.*, 3rd ed. (London: London County Council, 1921), 92–95. The full text of the guide is at https://www.archive.org/stream/hornimanguide00hornrich/hornimanguide00hornrich_djvu.txt (accessed July 14, 2019).

111 Ibid., 97.

112 Ibid., section "V: Magic and Religion," 54–70. The quotation is from 65.

113 The exhibit ran from October 13, 2018, through May 30, 2019, https://www.prm.ox.ac.uk/event/performing-tibetan-identities (accessed January 14, 2019).

114 Smith, "In Comparison a Magic Dwells," 35.

115 Chidester, *Empire of Religion*, 314.

116 Ibid., 312.

117 Richard H. Davis, *Lives of Indian Images* (Princeton and Oxford: Princeton University Press, 1997).

Chapter 2

1 Crispin Paine's edited volume *Godly Things: Museums, Objects & Religion* (London: Leicester University Press, 2000) and his *Religious Objects in Museums* have facilitated new understandings of religious objects in museums. New approaches to our understanding of objects by Graham Harvey, *Animism: Respecting the Living World* (London: Hurst & Co., 2005), Amy Whitehead, *Religious Statues and Personhood: Testing the Role of Materiality* (London and New York: Bloomsbury Academic, 2013) and others are helping to reconfigure our understanding of the role of the material in religion.

2 For the painting, see https://en.wikipedia.org/wiki/Christ_of_Saint_John_of_the_Cross. The painting was moved to the Kelvingrove Art Gallery in 2006.

3 The so-called "Dancing Śiva" has come to be the icon of Hinduism in the West. For an account of how this came to be, see Johannes Beltz, "The Dancing Shiva: South Indian Processional Bronze, Museum Artwork, and Universal Icon," *Journal of Religion in Europe*, 4 (2011): 204–22.

4 Related by Mark O'Neill, as quoted in Richard Sandell, *Museums, Prejudice, and the Reframing of Difference* (London and New York: Routledge, 2007), 54.

5 November 2, 2017, through April 8, 2018. The accompanying volume is by Neil Macgregor, *Living with the Gods: On Beliefs and Peoples* (New York: Alfred A. Knopf, Kindle edition, 2018).

6 "British Museum: Living with Gods," https://www.britishmuseum.org/about_us/past_exhibitions/2018/living_with_gods.aspx (accessed July 30, 2018).

7 The literature on secularization is extensive and arises in an articulate form in the early twentieth century as theorists such as Durkheim, Weber, and Freud postulated that the spread of education and science was leading to an erosion of religious belief. An important theoretical formulation is found in Peter L. Berger's now classic work, *The Sacred Canopy: Elements of a Sociological Theory of Religion* (New York: Anchor Books, 1969). Berger's more recent edited volume *The Desecularization of the World: Resurgent Religion and World Politics* (Grand Rapids: Wm. B. Eerdmans Publishing Company, 1999) provides perspective on the notion. Charles Taylor's *A Secular Age* (Cambridge, MA: Harvard University Press, 2007) presents a challenging view of the role of Protestantism in secularism in the West and the rise of individual kinds of spirituality from the 1960s onwards.

8 See, for instance, Linda Woodhead, Paul Heelas, and Benjamin Seel, *The Spiritual Revolution: Why Religion Is Giving Way to Spirituality* (Malden: Wiley-Blackwell, 2005).

9 For a trenchant critique, see Jeremy Carrette and Richard King, *Selling Spirituality: The Silent Takeover of Religion* (London and New York: Routledge, 2004). Jeff Wilson's *Mindful America: The Mutual Transformation of Buddhist Meditation and American Culture* (Oxford and New York: Oxford University Press, 2014) explores topics such as the medicalization of meditation as well as its commercial appropriation.

10 Crispin Paine, *Gods and Rollercoasters: Religion in Theme-parks Worldwide* (London and New York: Bloomsbury Academic, 2019). For the Creation Museum, see Susan L. Trollinger, Jr. and William Vance, *Righting America at the Creation Museum* (Baltimore: Johns Hopkins University Press, 2016).

11 For a list of some other museums that treat religions, or that are presently in planning stages, see note 5.

12 See, for instance, the National Football Museum in Manchester, https://www.nationalfootballmuseum.com/.

13 One is reminded of the fictional academicians of Lagado in chapter V of Jonathan Swift's *Gulliver's Travels into Several Remote Nations of the World*. The academicians there propose substituting objects for words, reducing all communication to material demonstration. The work is available at Gutenberg.org, https://www.gutenberg.org/files/829/829-h/829-h.htm.

14 Tylor's famous "minimum definition of Religion, the belief in Spiritual Beings" can be found in his *Primitive Culture*, 4th rev. ed., 2 vols. (London: John Murray, 1903), I: 424 (1st ed., 1873, I: 383).

15 Revised Standard Version.

16 For a discussion of key terms, see S. Brent Plate, ed., *Key Terms in Material Religion* (London: Bloomsbury Academic, 2015), and Mark C. Taylor, ed., *Critical Terms in Religious Studies* (Chicago: The University of Chicago Press, 1998).

17 The phrase appears in Exod. 7:3 and elsewhere in the biblical texts, indicating miraculous revelations of the spirit. Both Homi K. Bhabha's essay "Signs Taken for Wonders: Questions of Ambivalence and Authority under a Tree outside Delhi, May 1817," *Critical Inquiry*, 12, no. 1, "Race, Writing, and Difference" (Autumn 1985): 144–65 and Franco Moretti's *Signs Taken For Wonders: On the Sociology of Literary Forms* (London and New York: Verso, 1988) take up issues of representation and "a process of displacement, distortion, dislocation, repetition." Bhabha, "Signs," 147 alluding to Freud.

18 See Sandell, *Museums, Prejudice, and the Reframing of Difference*, esp. pp. 79 ff. As Sandell points out, not all visitors acquiesce to the narrative presented to them and there are those who either ignore the narrative framing or substitute an oppositional reading.

19 Anja Lüpken, "Politics of Representation—Normativity in Museum Practice," *Journal of Religion in Europe*, 4 (2011): 159.

20 Ibid. The original is from Timothy W. Luke, *Museum Politics: Power Plays at the Exhibition* (Minneapolis: University of Minnesota Press, 2002), 219–20.

21 Mary Louise Pratt, *Imperial Eyes: Travel Writing and Transculturation* (London and New York: Routledge, 1992), 6–7.

22 James Clifford, *Routes: Travel and Translation in the Late Twentieth Century* (Cambridge, MA: Harvard University Press, 1997), 192–93.

23 Cited in Tim Ingold, "Materials Against Materiality." Discussion article in *Archaeological Dialogues*, 14, no. 1 (2007): 1.

24 Maurice Merleau-Ponty, "Eye and Mind," in *The Primacy of Perception*, edited by James M. Eide (Evanston: Northwestern University Press, 1964), 158; 157. "Eye and Mind" was Merleau-Ponty's last publication before his death.

25 Mark Johnson and George Lakoff first articulated their theory of metaphor in *Metaphors We Live By* (Chicago: University of Chicago Press, 1980). Lakoff provides a report on advances in theory of metaphor more than a decade later in "The Contemporary Theory of Metaphor," in *Metaphor and Thought*, edited by Andrew Ortony, 2nd ed. (Cambridge: Cambridge University Press, 1993), 202–51. Lakoff and Johnson teamed up again in *Philosophy in the Flesh: The Embodied Mind and its Challenge to Western Thought* (New York: Basic Books, 1999). Further advances were made by Giles Fauconnier and Mark Turner in *The Way We Think: Conceptual*

Blending and the Mind's Hidden Complexity (New York: Basic Books, 2002). For an up-to-date bibliography consult, see Mark Turner's website on conceptual integration, http://markturner.org/blending.htm (accessed December 1, 2018).

26 Merleau-Ponty, *The Primacy of Perception*, 163.

27 David Morgan, "Thing," in *Key Terms in Material Religion*, 253–9. The quotation is from page 255.

28 Michel Foucault, *The Order of Things: An Archaeology of the Human Sciences* (London and New York: Taylor & Francis e-library, 2005), 183. Foucault describes the episteme as "the epistemological field, the episteme in which knowledge, envisaged apart from all criteria having reference to its rational value or to its objective forms, grounds its positivity and thereby manifests a history which is not that of its growing perfection, but rather that of its conditions of possibility," xxiii–xxiv.

29 Bruno Latour, *We Have Never Been Modern*, translated by Catherine Porter (Cambridge, MA: Harvard University Press, 1993), 27–8.

30 William James, *The Varieties of Religious Experience: A Study in Human Nature: Being the Gifford Lectures on Natural Religion Delivered at Edinburgh in 1901-1902* (New York: The Modern Library, 1929), 32.

31 James did note that such experience was authoritative for the individual, but not for others. For a critique on the notion of religious experience, see Robert Sharf, "The Rhetoric of Experience and the Study of Religion," *Journal of Consciousness Studies*, 7, no. 11–12 (2000): 267–87. The essay first appeared in Taylor's *Critical Terms*, 94–116. For an attempt at redeeming the category religious experience by introducing the qualifier "special," see Ann Taves, *Religious Experience Reconsidered: A Building Block Approach to the Study of Religion and other Special Things* (Princeton: Princeton University Press, 2011).

32 Adam S. Miller, *Speculative Grace: Bruno Latour and Object-Oriented Theology* (New York: Fordham University Press, 2013), 123. Also see the discussion by David Morgan, "Introduction: The Matter of Belief," in *Religion and Material Culture: The Matter of Belief*, edited by David Morgan (London and New York: Routledge, 2010), esp. 1–12.

33 Miller, *Speculative Grace*, 124.

34 Some would argue that such works amount to a kind of ventriloquism. For an astute discussion of the social and economic location of such works, see Mark Blackwell, *The Secret Life of Things: Animals, Objects, and It-narratives in Eighteenth-Century England* (Lewisburg: Bucknell University Press, 2007), and Laura Brown, *Homeless Dogs & Melancholy Apes: Humans and Other Animals in the Modern Literary Imagination* (Ithaca: Cornell University Press, 2010).

35 Davis, *Lives of Indian Images*, xi.

36 An early version of my discussion of animism was presented in December 2017 at the State Museum of the History of Religions in St. Petersburg, Russia.

37 For an excellent discussion of Tylor, his theories, and their reception, see Wheeler-Barclay, *The Science of Religion in Britain: 1860-1915*, 71–103.

38 J. G. Frazer, in his *Totemism and Exogamy: A Treatise on Certain Early forms of superstition and Society*, 4 vols. (London: Macmillan and Co., 1910) attributes certain features of "primitive" societies to an inability to distinguish between humans, plants, and so on.

39 Frazer, *Totemism and Exogamy*, IV: 61. Frazer continues noting that "the ultimate source of totemism is a savage ignorance of the physical process by which men and animals reproduce their kind." On *urdummheit* see F. R. Lehmann, "Der Begriff 'Urdummheit' in der ethnologischen und religionswissenschaftlichen Anschauungen von K. Th. Preuss, Ad. E. Jensen und G. Murray," *Sociologus* II (1952): 131–45.

40 Lucien Lévy-Bruhl, *Primitive Mentality*, translated by Lilian A. Clare (London: George Allen and Unwin, Ltd, 1923), 35.

41 Durkheim, writing in *The Elementary Forms of the Religious Life*, translated by Joseph Ward Swain (London: George Allen & Unwin, 1915), 238, is here referring to Lévy-Bruhl's *How Natives Think*, translated by Lilian A. Clare (London: George Allen and Unwin, Ltd, 1926), 78, that was originally published in French as *Les fonctions mentales dans les sociétés inférieures* in 1910. For an extended examination, see Dominique Merllié, "Durkheim, Lévy-Bruhl et la 'pensée primitive': quell différend?" *L'Année sociologique*, 62, no. 2 (2012): 429–46. Quotation from p. VI. The English version is translated by Cadenza Academic Translations and is at https://www.cairn.info/article-E_ANSO_122_0429--durkheim-levy-bruhl-and-primitivethink.htm.

42 Lévy-Bruhl, *How Natives Think*, 367–68.

43 Years ago, I explored the implications of drawing cosmological boundaries differently. See Charles D. Orzech, *Politics and Transcendent Wisdom: The Scripture for Humane Kings in the Creation of Chinese Buddhism* (University Park: The Pennsylvania State University Press, 1998), especially Chapter One, "Locating Authority: Cosmology and Complex Systems," 13–31.

44 Bill Brown, "Thing Theory," *Critical Inquiry*, 28, no. 1, Things (Autumn 2001): 1–22, traces some of these earlier discussions.

45 Mihaly Csikszentmihalyi, "Why We Need Things," in *History from Things, Essays on Material Culture*, edited by Steven Lubar and W. David Kingery (Washington: Smithsonian Institution Press, 1993), 20–29.

46 Ibid., 21.

47 Theodor Adorno, "Valery Proust Museum," in *Prisms* (Cambridge, MA: MIT Press, 1967), 175.

48 Adam B. Seligman, Robert P. Weller, Michael J. Puett, and Bennett Simon, *Ritual and Its Consequences: An Essay on the Limits of Sincerity* (Oxford and New York: Oxford University Press, 2008) make this argument. It depends, however, on

dismissing testimony from millions of believers and it assumes a modern, Western, episteme as universal.

49 For an account, see https://en.wikipedia.org/wiki/Pinocchio_(1940_film (accessed October 6, 2018).

50 Istvan Praet, *Animism and the Question of Life* (New York and London: Routledge, 2014).

51 Ibid., 35.

52 I am summarizing material from pp. 2–3; 15; 20; 35–6. Praet does not discuss icons but the implication is obvious. We might add here that such curating also transforms objects into museum objects.

53 Whitehead, *Religious Statues.*

54 For a concise discussion of relics, see Robert H. Sharf, "On the Allure of Buddhist Relics," *Representations*, 66 (1999): 75–99; a classic treatment is Peter Brown's *The Cult of the Saints: Its Rise and Function in Latin Christianity* (Chicago: University of Chicago Press, 2015).

55 Robert H. Sharf and Elizabeth Horton Sharf, eds., *Living Images: Japanese Buddhist Icons in Context* (Stanford: Stanford University Press, 2002); Donald K. Swearer, *Becoming the Buddha: The Ritual of Image Consecration in Thailand* (Princeton: Princeton University Press, 2004).

56 Whitehead, *Religious Statues*, 100–1. In a recent blog concerning the agency of religious objects, Whitehead relates a comment by David Morgan who "suggested that we might regard sacred things as tools with handles for both the human user and a nonhuman one. It is the simplest version of a network: three agents engaged in a dynamic set of relations that redefine the scope of each." http://materialrelig ions.blogspot.co.uk/2015/10/on-agency-of-religious-objects.html

57 David Morgan, Brent S. Plate, Jeremy Stolow, and Amy Whitehead, "On the Agency of Religious Objects: A Conversation," Web blog post. *Material Religions*, October 29, 2015, http://materialreligions.blogspot.co.uk/2015/10/on-agency-of-religious -objects.html (accessed May 8, 2018).

58 For a discussion, see Fabio Rambelli, *Buddhist Materiality: A Cultural History of Objects in Japanese Buddhism* (Stanford: Stanford University Press, 2007), especially his discussion of trees and the environment and *kuyō* for "inanimate" objects. Robert H. Sharf explores some of the Buddhist thinking about sentience and insentience in "How to Think with Chan Gong'an," in Charlotte Furth, Judith T. Zeitlin, and Ping-chen Hsiung, eds., *Thinking with Cases: Specialist Knowledge in Chinese Cultural History* (Honolulu: University of Hawai'i Press, 2007), 205–43.

59 Indeed, both Bruno Latour and Tim Ingold (discussed later) refer to the work of Merleau-Ponty.

60 Bruno Latour, "How Better to Register the Agency of Things," *Tanner Lectures*, Yale University, 2014, 22, http://www.bruno-latour.fr/sites/default/files/137-YALE -TANNER.pdf. (accessed January 19, 2019).

61 Bruno Latour, *Reassembling the Social: An Introduction to Actor-Network-Theory* (Oxford and New York: Oxford University Press, 2005). Latour's insistence on "irreductionism" and the need to trace action through description are humorously depicted in "On the Difficulty of Being an ANT: An Interlude in the Form of a Dialog," 141–56. For "irreduction not reduction," see 137–38.

62 Latour, "How Better to Register the Agency of Things," 7.

63 Ibid., 8.

64 Bruno Latour, "On Actor-Network Theory A Few Clarifications," *Soziale Welt*, 47. Jahrg., H. 4 (1996): 369.

65 Ibid., 373.

66 Ibid., 370.

67 Ibid., 373.

68 Ibid., 374.

69 Ibid., 378.

70 Beate Ochsner, "Talking about Associations and Descriptions or a Short Story about Associology," in *Applying the Actor-Network Theory in Media Studies*, edited by Markus Spöhrer and Beate Ochsner (Baden-Württemberg: University of Konstanz, 2016), 228.

71 Latour, "On Actor-Network Theory," 375.

72 This is also the case of the book published in concert with the display and a BBC series. For instance, "Every known society shares a set of beliefs and assumptions—a faith, an ideology, a religion—that goes far beyond the life of the individual, and is an essential part of a shared identity." This sort of speculation is exactly what Latour is inveighing against. MacGregor, *Living with the Gods*, xiii. This approach is taken throughout the book and is nowhere as blatant as with the discussion in Chapter 1, "The Beginnings of Belief" of the "Lion-Man of Ulm" an ivory theriomorphic carving radiocarbon dated to 40,000 years ago. According to Jill Cook of the British Museum, "we do not know whether the Lion Man was a deity, a spiritual experience, a being from a creation story or an avatar used to negotiate with the forces of nature. But it is an object that makes sense only if it is part of a story, what we might now call a myth. There must have been a narrative or a ritual to accompany the statue that would explain its appearance and its meaning." MacGregor, *Living with the Gods*, 22.

73 Latour, *Reassembling the Social*, 149.

74 Tim Ingold, "On Human Correspondence," *Journal of the Royal Anthropological Institute* (N.S.) 23 (2016): 10. The embedded reference is to Ingold, *The Life of Lines* (Abingdon: Routledge, 2015).

75 Ingold, "Materials against Materiality," 11.

76 Ibid., 14.

77 Ibid., 7. Further, "The forms of things, far from having been imposed from without upon an inert substrate, arise and are borne along—as indeed we are too—within this current of materials." Ingold, "Materials against Materiality," 7.

78 Ibid., 14.

79 Ibid., 12. Emphasis added.

80 Cited in Ingold, "On Human Correspondence," 23.
    Peter J. Candler, Jr., *Theology, Rhetoric, Manuduction, or Reading Scripture Together on the Path to God* (Grand Rapids: William B. Eerdmans, 2006), 30–40.

81 Ingold, "On Human Correspondence," 23.

82 Ibid., 24.

83 This was the Ackland Museum of Art at the University of North Carolina, Chapel Hill. Ironically, some years prior to the current dispensation I had participated in a three-year seminar at the museum funded by the Luce foundation and dedicated to bringing together curators, scholars, and community faith leaders to seek new ways of displaying religious objects and involving members of the community. It resulted in a handbook for curators to which I contributed. See Hughes and Wood, *A Place for Meaning*.

84 It ran from March 17 to May 30, 2016. The exhibit website is https://www.britishm useum.org/whats_on/exhibitions/containing_the_divine.aspx (accessed December 31, 2018).

85 Julie Adams, "A Celebrity Sculpture: New discoveries and Old Questions," in *A'a: A Deity from Polynesia*, edited by Julie Adams, Steven Hooper, and Maia Nuku (London: The British Museum Press, 2016), 9–27. Quotation on p. 14.

86 Steven Hooper, "Mysteries, Methods, and Meanings: On Looking Closely at A'a," in *A'a: A Deity from Polynesia*, 45–47.

87 Edward W. Soja, *Postmetropolis: Critical Studies of Cities and Regions* (Oxford: Basil Blackwell, 2000), 11. Soja first developed his theory in *Thirdspace: Journeys to Los Angeles and Other Real-and-Imagined Places* (Cambridge: Blackwell Publishers, 1996).

88 Soja, *Thirdspace*, 5.

Chapter 3

1 The church was founded by the order of the Teutonic Knights, and its website is available at https://www.elisabethkirche.de/. On St. Elizabeth, see http://saintelizabet hchurch.org/who-is-saint-elizabeth-of-hungry/. For Philipps-Universität, see https://www.uni-marburg.de/en

2 Religious Studies Department can be accessed at https://www.uni-marburg.de/fb03/ ivk/religionswissenschaft/welcome?set_language=en. For the Neue Kanzlei see https://www.uni-marburg.de/relsamm/kanzlei

3 *Kundliche sammlung* would be roughly any scientific collection or collection for systematic research.

4 *Das Heilige: Über das Irrationale in der Idee des Göttlichen und sein Verhältnis zum Rationalen*; in English, *The Idea of the Holy: An Inquiry into the Non-Rational Factor in the Idea of the Divine and Its Relation to the Rational*, translated by John W. Harvey (London: Oxford University Press, 1936).

5 See Otto, *The Idea of the Holy*, 11. Also see Friedrich Schleiermacher, *On Religion: Speeches to Its Cultured Despisers*, translated by John Oman with an introduction by Rudolf Otto (New York: Harper and Row, Publishers, 1958).

6 Otto, *The Idea of the Holy*, 7, 26 and indeed, the entire chapter.

7 See, for instance, Mircea Eliade, *The Sacred and the Profane: The Nature of Religion* (New York: Harcourt, Brace and World, 1959). Eliade discusses Otto's importance on pages 8–10.

8 Gregory D. Alles, "The Rebirth of Cultural Colonialism as *Religionswissenschaft*: Rudolf Otto's Import House," *Temenos* 43, no. 1 (2007): 34.

9 Ibid.

10 Peter J. Bräulein, "The Marburg Museum of Religions," in *Material Religion: The Journal of Objects, Art and Belief*, 3, no. 3 (November 2006): 285.

11 Konstanze Runge, "Studying, Teaching, and Exhibiting Religion: The Marburg Museum of Religions (Religionskundliche Sammlung)," in *Religion in Museums*, 156.

12 Quotations and summary from Runge, "Studying, Teaching, and Exhibiting Religion," 156.

13 Alles, "The Rebirth of Cultural Colonialism as *Religionswissenschaft*," 30.

14 Ibid., 40.

15 Ibid.

16 Otto, *The Idea of the Holy*, 33.

17 Bräulein, "The Marburg Museum of Religions," 284.

18 Runge, "Studying, Teaching, and Exhibiting Religion," 157.

19 Peter J. Bräulein, "Religion in 'kultlichen und rituellen Ausdrucksmitteln.' Die Religionskundliche Sammlung der Philipps-Universität Marburg," *Berliner Theologische Zeitschrift*, 23, no. 2 (2006): 263–4.

20 Runge, "Studying, Teaching, and Exhibiting Religion," 156–7.

21 For a biography of Heinrich Frick see his entry in Ingeborg Schnack, ed., *Marburger Gelehrt in der ersten Hälfte de 20. Jarhunderts* (Marburg: N. G. Elwert Verlag, 1977), 75–90.

22 Bräulein, "The Marburg Museum of Religions," 285–86.

23 Bräulein, "Religion in 'kultlichen und rituellen Ausdrucksmitteln,'" 265–6; Bräulein, "The Marburg Museum of Religions," 286.

24 Jacob Wilhelm Hauer's Arisches Institut (Aryan institute) in Tübingen met with more success. See the discussion in Gregory D. Alles, "The Science of Religions in a Fascist State: Rudolf Otto and Jacob Wilhem Hauer during the Third Reich," *Religion*, 32 (2002): 182. doi:10.1006/reli.2002.0401. The phrase from the proposal is

on 183. Alles's article is a detailed and nuanced account of the maneuvering of Otto and Frick and their involvement with the Nazi government. While Otto, Frick, and Hauer (among others) worked under the regime "Otto did not share the religious convictions of Nazi racialists, but he did share their fundamental goal: German national unification" (182). Notes Alles, "Otto rejected Hauer's racialist explanation of religious differences. He appealed instead to a different biological principle, which he called the 'convergence of types'" (191).

25 Ibid., 184.

26 Ibid.

27 Indeed, Alles notes that "Otto located the most profound encounter with the numinous in the experiences of ancient Judaism as handed down to, in his view, its contemporary successor, Christianity." Ibid., 193.

28 Bräulein, "The Marburg Museum of Religions," 286.

29 For a biography of Friedrich Heiler see his entry in *Marburger Gelehrt*, 153–68.

30 For a brief overview in English see https://en.wikipedia.org/wiki/Friedrich_Heiler (accessed October 24, 2018).

31 Bräulein, "The Marburg Museum of Religions," 286.

32 Kraatz reflects on the substantial undertaking of renovating the chancellery and making it suitable for a museum in "Some Short Considerations in Advance" in *Materiality in Religion and Culture: Tenri University—Marburg University Joint Research Project*, edited by Saburo Shawn Morishita (Zurich: LIT Verlag, 2016), 47–9.

33 Kraatz, "Some Short Considerations," 48.

34 Bräunlein, "Religion in 'kultlichen und rituellen Ausdrucksmitteln,'" 267.

35 Ibid., 269.

36 https://www.uni-marburg.de/fb03/ivk/religionswissenschaft/welcome?set_language=en (accessed July 8, 2018).

37 Runge, "Studying, Teaching, and Exhibiting Religion," 158.

38 Bräunlein, "Religion in 'kultlichen und rituellen Ausdrucksmitteln,'" 268.

39 Ibid.

40 To use the turn of phrase popularized by Dipesh Chakrabarty, see Dipesh Chakrabarty, *Provincializing Europe: Postcolonial Thought and Historical Difference* (Princeton: Princeton University Press, 2000).

41 Bräunlein, "Religion in 'kultlichen und rituellen Ausdrucksmitteln,'" 268.

42 Runge, "Studying, Teaching, and Exhibiting Religion," 157.

43 Ibid., also noted by Bräunlein, "Religion in 'kultlichen und rituellen Ausdrucksmitteln,'" 287.

44 Otto initially made the proposal after the First World War. See Alles, "The Science of Religions in a Fascist State," 181–82; 196.

45 Runge, "Studying, Teaching, and Exhibiting Religion," 160; 157.

46 Ibid., 160–1.

47 Ibid., 158.

48 Ibid.

49 For a summary of Tenrikyō, see the World Religions and Spirituality account at https://wrldrels.org/2015/03/22/tenrikyo/ which includes a substantial bibliography of primary and secondary work (accessed January 1, 2019).

50 Smith, "A Matter of Class," 400.

51 Ibid., 399.

52 The British Museum, "Living with Gods."

53 Ingold, "Materials against Materiality," 12.

54 Ibid.

55 Miller, *Speculative Grace*, 123.

56 This sort of labeling is fascinating for someone interested in the history of religious studies but it is inadequate for visitors.

57 Though one could argue that Christianity rightfully should be classed as a polytheistic system.

58 In storage like the Indian government storage vault mentioned by Richard H. Davis in his *Lives of Indian Images*, 256–9.

59 Ibid., 33.

60 Michael Pye, "Exhibiting Religion," in *Materiality in Religion and Culture*, 26; 28.

61 Soja, *Postmetropolis*, 11. "Thirdspace" is Soja's coinage.

62 Soja, *Thirdspace*, 5.

63 The exhibit opened in November of 2015. For a description, see Celica Fitz and Anna Matter, "SinnRäume—An Exhibition on Contemporary Religion in Germany: Exhibition Practice as a Medium in Religious Studies," *Journal for Religion, Film and Media*, www.jrfm.eu, 3, no. 2 (2017): 37.

64 The Religionskundliche Sammlung Exhibition page contains pages on permanent and special exhibitions, https://www.uni-marburg.de/relsamm/ausstellung (accessed January 15, 2019).

65 The main page is at https://www.uni-marburg.de/relsamm/ausstellung/permanen texhibition?set_language=en (accessed January 10, 2018).

66 The Special Exhibition page is at https://www.uni-marburg.de/relsamm/ausstellun g/sonderausst (accessed January 10, 2018).

67 The Facebook page is at https://www.facebook.com/relwiss.marburg/ (accessed January 10, 2018).

Chapter 4

1 Marianna Shakhnovich, "The Study of Religion in Russia: The Foundation of the Museum of the History of Religion," in *Contemporary Views on Comparative Religion*, 426.

2 For an examination of the Soviet attitudes toward museums and for the development of anti-religious museums, see Crispin Paine, "Militant Atheist Objects: Anti-Religion Museums in the Soviet Union," *Present Pasts*, 1, no. 1, p. None, doi: http://doi.org/10.5334/pp.13

3 Ekaterina Teryukova, "Display of Religious Objects in a Museum Space: Russian Museum Experience in the 1920s and 1930s," *Material Religion*, 10, no. 2 (2014): 255.

4 Paine, "Militant Atheist Objects."

5 Shakhnovich, "The Study of Religion in Russia," 429. An earlier anti-religious exhibition had been installed in the Kazan Cathedral in 1930. See Shakhnovich, "The Study of Religion in Russia," 426.

6 The Kazan Cathedral was one of the two major cathedrals dedicated to this instantiation of the Virgin, considered the protector of Russia. The St. Petersburg icon was transferred from Moscow in 1821 to commemorate the repulse of Napoleon's armies. It disappeared after the revolution. For a brief introduction, see https://en.wikipedia.org/wiki/Kazan_Cathedral,_Saint_Petersburg (accessed August 10, 2018), and https://orthodoxwiki.org/Our_Lady_of_Kazan (accessed August 10, 2018).

7 Lüpken, "Politics of Representation," 170. The handbook she is citing is M. С. Бутинова and Н. П. Красников, Музей Истории Религии и Атеизма: Справочнник-Путеводителъ (Москва and Ленинград: Издателъство.Наука., 1965). (M. S. Butinova and N. P. Krasnikov, *Museum of the History of Religion and Atheism: Handbook* [Moscow and Leningrad: publishing house "science," 1965]).

8 Paine, "Militant Atheist Objects."

9 Ibid. Bruce Lincoln, "Revolutionary Exhumations in Spain," in *Discourse and the Construction of Society: Comparative Studies of Myth, Ritual, and Classification* (New York and Oxford: Oxford University Press, 1989), 103–27. Lincoln is playing upon and inverting Eliade's notion of the sacred manifesting in "hierophanies."

10 Paine, "Militant Atheist Objects."

11 James Clifford is here borrowing the phrase contact zone from Mary Louise Pratt. See Clifford, *Routes,* 192–93. Pratt, *Imperial Eyes*, 6–7.

12 Perhaps because of ideological pressures and because of the language barrier, the extensive and important work on the study of religion done in prerevolutionary Russia and then in the Soviet Union is little known outside of Russia. For an overview, see MaryAnn M. Shakhnovich, "The Study of Religion in the Soviet Union," *Numen*, 40, no. 1 (January 1993): 67–81; also her essay on eighteenth- and nineteenth-century studies of religion in Russia, "At the Origin of the Study of Religion in Russia," *Вестник СПбГУ*, Вып. 4, Сер. 17 (2016): 135–43, doi: 10.21638/11701/spbu17.2016.415.

13 The Kunstkamera was intended to be a building in which the knowledge of the whole world was represented. Established by Peter the Great in 1727, it was the

first museum in Russia. For an account of its innovative role in educating the population in the eighteenth century, see Olga A. Baird, "I Want the People to Observe and to Learn! The St Petersburg Kunstkamera in the Eighteenth Century," *History of Education*, 37, no. 4 (2008): 531–47. For Lev Sternberg's role in the early twentieth-century transformation of the museum, see Sergei Kan, "Evolutionism and Historical Particularism at the St. Petersburg Museum of Anthropology and Ethnography," *Museum Anthropology*, 31, no. 1 (2008): 28–46. The Kunstkamera's own account is at http://www.kunstkamera.ru/en/museum/kunst_hist/ (accessed December 5, 2018).

14 Ekaterina Teryukova, "Collecting and Research in the Museum of the History of Religion," in *Religion in Museums*, 147. For the Kunstkamera's account of its own history, see http://www.kunstkamera.ru/en/museum/kunst_hist/ (accessed December 2, 2018).

15 Teryukova, "Collecting and Research in the Museum of the History of Religion," 147.

16 Shakhnovich, "The Study of Religion in Russia," 427. There is also a brief overview of the history of the museum on its website at http://www.gmir.ru/about/history/

17 Mikhail Shakhovnich as quoted in Shakhnovich, "The Study of Religion in Russia," 428. Mikhail Shakhovnich had an abiding interest in the occult, magic, and alternative forms of religion in Russia and did much of the pioneering work in this area. Classified as mysticism, Mikhail Shakhovnich published major works on these topics including *Contemporary Mysticism in the Light of Science* (Moscow: Nauka, 1965) and *Mysticism on the Stand of Science* (Moscow: Znanie, 1970) both in Russian.

18 Quoted in Shakhnovich, "The Study of Religion in Russia," 429–30.

19 Quotations from Shakhnovich, "The Study of Religion in Russia," 428, 429, and 430.

20 Shakhnovich, "The Study of Religion in Russia," 430.

21 Paine, "Militant Atheist Objects."

22 Shakhnovich, "The Study of Religion in Russia," 431.

23 Teryukova, "Display of Religious Objects in a Museum Space," 255–6.

24 Teryukova, "Collecting and Research in the Museum of the History of Religion," 148. For more on the ideological pressures facing the museum see Shakhnovich, "The Study of Religion in Russia," 431–2.

25 Cited in Paine, "Militant Atheist Objects."

26 The Kazan Cathedral housing the museum was returned to the jurisdiction of the Orthodox Church in 1988 and services restarted in 1992, and the two institutions shared quarters for a number of years.

27 Virtual Museum, http://www.gmir.ru/eng/virtual/ (accessed August 10, 2018).

28 Sukhavata: Pure Land of Amitabha Buddha, http://www.gmir.ru/exposition/budda/sukhavati/?action=show&category=64&id=3287 (accessed January 16, 2019).

29 Supersessionist or replacement theology advances the notion that god's covenant with the Israelites has been replaced with the new covenant in Christianity.

30 For instance, see "Walking and Bus Tours," http://www.gmir.ru/news/ (accessed January 16, 2019).

31 Teryukova, "Collecting and Research in the Museum of the History of Religion," 148.

32 Ibid.

33 Ibid., 147–8.

34 Ibid., 148–9.

35 For the research programs and publications, see the menu of "To the Researcher," http://www.gmir.ru/eng/special/festival/winners/. For the Library see http://www.gmir.ru/special/library/

36 Research Publications, http://www.gmir.ru/eng/special/public/ (accessed August 13, 2018).

37 Chinese Woodcuts, http://www.gmir.ru/eng/virtual/medialibrary/chinese-woo dcut-folk-pictures/ (accessed January 16, 2019). Also see E. Teryukova, P. Tugarinov, and E. Zavidovskaya, "On the Results of the International Conference 'Folk Images and Late Imperial China' (St. Petersburg, 29–30 June 2017)," *Manuscripta Orientalia*, 23, no. 1 (2017): 67–70, and *Study of Religion*, https://religio. amursu.ru/images/Volumes/2017/4/17/17--.pdf.

38 *Proceedings of the State Museum of the History of Religions*, http://www.gmir.ru/s pecial/research_editions/ (accessed January 16, 2019).

39 Museology: Restoration, Research Discussions, http://www.gmir.ru/eng/virtual/virt -discuss/ (accessed January 16, 2019).

40 Teryukova, "Collecting and Research in the Museum of the History of Religion," 150.

41 Ekaterina Teryukova, "The State Museum of the History of Religion, St Petersburg," *Material Religion*, 8, no. 4 (2012): 542.

42 Resources for Teachers and Outreach, http://www.gmir.ru/eng/virtual/resource/ (accessed January 16, 2019).

43 Museum for Children, http://www.gmir.ru/children/ (accessed January 16, 2019). Open University, with lectures on World Religions and other topics, http://www .gmir.ru/open_univer/open_university/ (accessed January 16, 2019). The Media Library, http://www.gmir.ru/eng/virtual/medialibrary/ (accessed January 16, 2019).

44 "Open Storage," http://www.gmir.ru/news/3/2706.html (accessed January 16, 2019).

45 Teryukova, "Collecting and Research in the Museum of the History of Religion," 150.

46 Teryukova, "The State Museum of the History of Religion, St Petersburg," 541.

47 Museum Open University for the History of the World Religions, http://www.gmir. ru/eng/open_univer/lectory/ (accessed January 16, 2019).

48 http://www.gmir.ru/virtual/

49 As of August 17, 2018, the English language main page list of exhibits has not been updated beyond 2015. The Russian page, however, is up to date.

50 http://www.gmir.ru/eng/ (accessed August 17, 2018).

51 The translations are not always perfectly idiomatic but Google Translate does a respectable job of conveying the information necessary.

52 Teryukova, "Collecting and Research in the Museum of the History of Religion," 151. For the regional virtual museums & accessibility, http://www.gmir.ru/representation/long-term-program/

53 Virtual Representation of the State Museum of the History of Religions, http://www.gmir.ru/representation/ (accessed January 16, 2019).

54 The translation provided for Музеефикация всей страны. The exhibit ran from June 2 until August 23, 2018, http://www.gmir.ru/vistavki/in_museum/vistavka_archive/vystavki_archiv2018/121/2638.html

55 For an example, see the website of the Ackland Art Museum Yoga in the Galleries, https://ackland.org/events-programs/adult-programs/yoga-in-the-galleries/ and Tai Chi in the Galleries, https://ackland.org/events-programs/adult-programs/tai-chi/ (accessed December 19, 2018).

56 Gregory Price Grieve, *Cyber Zen: Imagining Authentic Buddhist Identity, Community, and Practices in the Virtual World of Second Life* (Routledge, 2016), especially his discussions of "media practices" and "screening" in the Introduction, pp. 3–19.

57 Gilles Deleuze and Claire Parnet, *Dialogues* (New York: Columbia University Press, 1987), 148–53. Quoted in Grieve, *Cyber Zen*, 203.

58 See the discussion in Grieve, *Cyber Zen*, 201ff.

Chapter 5

1 Interview with Noémie Deschamps (Head of Expositions, Le Musée des Religions du Monde), Nicolet, April 24, 2017. Also present were Dominique Boucher (president of the Council) and Professor Mary Ellis Gibson (professor of English, Colby College).

2 According to the *Catholic Encyclopedia*: "The religious in the diocese are as follows: Soeurs de l'Assomption de la Sainte-Vierge, teachers, founded at St-Grégoire (Nicolet) in 1853, have eighteen houses in the diocese; Soeurs Grises (de Nicolet), hospitallers, three houses; Congrégation de Notre-Dame (of Montreal), teachers, at Arthabaskaville, and Victoriaville; Soeurs de la Présentation de la Bienheureuse Vierge Marie, teachers, at St-David and Drummondville; Soeurs Grises de la Croix (of Ottawa), teachers and nurses, with academy and school of house-keeping at

St-Francois du Lac, and a school at Pierreville (Abenaki Indian village); Religieuses hospitalières de St-Joseph (of Montreal), hospitallers, at Arthabaskaville; Soeurs du Précieux-Sang, and Soeurs de la Sainte-Famille at Nicolet; the Frères des Ecoles Chrétiennes have schools at Nicolet, Arthabaskaville, La Baie, and St-Grégoire; the Frères de la Charité are at Drummondville; and the Frères du Sacré-Coeur teach at Arthabaskaville, and Victoriaville," http://www.newadvent.org/cathen/11069a.htm (accessed July 5, 2018).

3 Website of the Sisters of the Assumption, http://www.sasv.ca/en/ (accessed January 16, 2019).

4 The Montfort Missionaries, http://www.montfort.org/content/index2.php?lang=EN (accessed January 16, 2019).

5 The shrine's website is https://www.sanctuaire-ndc.ca/en/nature-and-history/the -basilica/.

6 Museum website, "Who Are We," http://www.museedesreligions.qc.ca/who-are-we (accessed July 13, 2018).

7 Private correspondence with Michèle Paradis April 17, 2017, translated by Mathieu Fortin, Responsable de l'action educative. Nicolet sits on an unusual geological foundation that has led to disastrous landslips.

8 Private correspondence with Michèle Paradis April 17, 2017. The exhibit was organized on the theme of "4 natures"—that is, water, fire, earth, and air—as they appear in each of the local traditions. A description of the exhibition can be found at the museum website under "documents," www.museedesreligions.qc.ca/documen ts/symboles-4-temps.pdf.

9 Private correspondence with Michèle Paradis April 17, 2017.

10 Museum website, "Who Are We?"

11 Private correspondence with Michèle Paradis April 17, 2017.

12 Museum website, "Who Are We?"

13 Ibid. From 1991 until 2016 the Archives du séminaire de Nicolet were held in the museum basement, but these have since been moved to a site down the road from the museum, the Centre d'Archives Régionales Séminaire de Nicolet, https://archive sseminairenicolet.wordpress.com/ (accessed August 23, 2018).

14 http://www.museedesreligions.qc.ca/who-are-we (accessed July 4, 2018).

15 Jean-François Royal, "Protecting and Interpreting Québec's Religious Heritage: The Museum of Religions at Nicolet," *Material Religion: The Journal of Objects, Art and Belief*, 4, no. 1 (March 2007): 153–4.

16 Ibid., 154.

17 Interview with Noémie Deschamps (Head of Expositions, Le Musée des Religions du Monde), April 24, 2017. For examples see http://www.patrimoine-culturel.gouv. qc.ca/rpcq/detailInventaire.do?methode=consulter&id=1356&type=inv

18 Key objects in the collection can be viewed through the French language collections page, http://collection.mdrm.ca/collection/mdrm/ (accessed December 20, 2018).

19 For examples, see http://collection.mdrm.ca/collection/mdrm/page/5/ (accessed December 20, 2018).

20 Interview with Noémie Deschamps (Head of Expositions, Le Musée des Religions du Monde), April 24, 2017. The museum also collaborates with the Soeurs de l'assumption, and they help with collections maintenance and with supporting the archive which, until recently, was housed in the basement of the museum.

21 Current pricing is $12 Canadian for adults, http://www.museedesreligions.qc.ca/schedule-access-and-pricing (accessed September 02, 2018).

22 Interview with Noémie Deschamps (Head of Expositions, Le Musée des Religions du Monde), April 24, 2017.

23 Deschamps notes that the "boutique" is a popular gift shop for locals as well as visitors from further afield. Among the best sellers in the shop are Tibetan Buddhist objects, decorations, nice jewelry, singing bowls, Buddha sculptures, and yak wool shawls.

24 Royal, "Protecting and Interpreting Quebec's Religious Heritage," 153.

25 Ibid., 154.

26 "Plus vous vous situez près de cercle, symbol du divin, plus vous révélez la place importante que vous leur accordez."

27 http://www.museedesreligions.qc.ca/educational-programs. There are programs for 1st–3rd elementary cycles and for high school, as well as "à la carte services," "school trips," and "guided tours."

28 Interview with Noémie Deschamps, April 24, 2017.

29 The exhibit ran from May 16, 2014, through September 7, 2015. See http://www.museedesreligions.qc.ca/our-exhibitions/passed/i-still-remember-1984 (accessed December 17, 2018). Also see http://www.museedesreligions.qc.ca/our-exhibitions/passed/la-papamobile-a-nicolet.

30 Interview with Noémie Deschamps, April 24, 2017.

31 Ibid. For an example, see http://www.museedesreligions.qc.ca/our-exhibitions/passed/freedom-symphony.

32 The museum regularly cooperates with museums in Québec and New Brunswick (with history museums in particular), and the First World War exhibition (*Tu ne tueras point*) involved collaboration with the Ferrières (Tarn) museum in France. The exhibition on alcohol and religion (*Damn You Alcohol!*) will be traveling, and some exhibits such as *In Hockey We Trust* are rented to other museums.

33 Private email correspondence with Michèle Paradis April 19, 2017. For Andréanne Pâquet, see https://www.broadbentinstitute.ca/andreannepaquet. Frédéric Castel of the Université du Québec à Montréal can be found at http://ofde.ca/repertoire/frederic-castel/. The exhibit was Et Voilà! Le voile musulman dévoilé which ran from May 15, 2013, through September 7, 2014, http://www.museedesreligions.qc.ca/our-exhibitions/passed/et-voila-le-voile-musulman-devoile (accessed December 18, 2018).

34 For these and other exhibitions going back to 2010, see the "Exhibitions and Events" tab, http://www.museedesreligions.qc.ca/our-exhibitions.

35 The exhibit ran from June 10, 2016, through March 15, 2017, http://www.muse edesreligions.qc.ca/our-exhibitions/passed/museum--30-years-of-objects-and. The page also includes a link to a YouTube video on the exhibition, https://www.you tube.com/watch?v=6LqxEGfUO5M (accessed December 17, 2018).

36 The exhibit *À la vie, À la mort: Life before Death* ran from May 19 through September 6, 2011. For more on this work, see http://www.foto8.com/live/phot ographing-dying-walter-schels-and-beata-lakotta/ and https://www.standard.co.u k/arts/beforeand-after-6678514.html (accessed December 18, 2018).

37 The exhibit ran in 2011, http://www.museedesreligions.qc.ca/our-exhibitions/pass ed/tabarnak--a-look-at-swearing-in-Québec (accessed December 18, 2018).

38 The exhibit ran from February 20, 2018, through March 31, 2019. See http://www. museedesreligions.qc.ca/nos-expositions/a-affiche/larche-de-noe-selon-claude-la fortune.

39 Interview with Noémie Deschamps, April 24, 2017.

40 Ibid.

41 Ibid.

42 For these developments, see Tourisme Nicolet-Yamasaka, http://www.tourismen icoletyamaska.com/en/cycling/map-and-routes (accessed December 18, 2018).

43 Interview with Noémie Deschamps, April 24, 2017.

44 See the flyer at http://www.museedesreligions.qc.ca/upload/contenu-fichiers/Progra mmes_educatifs_depliants_secondaire2016_COURRIEL.pdf (accessed December 20, 2018).

45 http://www.museedesreligions.qc.ca/our-collections (accessed December 20, 2018).

46 http://collection.mdrm.ca/mdrm-accueil/ (accessed December 20, 2018).

47 It would, however, be helpful to put a link to these resources on the English language page.

48 http://collection.mdrm.ca/mdrm-a-propos/ (accessed December 20, 2018).

49 http://www.museedesreligions.qc.ca/nos-collections (accessed December 20, 2018).

50 The museum's Facebook page can be accessed at https://www.facebook.com/ museedesreligionsdumonde/ while its Twitter page is at https://twitter.com/ museereligions

51 See, for instance, Bruce M. Sullivan, "Reconsecrating the Icons: The New Phenomenon of Yoga in Museums," in *Sacred Objects in Secular Spaces: Exhibiting Asian Religions in Museums*, edited by Bruce M. Sullivan (London: Bloomsbury Academic, 2015), 35–48.

Chapter 6

1 The sectarian tensions have long manifested in marches and in the football rivalry between the Celtics and the Rangers. Adherents often valorize heritage in much the same way that supporters of the American Confederacy defend their displays of the Confederate flag and deny that the civil war was about slavery. The Glasgow City Council prepared a report on the problem (2003), http://www.glasgow.gov.uk/CHttpHandler.ashx?id=9735, and there have been many discussions of it. See also, Thomas M. Devine, ed., *Scotland's Shame?: Bigotry and Sectarianism in Modern Scotland* (Edinburgh: Mainstream Publishing, 2000).

2 Mark O'Neill, as quoted in Jemima W. Fraser, "Museums, Drama, Ritual and Power: A Theory of Museum Experience" (PhD thesis, University of Leicester, 2004), 84–85.

3 David Morgan, *The Sacred Gaze: Religious Visual Culture in Theory and Practice* (Berkeley: University of California Press, 2005).

4 The visitor comment cards have been studied by P. Michel, *La Religion au Musée* (Paris: l'Harmattan, 1999), and by Fraser, "Museums, Drama, Ritual and Power," 101ff. The didactic effect of the St. Mungo Museum and that of the Anne Frank House has been thoughtfully analyzed by Richard Sandell in *Museums, Prejudice and the Reframing of Difference* (London and New York: Routledge, 2007).

5 "Religion in Scotland," https://en.wikipedia.org/wiki/Religion_in_Scotland (accessed August 20, 2018).

6 Woodhead, Heelas, and Seel, *The Spiritual Revolution*. Richard E. King and Jeremy Carrette, *Selling Spirituality: The Silent Takeover of Religion* (Routledge, 2005).

7 The website of the Kagyu Samye Ling Monastery can be found at http://www.samyeling.org/. Wikipedia also has a good overview, https://en.wikipedia.org/wiki/Kagyu_Samye_Ling_Monastery_and_Tibetan_Centre.

8 For an overview of "Orange Walks" in Scotland, see https://en.wikipedia.org/wiki/Orange_walk. There have been repeated calls and petitions to ban such "walks." On August 30, 2019, Republican parade and counterdemonstration resulted in a riot.

9 Mark O'Neill, "Exploring the Meaning of Life: The St Mungo Museum of Religious Life and Art," *Museum International*, No. 185, 47, no. 1, UNESCO, Paris: Blackwell Publishers (1995): 50. See also the discussion by Sandell in *Museums, Prejudice and the Reframing of Difference*, 46–47 and again, by Mark O'Neill, "Religion and Cultural Policy: Two Museum Case Studies," *International Journal of Cultural Policy*, 17, no. 2 (2011): 229.

10 http://www.scotland-guide.co.uk/ALL_AREAS_IN_SCOTLAND/Glasgow/Areas/Centre/St_Mungo_Museum_of_Religious_Life_and_Art.htm. For the Callanish stones see https://www.historicenvironment.scot/visit-a-place/places/calanais-standing-stones

11 Clootie trees are associated with sacred wells across Brittany, the UK, and Ireland.
    Traditionally, a person with an ailment wishing to be healed dipped a piece of
    clothing into the well and then tied it to a nearby tree. As the fabric decomposed,
    the illness was supposed to be cured. There are important and popular such sites
    near Inverness and near the Culloden battlefield. A simple internet search turns up
    many YouTube videos of these sites. See, for instance, https://www.youtube.com/
    watch?v=iNPkLsxoSPU (accessed August 20, 2018). Wikipedia has an entry on
    "Clootie Wells" which offers links and bibliography, https://en.wikipedia.org/wiki/
    Clootie_well.

12 This particular image is of the "eleven-headed" Avalokiteśvara. Its many arms and
    heads are indicative of its efforts at aiding beings in distress.

13 The image of the dancing Śiva has become an icon of Hinduism generally. For
    an account of how this has happened, see Beltz, "The Dancing Shiva." Wikipedia
    provides a convenient introduction to the history and iconography of the image
    as well as further bibliography at https://en.wikipedia.org/wiki/Nataraja (accessed
    December 31, 2018).

14 The Festival dates were June 15–24, 2018. See the Refugee Festival Scotland,
    https://www.refugeefestivalscotland.co.uk/ (accessed August 22, 2018).

15 Cited from the Glasgow Life website, https://www.glasgowlife.org.uk/news/the-stori
    es-of-the-new-scots-to-be-told-at-st-mungo-museum-of-religious-art-and-life
    (accessed August 22, 2018).

16 Glasgow Life, https://www.glasgowlife.org.uk/event/1/new-scots-exhibition and
    http://www.glasgowist.com/stories-of-new-scots-are-being-told-at-st-mungo-m
    useum-of-religious-art-and-life/ (accessed August 22, 2018).

17 O'Neill, "Religion and Cultural Policy," 243.

18 Sandell, *Museums, Prejudice and the Reframing of Difference*, 48.

19 First quotation is from O'Neill, "Exploring the Meaning of Life." The second
    quotation is from O'Neill, "Religion and Cultural Policy," 231.

20 Ibid., 229.

21 Sandell, *Museums, Prejudice and the Reframing of Difference*, 52.

22 Mark O'Neill, "Serious Earth," *Museums Journal* (February 1994): 28, as quoted in
    Sandell, *Museums, Prejudice and the Reframing of Difference*, 53. Alexandra Greiser,
    Adrian Herman, and Katja Triplett have termed this process of rendering artifacts
    innocuous "museality." See "Museality as a Matrix of the Production, Reception, and
    Circulation of Knowledge Concerning Religion," *Journal of Religion in Europe*, 4
    (2011): 40–70.

23 Lüpken, "Politics of Representation," 178.

24 Sandell, *Museums, Prejudice and the Reframing of Difference*, 53, here quoting
    curator Harry Dunlap.

25 Lüpken, "Politics of Representation," 172–3. Also, see O'Neill, "Exploring the
    Meaning of Life."

26 Lüpken, "Politics of Representation," 178 and footnote 73.

27 The resulting handbook is by Amanda M. Hughes and Carolyn H. Wood, eds., *A Place for Meaning: Art, Faith, and Museum Culture* (University of North Carolina Press, 2009). The "Introduction" gives an overview of the project, 3–13.

28 Luepken, "Politics of Representation," 173.

29 Interview with David Page, architect, April 2003, cited in Fraser, "Museums, Drama, Ritual and Power," 95.

30 Interview with Harry Dunlop, curator, April 2003, cited in Fraser, Ibid., 84.

31 See my discussion in Visitor Reactions, Objects and Semiotics, and in Charles D. Orzech, "World Religions Museums: Dialogue, Domestication, and the Sacred Gaze," in *Sacred Objects in Secular Spaces*, edited by Bruce M. Sullivan (London and New York: Bloomsbury, 2015), 140–3.

32 O'Neill, "Religion and Cultural Policy," (1995): 229.

33 *Herald*, April 2, 1993, 14. See https://www.heraldscotland.com/news/12614842.city-museum-offers-a-unique-insight-to-religion-worldwide/ (accessed December 11, 2018).

34 The quotation is from an interview in *The Times* done by R. Gledhill "From Mungo to the Muslims; St Mungo Museum, Glasgow" which appeared on page 29 of the March 31, 1993, edition. Sandell, *Museums, Prejudice and the Reframing of Difference*, 48.

35 O'Neill, "Religion and Cultural Policy," (2011): 230.

36 Mark O'Neill, "The St Mungo Museum of Religious Life and Art," *Musées et Religions(s)*. Musées et Collections Publiques de France, Nr. 219 (1998): 87–88. As cited in Anja Lüpken, *Religion(en) im Museum: Eine vergleichende Analyse der Religionsmuseen in St. Petersburg, Glasgow und Taipeh* (Berlin: LIT Verlag, 2011): 110, n. 59. O'Neill has revisited the issue of tolerance, multiculturalism, and controversy in "Religion and Cultural Policy" (2011).

37 O'Neill, "Religion and Cultural Policy," (2011): 230.

38 Christopher Andrea, "Religious Emblems Find Unusual Niche." Boston, MA: *Christian Science Monitor*, August 4, 1993. The article is at https://www.csmonitor.com/1993/0804/04141.html (accessed December 12, 2018). A statue to the missionary David Livingstone is situated in the cathedral precinct almost next door to the museum.

39 Mark O'Neill, as quoted in Sandell, *Museums, Prejudice and the Reframing of Difference*, 54.

40 O'Neill, "Religion and Cultural Policy," 229.

41 Ibid.

42 Sandell, *Museums, Prejudice and the Reframing of Difference*, 49–50.

43 O'Neill, "Exploring the Meaning of Life," 50–51.

44 Cited in Sandell, *Museums, Prejudice and the Reframing of Difference*, 51.

45 Fraser, "Museums, Drama, Ritual and Power," 153.

46 Both comments cited in Fraser, "Museums, Drama, Ritual and Power," 122.

47 Sandell, *Museums, Prejudice, and the Reframing of Difference*, especially chapter four, "The Visitor Exhibition Encounter: Reconciling and Rethinking Museum Audience Agency," 71–104. See esp., 81–82.

48 Claussen as cited in Lüpken, "Politics of Representation," 173.

49 The exhibit opened on October 2, 2015, and had an extended run through the summer of 2017.

50 Charles Orzech, "The Material Representation of the Ethereal," *Material Religion*, 12, no. 3 (2016): 399–401, doi: 10.1080/17432200.2016.1192145.

51 https://www.glasgowlife.org.uk/ (accessed August 22, 2018).

52 St. Mungo Museum of Religious Life and Art Facebook page, https://www.facebook.com/StMungo.GlasgowMuseums (accessed January 16, 2019).

53 Orzech, "World Religions Museums," 140.

54 See my discussion of Whitehead in Chapter 2.

55 Diana L. Eck, "Dialogue and Method: Reconstructing the Study of Religion," in *A Magic Still Dwells*, 140.

56 Luke, *Museum Politics*, 219–20.

57 Slavoj Žižek (1997: 44) puts it well: "Liberal 'tolerance' condones the folklorist Other deprived of its substance—like the multitude of 'ethnic cuisines' in a contemporary megalopolis; however, any 'real' Other is instantly denounced for its 'fundamentalism,' since the kernel of Otherness resides in the regulation of its jouissance: the 'real Other' is by definition 'patriarchal,' 'violent,' never the Other of ethereal wisdom and charming customs." See "Multiculturalism or, the Cultural Logic of Multinational Capitalism," *New Left Review*, 225 (1997): 44.

58 The exception to this was complaints raised against the display in the Religious Life Gallery dealing with female genital mutilation as a coming of age ritual.

Chapter 7

1 For a biography of Hsin Tao, see the website of the "Lingjiou Mountain Buddhist Society," https://www.093ljm.org/index.aspx (accessed December 29, 2018).

2 There are two works, both in German, that treat the Museum of World Religions. The first, by Annette Wilke and Ester-Maria Guggenmos, eds., is *Im Netz des Indra: Das Museum of World Religions, sein buddhistisches Dialogkonzept und die neue Disziplin Religionsästhetik* (Berlin: LIT Verlag, 2008). The second work is by Lüpken, *Religion(en) im Museum*.

3 For a list of the hundreds of museums designed by the Appelbaum firm, see its website at http://www.raai.com/ (accessed December 29, 2018).

4 For Applebaum's account of his involvement, see the "He Turns the Past into Stories and the Galleries Fill Up," *New York Times*, April 21, 1999, https://www.nytimes.com/1999/04/21/arts/he-turns-the-past-into-stories-and-the-galleries-fill-up.html (accessed December 29, 2018).

5 Statement by Hsin Tao, cited on the "Founder" page of the museum, http://www.mwr.org.tw/content_en/introduction/fonder.aspx (accessed November 8, 2014).

6 https://www.mwr.org.tw/mwr_en/xmdoc/cont?xsmsid=0I052359411359500564 (accessed December 27, 2018).

7 "About the Museum: Origin," http://www.mwr.org.tw/content_en/introduction/origin-concept.aspx (accessed November 8, 2014).

8 https://www.mwr.org.tw/mwr_en/xcpmtexhi/cont?xsmsid=0I0523915777712117 47&sid=0I057612803752905496 (accessed December 27, 2018).

9 "Two HDS Staff On Hand for Opening of Museum of World Religions in Taipei" appeared in the Harvard Divinity School newsletter, Harvard University, 2002. The article describing Harvard's contribution can be found archived via the internet Archive or "Wayback Machine," July 5, 2008, http://www.hds.harvard.edu/news/article_archive/museum.html (accessed December 29, 2018).

10 Maria Reis Habito, "The Taipai, Taiwan, Museum of World Religions," *Buddhist-Christian Studies*, 22 (2002): 204.

11 For a treatment of the role of the *Avatamsaka Sutra* in the museum, see Esther-Maria Guggenmos, "Networking statt Inclusivism – Ein Dialog-Konzept im Anschluß an die Avatamsaka-Philosophie," in *Im Netz des Indra*, 177–204.

12 The full Sanskrit title is *Mahāvaipulya Buddhāvataṃsaka Sūtra*. The scripture is a composite and seems to have grown to its massive size by accretion. Pieces were translated into Chinese as early as the second century CE with the first full translation appearing in 420 CE.

13 Thomas Cleary, *The Flower Ornament Scripture: A Translation of the Avatamsaka Sutra* (Boston: Shambala Publications, 1993), 891–92.

14 Francis H. Cook, *Hua-Yen Buddhism: The Jewel Net of Indra* (University Park and London: The Pennsylvania State University Press, 1977), 2.

15 Admission pricing can be found at "Hours and Admission," https://www.mwr.org.tw/mwr_en/xmdoc/cont?xsmsid=0I052383560701707231 (accessed December 29, 2018). 150 NT is approximately US$5.

16 The Chinese phrase is *baiqian famen tonggui fangcun*百千法門 同歸方寸.

17 Hung Shu-yen, ed., *Museum of World Religions Guidebook* (Taipei: Museum of World Religions Foundation, 2004), 15.

18 Ibid.

19 The models of religious buildings occupying the central space on this floor were not part of the original plan but were added later. See Lüpken, *Religion(en) im Museum*, 49.

20 Ibid., 44.

21 Hung, *Guidebook*, 15.

22 Ibid., 17.

23 Lüpken, *Religion(en) im Museum*, 44.

24 Hung, *Guidebook*, 17.

25 Ibid.

26 The *jiao* or "offering" ritual performed by Daoist priests involves the periodic renewal of the universe. For a discussion, see Poul Andersen, "*Jiao,*" in *The Encyclopedia of Taoism*, edited by Fabrizio Pregadio, vol. 1 (London: Routledge, 2008), 539–44. The article is available online, http://www.goldenelixir.com/publica tions/eot_jiao.html (accessed December 29, 2018).

27 The *Yijing* or *Classic of Changes* is an ancient book of divination whose key components are combinations of solid and broken lines representing differing states of yang and yin. The lines, comprised eight figures of three lines and combined to make sixty-four figures of six lines, are sometimes arranged as a cosmogram. They also appear on the circumference of Chinese Fengshui compasses (*luopan*). For a translation of the *Yijing* see Edward L. Shaughnessy, *I Ching: the Classic of Changes* (New York: Ballantine Books, 1996). On Fengshui compasses and their use in Chinese geomancy, see Stephen Skinner, *Guide to the Feng Shui Compass: A Compendium of Classical Feng Shui* (Singapore: Golden Hoard Press, 2008) and the many online depictions.

28 Lüpken, *Religion(en) im Museum*, 45–46.

29 Hung, *Guidebook*, 23.

30 For examples from each of the stations see Hung, *Guidebook*, 25–33.

31 See Lüpken's discussion in *Religion(en) im Museum*, 46–47.

32 Hung, *Guidebook*, 34.

33 Ibid., 35.

34 Lüpken, *Religion(en) im Museum*, 47–48.

35 Hung, *Guidebook*, 37.

36 Lüpken, *Religion(en) im Museum*, 48.

37 Hung, *Guidebook*, 37.

38 The term "faiths" is a decidedly Christian term and many scholars in the religious studies field now restrict its use to Christian contexts. The poster and text are not reproduced in the *Guidebook* but can be seen in the Google Virtual Tour, https://www.mwr.org.tw/mwr_en/xmdoc/cont?xsmsid=0I052415740292978812 (accessed December 26, 2018).

39 Ibid., 40.

40 Ibid.

41 Habito, "The Taipai [*sic*], Taiwan, Museum of World Religions," 205.

42 For the classic account of the carvings, see Jan Fontein, *The Pilgrimage of Sudhana: A Study of Gandavyuha Illustrations in China, Japan and Java* (The Hague and Paris: Mouton, 1968).

43 Museum website, https://www.mwr.org.tw/mwr_en/xcpmtexhi/cont?xsmsid=0I0 52391577771211747&sid=0I057642718844073637 (accessed December 27, 2018).

44　There is a growing scholarly literature on religion and gaming culture. For a start, see Heidi Campbell and Gregory Price Grieve, eds., *Playing with Religion in Digital Games* (Bloomington: Indiana University Press, 2014).

45　The exhibit ran from November 9, 2018, through April 21, 2019. Its English website is at https://www.mwr.org.tw/mwr_en/xcspecexhi/cont?xsmsid=0I0573864341 70111747&sid=0I296411118315087325 (accessed December 28, 2018).

46　The ritual is a reenactment of the Buddha's preaching of the *Lotus Sutra* on "Vulture Peak." Hsin Tao's Lingjiou monastery is named after this famous mountain. The exhibit ran from September 4, 2018, through March 24, 2019. The website is https://www.mwr.org.tw/mwr_en/xcspecexhi/cont?xsmsid=0I057386434170111 747&sid=0I247354810107731972 (accessed December 28, 2018).

47　The exhibit ran from July 6, 2002, through October 6, 2002. The website is https://www.mwr.org.tw/mwr_en/xcspecexhi/cont?xsmsid=0I057386434170111 747&sid=0I058526971966881044 (accessed December 28, 2018).

48　This exhibit ran from October 15, 2007, through April 27, 2008. The website is https://www.mwr.org.tw/mwr_en/xcspecexhi/cont?xsmsid=0I057386434170111 747&sid=0I058599375857362760 (accessed December 28, 2018).

49　More on these exhibits can be found at https://www.mwr.org.tw/mwr_en/xcspe cexhi/old_index?xsmsid=0I057386434170111747.

50　These can be found at the website, https://www.mwr.org.tw/xcebook?xsmsid=0I 010370550014020867 (accessed December 28, 2018).

51　The Life Education Center is detailed at https://www.mwr.org.tw/mwr_en/xmdoc/ cont?xsmsid=0I057395935042119329 (accessed December 28, 2018).

52　The main website is at https://edu.ljm.org.tw/093en/index.html (accessed December 28, 2018).

53　https://edu.ljm.org.tw/093en/en1_rc.html (accessed December 28, 2018).

54　https://edu.ljm.org.tw/093en/en4_uwr.html (accessed December 28, 2018).

55　The journal, in Chinese, is available at the website https://www.ncrs.org.tw/# (accessed December 28, 2018).

56　For the website see http://www.gflp.org/ (accessed December 28, 2018).

57　See "Collections" at https://www.mwr.org.tw/mwr_en/xcalbum?xsmsid=0I057 390562444070288 (accessed December 28, 2018). The Chinese page (https://w ww.mwr.org.tw/xcalbum?xsmsid=0H305743751129902582) includes forty-five objects while the English page only incudes thirty-seven objects.

58　The video on the establishment of the museum is at https://www.youtube.com/w atch?v=RZXn9G5KN9s (accessed December 28, 2018).

59　Chanju Mun proposes that there are two styles of *panjiao*, one sectarian and one ecumenical. See *The History of Doctrinal Classification in Chinese Buddhism A Study of the Panjiao System* (Lanham, MD: University Press of America, 2005). For Kūkai's

Aims of the Three Teachings, see Yoshito S. Hakeda, trans., *Kūkai: Major Works* (New York: Columbia University Press, 1973), 101–39.

60 Statement by Hsin Tao, cited on the "Founder" page of the museum, http://www. mwr.org.tw/content_en/introduction/fonder.aspx (accessed November 8, 2014).

61 "Confucianism"—both the term and modern constructions of it—is indubitably a product of colonial encounter and, at base, Western sinology. The tradition of the "scholars" (*ru* 儒) and the various classical texts broadly classified as "Confucian" or "Neo-Confucian" by Western scholars is another matter. Nonetheless, the government of the People's Republic has vigorously embraced the sage and promulgates a version of his teaching as a "World Religion" in its many Confucius Institutes.

62 The Confucius temple website operated by the government, http://www.ct.taipei. gov.tw/en-us/Home.htm (accessed December 30, 2018).

63 For the Buddhist-Muslim Dialogues, see http://www.gflp.org/Buddhist-Muslim. html (accessed December 30, 2018).

Conclusion

1 https://www.britishmuseum.org/about_us/past_exhibitions/2018/living_with_ gods.aspx (accessed July 30, 2018).

2 Smith, "In Comparison a Magic Dwells," 35.

3 Runge, "Studying, Teaching, and Exhibiting Religion," 160–1.

4 Royal, "Protecting and Interpreting Quebec's Religious Heritage," 154.

5 O'Neill, as quoted in Fraser, "Museums, Drama, Ritual and Power," 84–85.

6 "Lingjiu Buddhist Monastery" website, https://edu.ljm.org.tw/093en/en4_uwr.html (accessed December 28, 2018).

7 Soja, *Thirdspace*, 5.

8 Eck, "Dialogue and Method: Reconstructing the Study of Religion," 140.

Bibliography

Adams, Julie. "A Celebrity Sculpture: New Discoveries and Old Questions." In *A'a: A Deity from Polynesia*, edited by Julie Adams, Steven Hooper, and Maia Nuku, 9–27. London: The British Museum Press, 2016.

Adorno, Theodor. "Valery Proust Museum." In *Prisms*, 173–85. Cambridge, MA: MIT Press, 1967.

Alles, Gregory D. "The Rebirth of Cultural Colonialism as *Religionswissenschaft*: Rudolf Otto's Import House." *Temenos* 43, no. 1 (2007): 29–51.

Alles, Gregory D. "The Science of Religions in a Fascist State: Rudolf Otto and Jacob Wilhem Hauer During the Third Reich." *Religion* 32 (2002): 177–204. doi: 10.1006/reli.2002.0401.

Andersen, Poul. "*Jiao*." In *The Encyclopedia of Taoism*, edited by Fabrizio Pregadio, vol. 1, 539–44. London and New York: Routledge, 2008.

Baird, Olga A. "I Want the People to Observe and to Learn! The St Petersburg Kunstkamera in the Eighteenth Century." *History of Education* 37, no. 4 (2008): 531–47.

Bazin, Germain. *The Museum Age*. Translated by Jane van Nuis Cahill. New York: Universe Books, 1967.

Bell, Catherine. *Ritual Theory, Ritual Practice*. New York: Oxford University Press, 1992.

Beltz, Johannes. "The Dancing Shiva: South Indian Processional Bronze, Museum Artwork, and Universal Icon." *Journal of Religion in Europe* 4 (2011): 204–22.

Bennett, Tony. *The Birth of the Museum: History, Theory, Politics*. London and New York: Routledge, 1995.

Berger, Peter L. *The Sacred Canopy: Elements of a Sociological Theory of Religion*. New York: Anchor Books, 1969.

Berger, Peter L., ed. *The Desecularization of the World: Resurgent Religion and World Politics*. Grand Rapids: Wm. B. Eerdmans Publishing Company, 1999.

Bergunder, Michael. "Comparison in the Maelstrom of Historicity: A Postcolonial Perspective on Comparative Religion." In *Interreligious Comparisons in Religious Studies and Theology: Comparison Revisited*, edited by Andreas Nehring and Perry Schmidt-Leukel, 34–52. London: Bloomsbury Academic, 2016.

Bhabha, Homi K. "Signs Taken for Wonders: Questions of Ambivalence and Authority under a Tree outside Delhi, May 1817". *Critical Inquiry* 12, no. 1, "Race, Writing, and Difference." (1985): 144–65.

Blackwell, Mark. *The Secret Life of Things: Animals, Objects, and It-Narratives in Eighteenth-Century England*. Lewisburg: Bucknell University Press, 2007.

Bräulein, Peter J. "The Marburg Museum of Religions." *Material Religion: The Journal of Objects, Art and Belief* 3, no. 3 (2006): 285–87.

Bräulein, Peter J. "Religion in 'kultlichen und rituellen Ausdrucksmitteln': Die Religionskundliche Sammlung der Philipps-Universität Marburg." *Berliner Theologische Zeitschrift* 23, no. 2 (2006): 263–70.

Bräulein, Peter J. "Thinking Religion Through Things: Reflections on the Material Turn in the Scientific Study of Religion\s." *Method and Theory in the Study of Religion* 28 (2016): 365–99.

Brown, Bill. "Thing Theory." *Critical Inquiry* 28, no. 1 (Autumn 2001): 1–22.

Brown, Laura. *Homeless Dogs & Melancholy Apes: Humans and Other Animals in the Modern Literary Imagination*. Ithaca: Cornell University Press, 2010.

Brown, Peter. *The Cult of the Saints: Its Rise and Function in Latin Christianity*. Chicago: University of Chicago Press, 2015.

Brunault, Joseph. "Nicolet." In *The Catholic Encyclopedia*, vol. 11. New York: Robert Appleton Company, 1911. http://www.newadvent.org/cathen/11069a.htm. Accessed July 5, 2018.

Buggeln, Gretchen, Crispin Paine, and S. Brent Plate, eds. *Religion in Museums: Global and Multidisciplinary Perspectives*. London: Bloomsbury Academic, 2017.

Burris, John P. *Exhibiting Religion: Colonialism and Spectacle at International Expositions 1851–1893*. Charlottesville and London: University Press of Virginia, 2001.

Cameron, William E. *History of the World's Columbian Exposition*. Chicago: Columbian History, 1893.

Campany, Robert Ford. "On the Very Idea of Religions (In the Modern West and in Early Medieval China)." *History of Religions* 42, no. 4 (May 2003): 287–319.

Candler, Peter J., Jr. *Theology, Rhetoric, Manuduction, or Reading Scripture Together on the Path to God*. Grand Rapids: William B. Eerdmans, 2006.

Carrette, Jeremy, and Richard E. King. *Selling Spirituality: The Silent Takeover of Religion*. London and New York: Routledge, 2004.

Chakrabarty, Dipesh. *Provincializing Europe: Postcolonial Thought and Historical Difference*. Princeton: Princeton University Press, 2000.

Chapman, William Ryan. "Arranging Ethnology: A.H.L.F. Pitt Rivers and the Typological Tradition." In *Objects and Others: Essays on Museums and Material Culture*, edited by George W. Stocking, Jr., 15–48. Madison: The University of Wisconsin Press, 1985.

Chidester, David. *Empire of Religion: Imperialism and Comparative Religion*. Chicago and London: University of Chicago Press, 2014.

Clarke, James Freeman. *Ten Great Religions: An Essay in Comparative Theology*. Boston and New York: Houghton Mifflin Co., 1871.

Cleary, Thomas. *The Flower Ornament Scripture: A Translation of the Avatamsaka Sutra*. Boston: Shambala Publications, 1993.

Clifford, James. *Routes: Travel and Translation in the Late Twentieth Century*. Cambridge, MA: Harvard University Press, 1997.

Colonial and Indian Exhibition, 1886: Official Catalogue. London: William Clowes and Sons, Limited, 1886.

Connor, Steven. "Myth and Meta-myth in Max Müller and Walter Pater." In *The Sun Is God: Painting, Literature, and Mythology in the Nineteenth Century*, edited by J. B. Bullen, 199–224. Oxford: Clarendon Press, 1988.

Cook, Francis H. *Hua-Yen Buddhism: The Jewel Net of Indra*. University Park and London: The Pennsylvania State University Press, 1977.

Cotter Christopher R., and David G. Robertson., eds. *After World Religions: Reconstructing Religious Studies*. London and New York: Routledge, 2016.

Council for a Parliament of the World's Religions. http://www.parliamentofreligions.or g/index.cfm?n=1. Accessed November 8, 2014.

Csikszentmihalyi, Mihaly. "Why We Need Things." In *History from Things, Essays on Material Culture*, edited by Steven Lubar and W. David Kingery, 20–29. Washington: Smithsonian Institution Press, 1993.

Davis, John R., and Angus Nicholls. "Friedrich Max Müller: The Career and Intellectual Trajectory of a German Philologist in Victorian Britain." *Publications of the English Goethe Society* 85, no. 2–3 (2016): 67–97.

Davis, Richard H. *Lives of Indian Images*. Princeton and Oxford: Princeton University Press, 1997.

Devine, Thomas M., ed. *Scotland's Shame?: Bigotry and Sectarianism in Modern Scotland*. Edinburgh: Mainstream Publishing, 2000.

Durkheim, Émile. *The Elementary Forms of the Religious Life*. Translated by Joseph Ward Swain. London: George Allen & Unwin, 1915.

Eck, Diana L. "Dialogue and Method: Reconstructing the Study of Religion." In *A Magic Still Dwells: Comparative Religion in the Postmodern Age*, edited by Kimberley C. Patton and Benjamin C. Ray, 131–49. Berkeley: University of California, 2000.

Eliade, Mircea. *Patterns in Comparative Religion*. Translated by Rosemary Sheed. Cleveland and New York: The World Publishing Company, 1970.

Eliade, Mircea. *The Sacred and the Profane: The Nature of Religion*. New York: Harcourt, Brace & World, Inc., 1959.

Elliot, George. *Middlemarch, A Study of Provincial Life*. Cleveland: The Burroughs Brothers Company, 1888. First published 1871 by William Blackwood and Sons (London).

Fauconnier, Giles, and Mark Turner. *The Way We Think: Conceptual Blending and the Mind's Hidden Complexity*. New York: Basic Books, 2002.

Feldman, Burton, and Robert D. Richardson, Jr., eds. *The Rise of Modern Mythology 1680–1860*. Bloomington: Indiana University Press, 1972.

Fielding, Henry, *The History of Tom Jones, a Foundling*, edited by R. P. C. Mutter. Baltimore: Penguin Books, Inc., 1966. First published 1749.

The First Amendment Center. http://www.firstamendmentschools.org/freedoms/faq. aspx?id=12823.

Fitz, Celica, and Anna Matter. "SinnRäume – An Exhibition on Contemporary Religion in Germany: Exhibition Practice as a Medium in Religious Studies." *JRFM Journal for Religion, Film, and Media* 3, no. 2 (2017): 37–51. http://doi.org/10.25364/05.3:2017.2.3.

Fitzgerald, Timothy. *The Ideology of Religious Studies*. New York: Oxford University Press, 2000.

Fontein, Jan. *The Pilgrimage of Sudhana: A Study of Gandavyuha Illustrations in China, Japan and Java*. The Hague and Paris: Mouton, 1968.

Foucault, Michel. *The Order of Things: An Archaeology of the Human Sciences*. London and New York: Taylor & Francis e-library, 2005.

Foulk, Griffith T. "The Ch'an *Tsung* in Medieval China: School, Lineage, or What?" *Pacific World*, n.s. 8 (1992): 18–31.

Fraser, Jemima W. "Museums, Drama, Ritual and Power: A Theory of Museum Experience." Ph.D thesis, University of Leicester, 2004.

Frazer, James George. *The New Golden Bough: A New Abridgment of the Classic Work*, edited by Theodore H. Gaster. New York: Mentor New American Library, 1964.

Frazer, James George. *Totemism and Exogamy: A Treatise on Certain Early Forms of Superstition and Society*, 4 vols. London: Macmillan and Co., 1910.

Fujiwara, Satoko. "Why the Concept of 'World Religion' has Survived in Japan: On the Japanese Reception of Max Weber's Comparative Religion." In *Contemporary Views on Comparative Religion in Celebration of Tim Jensen's 65th Birthday*, edited by Peter Antes, Armin W. Geertz, and Mikael Rothstein, 193–205. Sheffield and Bristol Connecticut: Eqinox, 2016.

Geertz, Clifford. *The Interpretation of Cultures*. New York: Basic Books, 1973.

Gennep, Arnold van. *The Rites of Passage*. Translated by Monika B. Vizedom and Gabrielle L. Caffee. Chicago: The University of Chicago Press, 1960.

Goethe, Johann Wolfgang von. *The Metamorphosis of Plants*. Translated by Douglas Miller. Cambridge, MA: MIT Press, 2009.

Greiser, Alexandra, Adrian Herman, and Katja Triplett. "Museality as a Matrix of the Production, Reception, and Circulation of Knowledge Concerning Religion." *Journal of Religion in Europe* 4 (2011): 40–70.

Grieve, Gregory Price. *Cyber Zen: Imagining Authentic Buddhist Identity, Community, and Practices in the Virtual World of Second Life*. London and New York: Routledge, 2016.

Guggenmos, Esther-Maria. "Networking statt Inclusivism – Ein Dialog-Konzept im Anschluß an die Avatamsaka-Philosophie." In *Im Netz des Indra*, edited by Annette Wilke and Esther-Maria Guggenmos, 177–204. Wein: LIT Verlag, 2008.

Guide to the Collections in the Horniman Museum and Library, Forest Hill, London, S.E., Third Edition. London: London County Council, 1921.

Habito, Maria Reis. "The Taipai [*sic*], Taiwan, Museum of World Religions." *Buddhist-Christian Studies* 22 (2002): 203–5.

Hakeda, Yoshito S., trans. *Kūkai: Major Works*. New York: Columbia University Press, 1973.

Harrison, Victoria S., Anna Bergqvist, and Gary Kemp, eds. *Philosophy and Museums: Essays on the Philosophy of Museums*. Series: Royal Institute of Philosophy supplement. Cambridge: Cambridge University Press, 2016.

Harvey, Graham. *Animism: Respecting the Living World*. London: Hurst & Co., 2005.

Hasmath, Reza, ed. *Managing Ethnic Diversity: Meanings and Practices from an International Perspective*. Surry: Ashgate, 2011.

Hedges, Paul. "Comparative Religion and the Religious Studies Toolkit." In *Interreligious Comparisons in Religious Studies and Theology: Comparison Revisited*, edited by Andreas Nehring and Perry Schmidt-Leukel, 17–33. London: Bloomsbury Academic, 2016.

Hoffenberg, Peter H. *Empire on Display: English, Indian, and Australian Exhibitions from the Crystal Palace to the Great War*. Berkeley: University of California Press, 2001.

Hooper, Steven. "Mysteries, Methods, and Meanings: On Looking Closely at A'a." In *A'a: A Deity from Polynesia*, edited by Julie Adams, Steven Hooper, and Maia Nuku, 29–47. London: the British Museum Press, 2016.

Horniman Museum History. https://www.horniman.ac.uk/about/museum-history. Accessed December 31, 2018.

Hughes Amanda M., and Carolyn H. Wood. *A Place for Meaning: Art, Faith, and Museum Culture*. Chapel Hill: University of North Carolina Press, 2010.

Hung, Shu-yen, ed. *Museum of World Religions Guidebook*. Taipei: Museum of World Religions Foundation, 2004.

Huxley, Aldous. *The Perennial Philosophy*. New York and London: Harper & Brothers, 1945.

Idinopulos, Thomas A., and Edward A. Yonan, eds. *Religion and Reductionism: Essays on Eliade, Segal, and the Challenge of the Social Sciences for the Study of Religion*. Leiden: E. J. Brill, 1994.

Impey, Oliver, and Arthur MacGregor, eds. *The Origins of Museums: The Cabinet of Curiosities in Sixteenth and Seventeenth-Century Europe*. Oxford: Clarendon, 1985; reprint Ashmolean Museum, 2018.

Ingold, Tim. *Being Alive: Essays on Movement, Knowledge and Description*. London and New York: Routledge, 2011.

Ingold, Tim. "Materials against Materiality." Discussion article in *Archaeological Dialogues* 14, no. 1 (2007): 1–16.

Ingold, Tim. "On Human Correspondence." *Journal of the Royal Anthropological Institute (N.S.)* 23, (2016): 9–27.

James, William. *The Varieties of Religious Experience: A Study in Human Nature: Being the Gifford Lectures on Natural Religion Delivered at Edinburgh in 1901–1902*. New York: The Modern Library, 1929.

Johnson, Mark, and George Lakoff. *Metaphors We Live By*. Chicago: University of Chicago Press, 1980.

Johnson, Mark, and George Lakoff. *Philosophy in the Flesh: The Embodied Mind and Its Challenge to Western Thought*. New York: Basic Books, 1999.

Kamel, Susan. *Wege zur Vermittlung von Religionen in Berliner Museen: Black Kaaba Meets White Cube*. Wiesbaden: Verlag für Sozialwissenschaften, 2004.

Kan, Sergei. "Evolutionism and Historical Particularism at the St. Petersburg Museum of Anthropology and Ethnography." *Museum Anthropology* 31, no. 1 (2008): 28–46.

Kant, Immanuel. "Fourth Essay: Service and Pseudo-Service Under the Sovereignty of the Good Principle, or Religion and Pfaffentum." In *Religion within the Limits of Bare Reason*. Translated by Jonathan Bennett (2017), 83–119. The version consulted is published at https://www.earlymoderntexts.com/assets/pdfs/kant1793.pdf. Accessed December 30, 2018.

King, Richard. *Orientalism and Religion: Post-Colonial Theory, India and "The Mystic East."* London and New York: Routledge, 1999.

Kraatz, Martin. "Some Short Considerations in Advance." In *Materiality in Religion and Culture: Tenri University—Marburg University Joint Research Project*, edited by Saburo Shawn Morishita, 47–49. Zurich: LIT Verlag, 2016.

Kunstkamera History. http://www.kunstkamera.ru/en/museum/kunst_hist/. Accessed December 05, 2018.

Lakoff, George. "The Contemporary Theory of Metaphor." In *Metaphor and Thought*, 2nd ed., edited by Andrew Ortony, 202–51. Cambridge: Cambridge University Press, 1993.

Latour, Bruno. "Fetish-Factish." In *Key Terms in Material Religion*, edited by S. Brent Plate, 87–94. London: Bloomsbury Academic, 2015.

Latour, Bruno. "How Better to Register the Agency of Things." *Tanner Lectures*, Yale University, 2014. http://www.bruno-latour.fr/sites/default/files/137-YALE-TANN ER.pdf. Accessed January 19, 2019.

Latour, Bruno. "On Actor-Network Theory: A Few Clarifications." 369 *Soziale Welt*, 47. Jahrg., H. 4 (1996): 369–81.

Latour, Bruno. *Reassembling the Social: An Introduction to Actor-Network-Theory*. Oxford and New York: Oxford University Press, 2005.

Latour, Bruno. *We Have Never Been Modern*. Translated by Catherine Porter. Cambridge: Harvard University Press, 1993.

Leeuw, Gerardus van der. *Religion in Essence and Manifestation: A Study in Phenomenology*, 2 vols. New York: Harper and Row, 1963.

Lehmann, Friedrich R. "Der Begriff 'Urdummheit' in der ethnologischen und religionswissenschaftlichen Anschauungen von K. Th. Preuss, Ad. E. Jensen und G. Murray." *Sociologus* II (1952): 131–45.

Levi-Strauss, Claude. *Structural Anthropology*. New York: Basic Books, 1963.

Lévy-Bruhl, Lucien. *How Natives Think*. Translated by Lilian A. Clare. London: George Allen and Unwin, Ltd., 1926.

Lévy-Bruhl, Lucien. *Primitive Mentality*. Translated by Lilian A. Clare. London: George Allen and Unwin, Ltd., 1923.

Lincoln, Bruce. *Discourse and the Construction of Society: Comparative Studies of Myth, Ritual, and Classification*. New York and Oxford: Oxford University Press, 1989.

Lings, Martin, and Clinton Minnaar, eds. *The Underlying Religion: An Introduction to Perennial Philosophy*. Bloomington: World Wisdom, 2007.

Liu, Shiyin. "Deciphering James Legge's Confucianism." PhD thesis, University of Glasgow, 2020.

"Living with Gods." https://www.britishmuseum.org/about_us/past_exhibitions/2018/living_with_gods.aspx. Accessed July 30, 2018.

Lubar, Steven. "Cabinets of Curiosity: What they Were, Why they Disappeared, and Why they're so Popular Now." https://medium.com/@lubar/cabinets-of-curiosity-a134f65c115a. Accessed November 12, 2018.

Luke, Timothy W. *Museum Politics: Power Plays at the Exhibition*. Minneapolis: University of Minnesota Press, 2002.

Lüpken, Anja. "Politics of Representation—Normativity in Museum Practice." *Journal of Religion in Europe* 4 (2011): 157–83.

Lüpken, Anja. *Religion(en) im Museum: Eine vergleichende Analyse der Religionsmuseen in St. Petersburg, Glasgow und Taipeh*. Berlin: LIT Verlag, 2011.

MacGregor, Neil. *Living with the Gods: On Beliefs and Peoples*. New York: Alfred A. Knopf, Kindle edition 2018.

Masuzawa, Tomoko. *The Invention of World Religions*. Chicago and London: University of Chicago Press, 2005.

Merleau-Ponty, Maurice. "Eye and Mind" translated by C. Dallery. In *The Primacy of Perception*, edited by James M. Eide, 159–90. Evanston: Northwestern University Press, 1964.

Merllié, Dominique. "Durkheim, Lévy-Bruhl et la 'pensée primitive': quell différend?" *L'Année sociologique* 62, no. 2 (2012): 429–46. English version at Cadenza Academic Translations. https://www.cairn.info/article-E_ANSO_122_0429--durkheim-levy-bruhl-and-primitivethink.htm.

Michel, P. *La Religion au Musee*. Paris: I'Harmattan, 1999.

Miles, Jack, Donald S. Lopez, Jr., and James Robson, eds. *The Norton Anthology of World Religions*, 2 vols. New York: W. W. Norton & Company, 2014.

Miller, Adam S. *Speculative Grace: Bruno Latour and Object-Oriented Theology*. New York: Fordham University Press, 2013.

Molendijk, Arie L. *The Emergence of the Science of Religion in the Netherlands*. Leiden: E.J. Brill, 2005,

Moretti, Franco. *Signs Taken For Wonders: On the Sociology of Literary Forms*, Rev. ed. London and New York: Verso, 1988.

Morgan, David. "Introduction: The Matter of Belief." In *Religion and Material Culture: The Matter of Belief*, edited by David Morgan, 1–18. London and New York: Routledge, 2010.

Morgan, David. *The Sacred Gaze: Religious Visual Culture in Theory and Practice*, Berkeley: University of California Press, 2005.

Morgan, David. "Thing." In *Key Terms in Material Religion*, edited by S. Brent Plate, 253–9. London: Bloomsbury, 2015.

Morgan, David, S. Brent Plate, Jeremy Stolow, and Amy Whitehead. "On the Agency of Religious Objects: A Conversation." Web blog post. *Material Religions*, October 29, 2015. http://materialreligions.blogspot.co.uk/2015/10/on-agency-of-religious-obje cts.html. Accessed May 8, 2018.

Mun, Chanju. *The History of Doctrinal Classification in Chinese Buddhism A Study of the Panjiao System*. Lanham, MD: University Press of America, 2005.

"Museum of World Religions: The Hall of Life's Journey." https://www.mwr.org.tw/mw r_en/xcpmtexhi/cont?xsmsid=0I0523915777771211747&sid=0I0576128037529054 96. Accessed October 1, 2018.

National Football Museum (Manchester). https://www.nationalfootballmuseum.com/.

Noss, David S., and Blake Gangaard, *A History of the World's Religions*, 13th ed., Upper Saddle River, NJ; Harlow: Pearson Education, 2011; originally *Man's Religions* by John B. Noss 1956.

Ochsner, Beate. "Talking about Associations and Descriptions or a Short Story about Associology." In *Applying the Actor-Network Theory in Media Studies*, edited by Markus Spöhrer and Beate Ochsner, 220–33. Baden-Württemberg, Germany: University of Konstanz, 2016.

O'Hanlon, Michael. *The Pitt Rivers Museum: A World Within*. London: Scala Arts and Heritage, 2014.

O'Neill, Mark. "Exploring the Meaning of Life: The St Mungo Museum of Religious Life and Art." *Museum International, No. 185* 47, no. 1 (1995): 50–3. https://doi.org/10.1 111/j.1468-0033.1995.tb01225.x.

O'Neill, Mark. "Religion and Cultural Policy: Two Museum Case Studies." *International Journal of Cultural Policy* 17, no. 2 (2011): 225–43. http://dx.doi.org/10.1080/1028 6632.2010.545401.

Orzech, Charles D. "The Material Representation of the Ethereal." *Material Religion* 12, no. 3 (2016): 399–401. doi: 10.1080/17432200.2016.1192145.

Orzech, Charles D. *Politics and Transcendent Wisdom: The Scripture for Humane Kings in the Creation of Chinese Buddhism*. University Park: The Pennsylvania State University Press, 1998.

Orzech, Charles D. "World Religions Museums: Dialogue, Domestication, and the Sacred Gaze." In *Sacred Objects in Secular Spaces*, edited by Bruce M. Sullivan, 133–44. London and New York: Bloomsbury, 2015.

Otto, Rudolf. *The Idea of the Holy: An Inquiry into the Non-Rational Factor in the Idea of the Divine and Its Relation to the Rational*. Translated by John W. Harvey. London: Oxford University Press, 1936.

Oxtoby, Willard G., and Alan F. Segal. *A Concise Introduction to World Religions*, 2nd ed. Oxford: Oxford University Press, 2011.

Paine, Crispin, ed. *Godly Things: Museums, Objects & Religion*. London: Leicester University Press, 2000.

Paine, Crispin, ed. *Gods and Rollercoasters: Religion in Theme-Parks Worldwide*. London and New York: Bloomsbury Academic, 2019.

Paine, Crispin, ed. "Militant Atheist Objects: Anti-Religion Museums in the Soviet Union." *Present Pasts* 1, no. 1. https://presentpasts.info/articles/10.5334/pp.13/. Accessed January 19, 2019. doi: http://doi.org/10.5334/pp.13.

Paine, Crispin, ed. *Religious Objects in Museums: Private Lives and Public Duties.* London: Bloomsbury, 2013.

Patton, Kimberley C., and Benjamin C. Ray, eds. *A Magic Still Dwells: Comparative Religion in the Postmodern Age.* Berkeley: University of California Press, 2000.

Pietz, William. "The Problem of the Fetish, I." *RES: Anthropology and Aesthetics* 9 (Spring 1985): 5–17.

Pietz, William. "The Problem of the Fetish, II: The Origin of the Fetish." *RES: Anthropology and Aesthetics* 13 (Spring 1987): 23–45.

Pietz, William. "The Problem of the Fetish, IIIa: Bosman's Guinea and the Enlightenment Theory of Fetishism." *RES: Anthropology and Aesthetics* 16 (Autumn 1988): 105–24.

Pitt-Rivers, A. Lane Fox. "The Evolution of Culture." In *The Evolution of Culture and Other Essays*, edited by J. L. Myers, 20–44. Oxford: Clarendon Press, 1906.

Plate, S. Brent, ed. *Key Terms in Material Religion.* London: Bloomsbury Academic, 2015.

Pomian, Krzysztof. *Collectors and Curiosities: Paris and Venice, 1500–1800.* Cambridge: Polity Press, 1990.

Praet, Istvan. *Animism and the Question of Life.* New York and London: Routledge, 2014.

Pratt, Mary Louise. *Imperial Eyes: Travel Writing and Transculturation.* London and New York: Routledge, 1992.

Pye, Michael. "Exhibiting Religion." In *Materiality in Religion and Culture: Tenri University – Marburg University*, edited by Saburo Shawn Morishita, 25–43. Zürich: LIT Verlag, 2017.

Rambelli, Fabio. *Buddhist Materiality: A Cultural History of Objects in Japanese Buddhism.* Stanford: Stanford University Press, 2007.

Royal, Jean-François. "Protecting and Interpreting Quebec's Religious Heritage: The Museum of Religions at Nicolet." *Material Religion: The Journal of Objects, Art and Belief* 4, no. 1 (March 2007): 153–54.

Runge, Konstanze. "Studying, Teaching, and Exhibiting Religion: The Marburg Museum of Religions (Religionskundliche Sammlung)." In *Religion in Museums: Global and Multidisciplinary Perspectives*, edited by Gretchen Buggeln, Crispin Paine, and S. Brent Plate, 155–62. London: Bloomsbury Academic, 2017.

Sandell, Richard. *Museums, Prejudice, and the Reframing of Difference.* London and New York: Routledge, 2007.

Saussaye, Pierre D. Chantepie de la. *Manual of the Science of Religion.* London: Longmans, Green, 1891.

Schleiermacher, Friedrich. *On Religion: Speeches to Its Cultured Despisers.* Translated by John Oman with an introduction by Rudolf Otto. New York: Harper & Row, Publishers, 1958.

Schnack, Ingeborg, ed. *Marburger Gelehrt in der ersten Hälfte de 20. Jarhunderts.* Marburg: N. G. Elwert Verlag, 1977.

Seager, Richard Hughes. *The World's Parliament of Religions: The East/West Encounter, Chicago 1893.* Bloomington: Indiana University Press, 1995.

Seligman, Adam B., Robert P. Weller, Michael J. Puett, and Bennett Simon. *Ritual and Its Consequences: An Essay on the Limits of Sincerity.* Oxford and New York: Oxford University Press, 2008.

Seton, Rosemary. "Reconstructing the Museum of the London Missionary Society." *Material Religion* 8, no. 1 (2012): 98–102.

Shakhnovich, Marianna. "At the Origin of the Study of Religion in Russia." *Вестник СПбГУ.* Вып. 4, Сер. 17 (2016): 135–43. doi: 10.21638/11701/spbu17.2016.415.

Shakhnovich, Marianna. "The Study of Religion in Russia: The Foundation of the Museum of the History of Religion." In *Contemporary Views on Comparative Religion: In Celebration of Tim Jensen's 65th Birthday,* edited by Peter Antes, Armin W. Geertz, and Mikael Rothstein, 425–37. Sheffield: Equinox Publishing, Ltd., 2016.

Shakhnovich, Marianna. "The Study of Religion in the Soviet Union." *Numen* 40, no. 1 (January 1993): 67–81.

Sharf, Robert H. "How to Think with Chan Gong'an." In *Thinking with Cases: Specialist Knowledge in Chinese Cultural History,* edited by Charlotte Furth, Judith T. Zeitlin, and Ping-chen Hsiung, 205–43. Honolulu: University of Hawai'i Press, 2007.

Sharf, Robert H. "On the Allure of Buddhist Relics." *Representations* 66 (1999): 75–99.

Sharf, Robert H. "The Rhetoric of Experience and the Study of Religion." *Journal of Consciousness Studies* 7, no. 11–12 (2000): 267–87.

Sharf, Robert H., and Elizabeth Horton Sharf, eds. *Living Images: Japanese Buddhist Icons in Context.* Stanford: Stanford University Press, 2002.

Sharpe, Eric J. *Comparative Religion: A History.* London: Duckworth, 1975; 2nd revised edition 1986.

Shaughnessy, Edward L. *I Ching: the Classic of Changes.* New York: Ballantine Books, 1996.

Silva, Neysela da. "Religious Displays: An Observational Study with a Focus on the Horniman Museum." *Material Religion* 6, no. 2 (2010): 166–91.

Skinner, Stephen. *Guide to the Feng Shui Compass: A Compendium of Classical Feng Shui.* Singapore: Golden Hoard Press, 2008.

Smart, Ninian. *Worldviews: Crosscultural Explorations of Human Beliefs,* 3rd ed. Englewood Cliffs: Prentice Hall, 1999.

Smith, Huston. *The World's Religions.* New York: Harper Collins, 2008; Reissue of 1991 edition.

Smith, Jonathan Z. "Acknowledgments: Morphology and History in Mircea Eliade's 'Patterns in Comparative Religion (1949–1999)' 'Part 1: The Work and Its Contexts' and 'Part 2: The Texture of the Work.'" *History of Religions* 39, no. 4 (2000): 315–31 and 332–51.

Smith, Jonathan Z. "Adde Parvum Parvo Magnus Acervus Erit." *History of Religions* 11, no. 1 (August 1971): 67–90.

Smith, Jonathan Z. "In Comparison a Magic Dwells." In *Imagining Religion: From Babylon to Jonestown*, 19–35. Chicago and London: University of Chicago Press, 1982.

Smith, Jonathan Z. "The 'End' of Comparison: Redescription and Rectification." In *A Magic Still Dwells: Comparative Religion in the Postmodern Age*, edited by Kimberly C. Patton and Benjamin C. Ray, 237–42. Berkeley: University of California Press, 2000.

Smith, Jonathan Z. "The Glory, Jest, and Riddle: James George Frazer and the Golden Bough." Ph.D dissertation, Yale University, 1969.

Smith, Jonathan Z. *Imagining Religion: From Babylon to Jamestown*. Chicago and London: University of Chicago Press, 1982.

Smith, Jonathan Z. *Map is Not Territory*. Leiden: E. J. Brill, 1978.

Smith, Jonathan Z. "A Matter of Class: Taxonomies of Religion." *The Harvard Theological Review* 89, no. 4 (October 1996): 387–403.

Smith, Jonathan Z. "Religion, Religions, Religious." In *Critical Terms for Religious Studies*, edited by Mark C. Taylor, 269–84. Chicago: University of Chicago Press, 1998.

Smith, Jonathan Z. "Sacred Persistence: Toward a Redescription of Canon." In *Imagining Religion: From Babylon to Jonestown*, 36–52. Chicago and London: University of Chicago Press, 1982.

Smith, Jonathan Z. "When the Bough Breaks." *History of Religion* 12, no. 4 (1973): 342–71.

Smith, Jonathan Z., and William Scott Green, eds. *The Harper Collins Dictionary of Religion*. New York: Harper Collins, 1995.

Soja, Edward W. *Postmetropolis: Critical Studies of Cities and Regions*, 11. Oxford: Basil Blackwell, 2000.

Soja, Edward W. *Thirdspace: Journeys to Los Angeles and Other Real-and-Imagined Places*. Cambridge: Blackwell Publishers, 1996.

Stanford Encyclopedia of Philosophy, Max Weber (5.2: Ideal Type). https://plato.stanford.edu/entries/weber/#IdeTyp. New York: Oxford University Press, 2010.

Stone, Jon R. *The Essential Max Müller: On Language, Mythology, and Religion*. London: Palgrave Macmillan, 2002.

Strenski, Ivan. "The Magic and Drudgery in J. Z. Smith's Theory of Comparison." In *Contemporary Views on Comparative Religion in Celebration of Tim Jensen's 65th Birthday*, edited by Peter Antes, Armin W. Geertz, and Michael Rothstein, 7–16. Yorkshire: Equinox Publishing Company, 2016.

Sullivan, Bruce M. "Reconsecrating the Icons: The New Phenomenon of Yoga in Museums." In *Sacred Objects in Secular Spaces: Exhibiting Asian Religions in Museums*, edited by Bruce M. Sullivan, 35–48. London: Bloomsbury Academic, 2015.

Sullivan, Lawrence E., ed., with Julien Ries, Andrea R. Jain, Nikky-Guninder Kaur Singh, Todd Curcuru, Yong Huang, Oliver Clément, Anthony Cerulli, and Marie W. Dallam. *Religions of the World: An Introduction to Culture and Meaning*. Minneapolis: Fortress Press, 2013.

Sun, Anna. *Confucianism as a World Religion: Contested Histories and Contemporary Realities*. Princeton, Princeton University Press, 2013.

Swearer, Donald K. *Becoming the Buddha: The Ritual of Image Consecration in Thailand*. Princeton: Princeton University Press, 2004.

Swift, Jonathan. *Gulliver's Travels into Several Remote Nations of the World*. George Bell and Sons, 1892. Available at Gutenberg.org: https://www.gutenberg.org/files/829/829-h/829-h.htm.

Taves, Ann. *Religious Experience Reconsidered: A Building Block Approach to the Study of Religion and other Special Things*. Princeton: Princeton University Press, 2011.

Taylor, Charles. *A Secular Age*. Cambridge, MA: Harvard University Press, 2007.

Taylor, Mark C., ed. *Critical Terms in Religious Studies*. Chicago: The University of Chicago Press, 1998.

"Tenrikyō." *World Religions and Spirituality*. https://wrldrels.org/2015/03/22/tenrikyo/. Accessed January 1, 2019.

Teryukova, Ekaterina. "Collecting and Research in the Museum of the History of Religion." In *Religion in Museums: Global and Multidisciplinary Perspectives*, edited by Gretchen Buggeln, Crispin Paine, and S. Brent Plate, 147–53. London: Bloomsbury Academic, 2017.

Teryukova, Ekaterina. "Display of Religious Objects in a Museum Space: Russian Museum Experience in the 1920s and 1930s." *Material Religion* 10, no. 2 (2014): 255–58. http://dx.doi.org/10.2752/175183414X13990269049761.

Teryukova, Ekaterina, Pavel Tugarinov, and Ekaterina Zavidovskaya, "On the Results of the International Conference 'Folk Images and Late Imperial China (St. Petersburg, 29–30 June 2017).'" *Manuscripta Orientalia* 23, no. 1 (2017): 67–70.

Tiele, Cornelis Petrus. *Outline of the History of Religion to the Spread of Universal Religion*. London: Trübner & Company, 1888. Available at Archive.org: https://archive.org/details/outlinesofthehi00tieluoft/page/n26.

Troeltsch, Ernst. "The Place of Christianity Among the World Religions." In *Christian Thought: Its History and Application*, edited by Baron F. von Hugel, 1–35. London: University of London Press, 1923.

Trollinger Jr., Susan L., and William Vance. *Righting America at the Creation Museum*. Baltimore: Johns Hopkins University Press, 2016.

Turner, Mark. "Conceptual Integration." http://markturner.org/blending.htm. Accessed December 1, 2018.

Turner, Victor W. *The Ritual Process: Structure and Anti-structure*. Harmondsworth: Penguin Books, 1969.

Tylor, E. B. *Primitive Culture*, 4th revised ed., 2 vols. London: John Murray, 1903.

Weber, Max. *The Methodology of the Social Sciences*. Translated and edited by Edward A. Shils and Henry A. Finch. Glencoe: The Free Press, 1949.

Wedemeyer, Christian K., and Wendy Doniger, eds. *Hermeneutics, Politics, and the History of Religions: The Contested Legacies of Joachim Wach and Mircea Eliade*. Oxford and New York: Oxford University Press, 2010.

Wheeler-Barclay, Marjorie. *The Science of Religion in Britain: 1860–1915.* Charlottesville and London: University of Virginia Press, 2010.

Whitehead, Amy. *Religious Statues and Personhood: Testing the Role of Materiality.* London and New York: Bloomsbury Academic, 2013.

Wilke, Annette, and Ester-Maria Guggenmos, eds. *Im Netz des Indra: Das Museum of World Religions, sein buddhistisches Dialogkonzept und die neue Disziplin Religionsästhetik.* Berlin: LIT Verlag, 2008.

William Blake Archive at http://www.blakearchive.org/work/aro and http://www.blakearchive.org/work/nnr. Accessed December 30, 2018.

Wilson, Jeff. *Mindful America: The Mutual Transformation of Buddhist Meditation and American Culture.* Oxford and New York: Oxford University Press, 2014.

Wingfield, Chris. "'Scarcely More than a Christian Trophy Case'? The Global Collections of the London Missionary Society Museum (1814–1910)." *Journal of the History of Collections* 29, no. 1 (2017): 109–28.

Woodhead, Linda, Paul Heelas, and Benjamin Seel. *The Spiritual Revolution: Why Religion Is Giving Way to Spirituality.* Hoboken: Wiley-Blackwell, 2005.

Załęski, Paweł. "Ideal Types in Max Weber's Sociology of Religion: Some Theoretical Inspirations for A Study of the Religious Field." *Polish Sociological Review* 171 (2010): 319–25.

Ziolkowski, Eric J., ed. *A Museum of Faiths: Histories and Legacies of the 1893 World's Parliament of Religions.* Atlanta: Scholars Press, 1993.

Žižek, Slavoj. "Multiculturalism or the Cultural Logic of Multinational Capitalism?" *New Left Review*, I/225, 44 (September–October 1997): 28–51.

Index